THE COURAGE TO FIGHT VIOLENCE AGAINST WOMEN

Psychoanalysis & Women Series
Series Editor: Frances Thomson-Salo

Feminine Sensuality
Alcira Mariam Alizade

The Embodied Female
Edited by Alcira Mariam Alizade

Studies on Femininity
Edited by Alcira Mariam Alizade

Masculine Scenarios
Edited by Alcira Mariam Alizade

On Incest: Psychoanalytic Perspectives
Edited by Giovanna Ambrosio

Motherhood in the Twenty-First Century
Edited by Alcira Mariam Alizade

Masculinity and Femininity Today
Edited by Ester Palerm Marí and Frances Thomson-Salo

Women and Creativity: A Psychoanalytic Glimpse through Art, Literature, and Social Structure
Edited by Laura Tognoli Pasquali and Frances Thomson-Salo

Homosexualities: Psychogenesis, Polymorphism, and Countertransference
Edited by Elda Abrevaya and Frances Thomson-Salo

Myths of Mighty Women: Their Application in Psychoanalytic Psychotherapy
Edited by Arlene Kramer Richards and Lucille Spira

Medea: Myth and Unconscious Fantasy
Edited by Esa Roos

The Status of Women: Violence, Identity, and Activism
Edited by Vivian B. Pender

Changing Sexualities and Parental Functions in the Twenty-First Century
Candida Sé Holovko and Frances Thomson-Salo

THE COURAGE TO FIGHT VIOLENCE AGAINST WOMEN

Psychoanalytic and
Multidisciplinary Perspectives

edited by

Paula L. Ellman and Nancy R. Goodman

KARNAC

First published in 2017 by
Karnac Books Ltd
118 Finchley Road, London NW3 5HT

Copyright © 2017 to Paula L. Ellman and Nancy R. Goodman for the edited collection and to the individual authors for their contributions.

The rights of the contributors to be identified as the authors of this work have been asserted in accordance with §§77 and 78 of the Copyright Design and Patents Act 1988.

All rights reserved. No part of this publication may be reproduced, stored in a retrieval system, or transmitted, in any form or by any means, electronic, mechanical, photocopying, recording, or otherwise, without the prior written permission of the publisher.

British Library Cataloguing in Publication Data

A C.I.P. for this book is available from the British Library

ISBN 978 1 78220 473 2

Edited, designed and produced by The Studio Publishing Services Ltd
www.publishingservicesuk.co.uk
email: studio@publishingservicesuk.co.uk

Printed in Great Britain

www.karnacbooks.com

CONTENTS

LIST OF FIGURES AND ILLUSTRATIONS	ix
ACKNOWLEDGMENTS	xiii
ABOUT THE EDITORS AND CONTRIBUTORS	xvii
SERIES EDITOR'S FOREWORD Frances Thomson-Salo	xxvii
PREFACE Gertraud Schlesinger-Kipp	xxix

OPENING WORDS BY THE SPONSORS
OF THE CONFERENCE "THE COURAGE TO FIGHT
VIOLENCE AGAINST WOMEN"
    Alexandra Billinghurst, Jack Rasmussen, Peter Starr, and
    Cecile Bassen
	xxxi

INTRODUCTION The courage to fight violence against women Paula L. Ellman and Nancy R. Goodman	xxxvii

CHAPTER ONE
Unconscious fantasy and the courage to fight
violence against women
Paula L. Ellman 1

CHAPTER TWO
Witnessing and resilience: commentary on being involved
in "The courage to fight violence against women"
Nancy R. Goodman 9

CHAPTER THREE
Human sex trafficking: extreme violence against women
and children
Vivian B. Pender 17

CHAPTER FOUR
How art imitates life
Diana Romero 29

CHAPTER FIVE
Sex trafficking: commentary on Chapters Three and Four
Margarita Cereijido 41

CHAPTER SIX
Girls at risk: paths to safety, interventions with female
adolescents at sexual risk in Quintana Roo, Mexico
Raquel Berman 47

CHAPTER SEVEN
Sew to speak: story cloth healing with survivors
of sexual violence
Rachel A. Cohen and Ana Maria Ramirez 63

CHAPTER EIGHT
Commentary on "Girls at risk" and "Sew to speak"
Carla Neely 83

CHAPTER NINE
Violation: a poem
Myra Sklarew with Introduction by *Nancy R. Goodman* 87

CHAPTER TEN
Anatomy of a man's assault on a woman 91
Donald Campbell

CHAPTER ELEVEN
Commentary on Donald Campbell's "Anatomy of a 99
man's assault on a woman"
Justine Kalas Reeves

CHAPTER TWELVE
End Rape on Campus (EROC) and the making 103
of *The Hunting Ground*
Annie Clark

CHAPTER THIRTEEN
Sexual abuse of women in United States prisons: 107
a modern corollary of slavery
Brenda V. Smith, with Introduction by *Paula L. Ellman*

CHAPTER FOURTEEN
Commentary on "End Rape on Campus (EROC)" and 129
"Sexual abuse of women in United States prisons"
Joy Kassett

CHAPTER FIFTEEN
Combatting femicide in Mexico: achievements and 133
ongoing challenges
Maureen Meyer

CHAPTER SIXTEEN
Justice matters: scaling up the response to sexual 149
violence in areas of conflict and unrest
Hope Ferdowsian

CHAPTER SEVENTEEN
Women seeking asylum due to gender-based violence 161
Katalin Roth

CHAPTER EIGHTEEN
Violence against women worldwide: a commentary 167
on Chapters Fifteen to Seventeen
Louis W. Goodman

CHAPTER NINETEEN
Poems on violence against women 171
   E. Ethelbert Miller, Poet Laureate
   with Introduction by *Louis W. Goodman*

CHAPTER TWENTY
Violence against women in the work of women artists 177
   Janice S. Lieberman

CHAPTER TWENTY-ONE
Woman: power and representation in pre-Columbian societies in the Andean region 189
   Moisés Lemlij

CHAPTER TWENTY-TWO
Maternal imago and bodily symptoms 209
   Rosine Jozef Perelberg

CHAPTER TWENTY-THREE
Discussion of Lemlij and Perelberg: women of power 227
   Arlene Kramer Richards

CHAPTER TWENTY-FOUR
Introduction to *Traces in the Wind* 231
   Robin Dean

CHAPTER TWENTY-FIVE
A staged reading for remembrance, reminder, and inspiration: *Traces in the Wind* 233
   Gail Humphries Mardirosian

INDEX 252

LIST OF FIGURES AND ILLUSTRATIONS

CHAPTER SEVEN

7.1   Esther Weisenthal Krinitz: "The Nazis beat up my father."

7.2   Amazwi Abesifazane (Voices of Women) project in South Africa—experiences under apartheid.
Courtesy of Coral Bijoux, Voices of Women, South Africa.

7.3   Sewing circle.
Courtesy of Pilar Pena, ACNUR.

7.4   "This is a moment I will never forget." Maria depicts the day her village was attacked and her life destroyed.
Courtesy of Pilar Pena, ACNUR.

7.5   "This is what I cannot say." Pilar forced to flee for her life and no chance to say goodbye to her father.
Courtesy of Pilar Pena, ACNUR.

7.6   "This is what I need you to know." Rosa sewed the scene of her children being shot at on the river in front of their home, her husband holding a bottle of alcohol in his hand.
Courtesy of Pilar Pena, ACNUR.

7.7   "This is what the cloth is trying to say." Blanca's daughter is being raped and murdered by soldiers.
Courtesy of Pilar Pena, ACNUR.

7.8 "This is what I hope for the future." Carla created a vision of her future—grandchildren playing in her garden, bright colors, a house, and the pastoral scene of a peaceful life; the mango tree is where she hid when her father came to beat her.
Courtesy of Pilar Pena, ACNUR.

7.9 Graph of research results.

CHAPTER TWENTY

20.1 Artemesia Gentileschi (1610) *Susannah and Her Elders.*

20.2 Frieda Kahlo (1935) *A Few Small Nips: Passionately in Love.*

20.3 Kiki Smith (1992) *Tale.*
Photograph courtesy of the artist and Pace Gallery.

20.4 Kiki Smith (1992) *Blood Pool.*
Courtesy of the Art Institute of Chicago.

20.5 Kiki Smith (1992) *Pee Body.*
Harvard Art Museums / Fogg Museum, gift of Barbara Lee, promised gift of Emily Rauh Pulitzer and purchase in part from the Joseph A. Baird, Jr., Francis H. Burr Memorial and Director's Acquisition Funds, 1997.82
Copyright © Kiki Smith. Photo: Imaging Department
Copyright © President and Fellows of Harvard College.

20.6 Kiki Smith (2001) *Rapture.*
Photograph courtesy of the photographer Richard-Max Tremblay and Pace Gallery.

20.7(a,b) Kiki Smith (2000) *Geneviève and the May Wolf.*
Photograph courtesy of the Shoshana Wayne Gallery and the Denver Art Museum.

CHAPTER TWENTY-ONE

21.1 Representations of genitalia and sexual pleasures related to life and creation for women and men in Mochica art: male.
Courtesy of the Peruvian National Museum of Archeology, Anthropology and History.

21.2 Representations of genitalia and sexual pleasures related to life and creation for women and men in Mochica art: female.
Photograph by Yutaka Yoshii. Courtesy of Museo Larco.

LIST OF FIGURES AND ILLUSTRATIONS   xi

21.3   Ceramic plate with representation of women with genitalia. Courtesy of the Peruvian National Museum of Archeology, Anthropology and History.
21.4   Representations of genitalia and sexual pleasures related to life and creation for women and men in Mochica art: male and female.
Photograph by Yutaka Yoshii. Courtesy of Museo Larco.
21.5   Scene of sacrifice on a piece of Mochica pottery showing the preeminence of a priestess.
Courtesy of Museo Larco.
21.6   Arms.
Courtesy of Régulo Franco Jordán, Director of the Complejo Arqueológico y Museo de Sitio El Brujo.
21.7   Inca pot, with geometric design.
Photographer: Moisés Lemlij.
21.8   Drawings of functions of women in Inca representations. Drawing by Felipe Guamán Poma de Ayala (circa 1650), *Nueva corónica y buen gobierno*
21.9   Drawings of functions of women in Inca representations. Drawing by Felipe Guamán Poma de Ayala (circa 1650), *Nueva corónica y buen gobierno*
21.10 Drawings of functions of women in Inca representations. Drawing by Felipe Guamán Poma de Ayala (circa 1650), *Nueva corónica y buen gobierno*

CHAPTER TWENTY-FIVE
25.1   Audience's ages.
25.2   Audience's gender.
25.3   Audience responses to the first set of questions.
25.4   Response to whether the stories evoked emotional connection.
25.5   Response to whether the music evoked empathy.
25.6   Response to whether enactment of the writing generated emotional reactions.
25.7   Strength of reactions in specific categories of emotions.

25.8 Connections to the women's stories.
25.9 Responses to how the arts contributed to the audience members' connection.
25.10 Response as to whether the performance would be as effective without music.

ACKNOWLEDGMENTS

We are tremendously grateful to all of the contributors to this volume. We appreciate your courage to fight violence against women and your willingness to write about your important creative work for this volume of *The Courage to Fight Violence against Women*. We thank Frances Thomson-Salo, Past Overall Chair of COWAP, for her support on this book.

Karnac Books has been wonderfully receptive to this topic and we thank Oliver Rathbone, Rod Tweedy and Kate Pearce for welcoming our work and responding to our many questions.

At American University, we found support and encouragement and thank Peter Starr, Jack Rasmussen, Kristi-Anne Caisse, Lisa Ager, Sarah Wedgewood, and Ethan Hicks. The gallery exhibition at American University Museum Katzen Arts Center was a perfect accompaniment to the conference on which this book is based.

Paula L. Ellman: I extend my loving appreciation to my husband, Douglas A. Chavis, and my children, Jennie Chavis, Sam Chavis, and Anna Chavis and Karl Rodger, for their ongoing support of my work. I appreciate my co-editor and collaborator, Nancy Goodman, for our thinking, learning, and working together, along with our Courage Conference Planning Committee: Margarita Cereijido, Robin Dean,

Joy Kasnett, Lizbeth Moses, Carla Neely, and Justine Kalas Reeves. I thank all our contributors, the courageous women and men whose work has been to fight violence against women and who wrote for this volume. Finally, I thank my many Contemporary Freudian Society colleagues for serving as my analytic home.

Nancy R. Goodman: I thank my husband, Louis Goodman, and my children and grandchildren for their love and support: Elizabeth Goodman, David Brown, and Ella, Isaiah, and Julian and Jennifer Goodman, and Fred Yturralde and Kaia and Sophia. I am grateful to each brave woman who speaks out about violence experienced and, in doing so, brings courage to others. The women and men who presented at the Conference and have contributed to this book are active witnesses who are unwavering in their own professional and creative endeavors to bring light to the darkness of violence against women. My enactment group colleagues, Raquel Berman, Batya Monder, Elizabeth Reese, and Marilyn Meyers, my friend and co-editor of *The Power of Witnessing*, are particular encouragement for me to write about hatred and atrocity through our reading and thinking together on these topics. Thank you, Paula Ellman, for being the engine for the Conference and the book and being my friend, colleague, and writing partner. Our planning committee was able to hold and contain the violence and the courage we gathered together. Thank you Margarita Cereijido, Robin Dean, Joy Kasnett, Lizbeth Moses, Carla Neely, and Justine Kalas Reeves.

Acknowledgments of artwork

We are grateful to the artists whose images we include here. They represent the courage to depict representations of the power of women, of violence against women, and instances of the resilience found in women making art. Moisés Lemlij was generous with his time to gather together permissions for the use of Mochican and Incan artwork. Pilar Pena and Rachel Cohen helped arrange the photographs of sewing panels created by traumatized women. We thank Art and Remembrance for granting us the use of the sewing panel by Esther Weisenthal Krinitz, and Coral Bijoux, of Voices for Women in South Africa. Pace Gallery granted us permission to use Kiki Smith artwork and guided us to the museums and photographers who then granted the next level of permission to use the artwork. The Fogg Museum at Harvard, Shoshanna Gallery and the Denver Art Museum, and the Art Institute of Chicago waived fees for use of images of Kiki Smith's sculptures and provided images for us. Richard-Max Tremblay granted us use of his photographs of *Rapture*, by Kiki Smith. In particular, we thank Lindsay McGuire of Pace Gallery, Isabella Donadio of The Harvard Art Museums, and Aimee L. Marshall of The Art Institute of Chicago.

ABOUT THE EDITORS AND CONTRIBUTORS

Editors

Paula L. Ellman, PhD, ABPP, is a training and supervising analyst in the Contemporary Freudian Society (CFS) and the IPA, Vice President of the CFS Board, past institute director of the Washington Program of CFS, a Member of the Committee on Women and Psychoanalysis of the IPA (COWAP), and a Board Member of the North America Psychoanalytic Confederation (NAPsaC). She is Visiting Professor at the Sino-American Continuing Training Project for Wuhan Hospital for Psychotherapy, Wuhan China. She has written and presented in the areas of female psychology, enactment, terror, sadomasochism, and unconscious fantasy. Recent publications include: "Donald Winnicott Today: Book Review" (co-authored with Nancy Goodman); *Division Review* (2014); *Battling the Life and Death Forces of Sadomasochism: Clinical Perspectives* (co-edited with Harriet Basseches and Nancy Goodman, Karnac, 2013); and *Finding Unconscious Fantasy in Narrative, Trauma and Body Pain: A Clinical Guide* (co-edited with Nancy Goodman, Routledge Press, 2017). She has a psychoanalytic practice in North Bethesda, Maryland and Washington, DC.

Nancy R. Goodman, PhD, is a training and supervising analyst with the CFS and the IPA. She is on the permanent faculty of the CFS and has served as Institute Director of the CFS Washington, DC Program. She writes on female development, analytic listening, Holocaust trauma, enactments and sadomasochism, and unconscious fantasy. Her most recent publications include: "Donald Winnicott today": Book Review (co-authored with Paula Ellman), *Division Review* (2014); *Battling the Life and Death Forces of Sadomasochism: Clinical Perspectives* (co-edited with Harriet Basseches and Paula Ellman, Karnac, 2013); "Psychoanalysis: listening to understand, selection of readings of Arlene Kramer Richards", editor Nancy R. Goodman (IP Books, 2013); and *Finding Unconscious Fantasy in Narrative, Trauma and Body Pain: A Clinical Guide* (co-edited with Paula Ellman) published by Routledge Press, 2017. She is Director of The Virtual Psychoanalytic Museum (IP Books www.thevirtualpsychoanalytic museum.org). Dr. Goodman has a psychoanalytic practice in Bethesda, MD.

Contributors

Cecile R. Bassen, MD, has a longstanding interest in the psychology of gender, and is the North American Co-Chair of the IPA Committee on Women and Psychoanalysis (COWAP). She is a training and consulting analyst at the Seattle Psychoanalytic Society and Institute, and the Northwestern Psychoanalytic Society and Institute, and is also on the clinical faculty of the Department of Psychiatry of the University of Washington. She sees adolescents and adults in her private practice in Seattle.

Raquel Berman, PhD, is a training analyst at the Mexican Association for Psychoanalytic Practice, Training and Research (MAPPTR) IPA, and founder of the study group "Father's Imprint on Daughter's Development". She is a Fellow of IPTAR, CIPS Study Group member on Enactment, member of the Latin American COWAP, member of the Cultural Committee IPA, and heads the Pilot Project on Female Adolescent Sexual Risks. She has written about women's introjection of machismo, femicide, and female leadership issues in psychoanalytic organizations.

Alexandra Billinghurst, PhD, is Vice President of the International Psychoanalytical Association. She is past president of the Swedish Psychoanalytical Association as well as past treasurer and chair of the Outreach Committee. She conducts private practice in Stockholm in addition to supervising analysts and teaching psychoanalytic theory, psychotherapy practice, and supervising supervision.

Donald Campbell is a past President of the British Psychoanalytical Society, former Secretary General of the International Psychoanalytical Association, and served as Chair of the Portman Clinic in London, where he worked as a child, adolescent, and adult analyst for thirty years. He has published on such subjects as violence, suicide, perversion, child sexual abuse and adolescence.

Margarita Cereijido, PhD, is a supervising and training analyst at the Washington Psychoanalytic Institute. She has taught, lectured, and written on, among other issues, gender, culture, and conflict. She organizes the annual conference on culture and psychoanalysis at the Washington psychoanalytic institute. She is in private practice in Washington DC.

Annie E. Clark is Co-Founder, End Rape On Campus and lead complainant in the Title IX and Clery Act violations against UNC-Chapel Hill, featured in the documentary, *The Hunting Ground*. Contributing writers, *Huffington Post*, *MSNBC*, *The Chronicle Vitae*. With Sen. Kirsten Gillibrand (D-NY), she wrote the *Bi-Partisan Campus Safety and Accountability Act*. In 2013, she was listed, alongside President Barack Obama, as one of the most influential forces in higher education.

Rachel Cohen, PhD, is a clinical psychologist who has been in practice for over thirty years. She founded Common Threads in Geneva, Switzerland in 2012. Now based in New York, she is a consultant specializing in psychological support for survivors of sexual violence, especially in conflict-affected regions. She has designed recovery projects in the developing world, training local staff and implementing interventions in Bosnia-Herzegovina, South Sudan, Kenya, Uganda, Ecuador, and Nepal. She earned her doctorate from the University of Michigan in 1986, and a certificate in global mental health from the Harvard Program in Refugee Trauma in 2010.

Robin Dean, PsyD, is a psychoanalyst with the Contemporary Freudian Society (CFS) and a member of the IPA. She is the Faculty Chair for the Washington, DC CFS Institute. She completed a law degree at the University of Texas School of Law, then pursued her psychology degree after a career as an attorney. She is also an Assistant Clinical Professor of Clinical Psychology at The George Washington University. She has a private practice in psychotherapy and psychoanalysis in Washington, DC.

Carla Elliott-Neely, PhD, is a teaching analyst at the Washington Center for Psychoanalysis, trained in child and adult psychoanalysis. She is past President and current Secretary-Elect of the Association for Child Psychoanalysis. She is a consulting psychoanalyst to Jubilee Jumpstart, a Washington, DC daycare and pre-kindergarten program. Her publications include articles on Anna Freud, developmental disharmony, parent loss in childhood, creativity, adolescence, and pre-latency psychopathology, as well as books on sublimation and the collected writings of Hansi Kennedy. She is in private practice in Washington, DC.

Hope Ferdowsian, MD, MPH, FACP, FACPM, is an internist and preventive medicine and public health physician. Her expertise spans the fields of medicine, human rights, animal protection, public health, and ethics. For more than a decade, she has evaluated and cared for survivors of torture and sexual violence. Internationally, she has worked in Sub-Saharan Africa and the Federated States of Micronesia. Domestically, she has worked with non-profit organizations providing health care for underserved populations.

Louis W. Goodman, PhD, is Professor of International Relations and Dean Emeritus of American University's School of International Service. He is a sociologist who has researched and published for decades on social change and economic development, first in Latin America and, more recently, in Asia and Africa. Since his student days, he had understood changing gender roles and the erosion of patriarchy as one of the most promising opportunities for humanity, and that confronting violence against women is central to engagement with this process.

Gail Humphries Mardirosian, PhD, is Dean of the Stephens College School of Performing Arts and Artistic Director of the college's Okoboji Summer Theatre. She is Professor Emeritus at American University in Washington, DC and served as Chair of the Department of

Performing Arts. Her directing credits include over 140 productions in national and international venues. Her new book, entitled *Arts Integration in Education: Teachers and Teaching Artists as Agents of Change*, will be published in 2016 by Intellect Books.

Justine Kalas Reeves, DPsych, is a child, adolescent, and adult psychoanalyst in Washington, DC. She is presently writing about a revision of Anna Freud's diagnostic profile, work with parents of adolescents and young adults in analysis, and work with transgender young adults and adolescents.

Joy Kassett, PhD, is a teaching analyst, Executive Board Member and Clinic Co-Director, Baltimore Washington Center for Psychotherapy and Psychoanalysis. She is also Assistant Clinical Professor of Clinical Psychology, George Washington University Center for Professional Psychology and a member of the clinical faculty, Washington School of Psychiatry, Child and Adolescent Training Program. She maintains a private practice in adult, adolescent, and child psychotherapy and psychoanalysis and provides mental health consultation to community organizations working with underserved families and children in the District of Columbia.

Arlene Kramer Richards, EdD, is a psychoanalyst and a poet. She is a training analyst with the Contemporary Freudian Society and the IPA. She teaches and supervises in Wuhan, China. She writes about female development, perversion, loneliness, and the internal world of artists and poets. Her most recent books are: *Encounters With Loneliness* (co-edited) and *Psychoanalysis: Listening to Understand* (her selected writings). She serves as elected representative to the IPA and practices in New York City.

Moisés Lemlij, MD, DPM, FRC Psych, has been Vice-President and Treasurer of the International Psychoanalytical Association, President of the Peruvian Psychoanalytical Society, Visiting Professor of the Elliot School of International Affairs and of the Guy's London School of Medicine. He has been distinguished with the Mary S. Sigourney's Award for his outstanding contributions to psychoanalysis and the Medal for Exceptional Merits of the Peruvian Medical College. He is the author of *The Tablas of Sarhua: Art, Violence and History in Peru*, and

Cara a cara: Entrevistas Profanas (Face to Face: Profane Interviews), among other books.

Janice S. Lieberman, PhD, is a psychoanalyst in private practice in New York City. She is a training and supervising analyst, and faculty member at IPTAR (Institute for Psychoanalytic Training and Research), where she teaches a course on "The Contemporary Dream". She has served on the Editorial Boards of *JAPA*, the *PANY Bulletin*, and *The American Psychoanalyst*. She chairs an annual discussion group on masculinity at the Winter Meetings of the American Psychoanalytic Association. She has written two books: *The Many Faces of Deceit: Omissions, Lies and Disguise* (with Helen Gediman) (1996), and *Body Talk: Looking and Being Looked at in Psychotherapy* (2000), and has published and presented numerous papers on gender, body narcissism, deception, greed and envy, art and psychoanalysis, loneliness, and the digital age and its effects on relationships.

Maureen Meyer directs WOLA's (Washington Organization for Latin America) Mexico program with a special focus on analyzing US–Mexico security policies and their relation to organized crime-related violence, corruption, and human rights violations in Mexico. She promotes justice for human rights violations in Mexico, including women's rights and migrant rights, and carries out advocacy work regarding US security assistance to Mexico through the Merida Initiative.

E. Ethelbert Miller is a writer and literary activist. He is the author of several collections of poems and two memoirs and serves as a board member for The Community Foundation for the National Capital Region. Miller is an inductee of the 2015 Washington, DC Hall of Fame and recipient of the AWP 2016 George Garrett Award for Outstanding Community Service in Literature and the 2016 DC Mayor's Arts Award for Distinguished Honor. His most recent book is *The Collected Poems of E. Ethelbert Miller*, edited by Kirsten Porter and published by Willow Books.

Vivian Pender, MD, is Clinical Associate Professor of Psychiatry, Weill Cornell Medical College, and Training Analyst, Columbia University Psychoanalytic Center. She chairs the NGO Committee on Mental Health and the UN Committee of the International Psychoanalytical Association. She is the founder of Healthcare Against Trafficking and a research group on Human Trafficking at Weill Cornell. She is editor of a book, *The Status of Women*, published in 2016.

Rosine Jozef Perelberg is a Fellow and Training Analyst of the British Psychoanalytic Society, Visiting Professor in the Psychoanalysis Unit at University College London and Corresponding Member of the Paris Psychoanalytical Society. She has published widely, especially in the *International Journal of Psychoanalysis* and *Revue Française de Psychanalyse*. She edited *Gender and Power in Families* (with Ann Miller, 1990); *Psychoanalytic Understanding of Violence and Suicide* (1997); *Female Experience: Four Generations of British Women Psychoanalysts on Work with Women* (1998, 2008) (with Joan Raphael-Leff); *Freud: A Modern Reader* (2006); *Time and Memory* (2007); *Dreaming and Thinking* (2000); *The Greening of Psychoanalysis* (2017, with Gregorio Kohon); and *Bisexuality: The British–French Colloquium on Sexuality* (forthcoming). She is the author of *Time, Space and Phantasy* (2008), and *Murdered Father, Dead Father: Revisiting the Oedipus Complex* (2015). In 2007 she was named one of the ten women of the year by the Brazilian National Council of Women.

Ana Maria Ramirez, MPH, is a public health researcher who has worked in the area of sexual and reproductive health, HIV and AIDS, and global health. Her research as been primarily qualitative, looking at how the perceptions and experiences of girls during menarche impact their health and education options. She has recently lived in Brazil and worked on issues of HIV and AIDS prevention literacy and access. Her work there will be presented in partnership with the Brazilian organization, ABIA, at the 2016 AIDS conference in Durban, South Africa. Now based in the San Francisco Bay Area, she is a research assistant at Ibis Reproductive Health, specializing in research on stigma and access to abortion services, HIV, and contraception in Latin America, South East Asia, and the USA. She earned her Masters in Public Health from the Columbia University's Mailman School of Public Health with a certificate in global health and received the Award for Excellence in Global Health.

Jack Rasmussen, PhD, is Director and Curator of the American University Museum, a 30,000 square foot exhibition space in the new Katzen Arts Center, dedicated to putting Washington-based art in a global context. He served for ten years as the Executive Director of Maryland Art Place in Baltimore, and three years as Executive Director of di Rosa, a contemporary art museum and natural habitat in Napa, California, Rasmussen currently serves on the Maryland State Arts Council and on the board of the Association of Academic Museums and Galleries.

Diana Romero, an award winning producer and writer, started working in film production in 1996. Several films later, Diana attended the prestigious American Film Institute and earned an MFA in Producing. At AFI, she wrote and produced the award-winning *Niña Quebrada* (2007). The film screened in film festivals and other venues throughout the world. To this day, the film is still screened worldwide. Currently, Diana is in development of the sequel to *Nina Quebrada*: *Chasing Ghosts*.

Katalin Roth, JD, MD, is Associate Professor of Internal Medicine at the George Washington University School of Medicine. She is board-certified in internal medicine, geriatrics, and palliative medicine. Interests include medical ethics, women's health, under-served populations, HIV, international health, and medical humanities. She is currently Director of the GW Division of Geriatrics and Palliative Medicine and a volunteer physician for the Washington Asylum Network and Physicians for Human Rights.

Gertraud Schlesinger-Kipp, PhD, member and training analyst of German Psychoanalytic Association (IPA), is a member and consultant of COWAP since 2002 and organizer and panelist of many COWAP events. Since 2015 she is overall Chair of COWAP. She has published on female development, sexuality, dreams and the unconscious She is past president of Alexander-Mitscherlich-Insitut of Psychoanalysis and Psychotherapy (IPA), past president of German Psychoanalytic Association and past member of the IPA board. Other emphasis of her psychoanalytic work is the psychotherapeutic treatment of transgender, refugees, and research on Children of World War II.

Myra Sklarew, former president of Yaddo Artists Community, Professor Emerita, American University, and founder of the MFA Program in Creative Writing, has published seventeen books, including poetry, fiction, and essays. A forthcoming title, *A Survivor Named Trauma: Holocaust and the Construction of Memory* is to be published by SUNY Press. "Monuments" was performed at the Kennedy Center for the Performing Arts in celebration of the millennium. Recent publications include "Imagine a village," *About Place Journal*; "Scars of last year's leaves," *Beltway Poetry Quarterly*; "My mother and the Golem," *Blue Lyra Review*. Her poetry has twice been recorded for the Library of Congress Contemporary Poet's Series. She was educated at Tufts University, Johns Hopkins University, Cold Spring Harbor Biological Institute, the Radcliffe Institute, and the National Institutes of Health. She recently presented a paper, "The (impossible) reconciliation of time," at Rice University.

Brenda Smith, JD, is a professor at the American University Washington College of Law. Community and Economic Development Law Clinic. She is also the Director of Project on Addressing Prison Rape. Political appointments include the National Prison Rape Elimination Commission and the Advisory Committee on Women's Services for the Substance Abuse and Mental Health Services Administration (SAMHSA). Professor Smith is an expert on issues at the intersection of gender, crime, class, and sexuality. She is widely published and has received numerous awards for her work, including the Emmalee C. Godsey Research Award for her article, "Battering, forgiveness, and redemption", 12 *Am. Un. J. Gender Soc. Pol'y & L. 1*, 921 (2003).

Peter Starr, PhD, joined American University as Dean of the College of Arts and Sciences in July 2009. In this role, he is responsible for 324 full-time faculty in seventeen departments. His primary goals for the college include recruiting and supporting a more research-active and diverse faculty, growing the college's endowment, developing outstanding new curricula in a variety of fields, and building bridges to partner organizations in the district and around the globe. Before coming to AU, Dean Starr was a professor of French and Comparative Literature at the University of Southern California.

SERIES EDITOR'S FOREWORD

Frances Thomson-Salo

I am very pleased, both as Series Editor and former overall Chair of the International Psychoanalytical Association's Committee on Women and Psychoanalysis (COWAP), to write this Foreword in the growing series of Psychoanalysis and Women. Otto Kernberg, when he was President of the IPA, set up COWAP in 1998 with Joan Raphael-Leff as foundational chair to explore scientific and political issues about women and men; and a hallmark of COWAP has always been a willingness to engage with other organizations. On behalf of COWAP and its wider community, we are grateful to Paula L. Ellman and Nancy R. Goodman for their thoughtful and unstinting hard work in enabling this book to come to fruition.

The chapters in this very important book represent enormous breadth as well as an enormous amount of work. The powerful writing is often very painful, partly in trying to make meaningful something that from the outside seems almost at times to have lost touch with what is sane and real.

The commentaries or introductions act to form a holding for the reader in the face of so much violence.

All those who have been violated need a rapid response so that early results of shame do not have to be enduringly activated, to assist healing and develop resilience; mothers and carers of children, to counteract transgenerational transmission of this.

The book offers a tumultuous experience of scientific interest, covering worldwide issues, particularly currently, but also long ago to cast an additional illuminating perspective on them.

I am proud on behalf of the IPA to have supported Paula Ellman and Nancy Goodman in organizing the conference and the book.

Frances Thomson-Salo
Series Editor for Psychoanalysis and Women series

PREFACE

Gertraud Schlesinger-Kipp

COWAP was established in 1998 by the IPA to provide a framework for the exploration of topics related to issues primarily about women. In 2001, it shifted to the relations between women and men, masculinity and femininity (and others) because in this world we all are interconnected and, as we learn more and more, it is not possible to see the individual—be it woman, man, or child—just by itself.

Our approach is theoretical and clinical psychoanalysis, and we emphasize also the socio-cultural viewpoint. Therefore, we listen to psychoanalysts, medical doctors, artists, film makers, poets, and sociologists from all over the world.

I come from Germany and the topic of violence against women is, at the moment, in a very sad and tragic state at the center of our attention. After the disclosure of the enormous and terrifying abuse of children in Catholic residential schools and in alternative reformative boarding schools, the sexual attacks on, and harassment of, women and girls came to be known to the public. Currently, the government is creating a new, stronger laws concerning sexual violence and attacks.

In our free and democratic republic of Germany, women and men have equal rights and equal obligation to stand for the perseveration of the basic democratic law. It is the duty of civil societies to guarantee that women and girls can feel secure from violence wherever they are. This is, sadly, not always the case, wherever the perpetrators come from or whoever they are.

Some attacks are grist to the mill of right-wing people in Germany who never before served as fighters for the rights of women. We are tempted to place under suspicion all people who now live as migrants among us and who, at the moment, are seeking shelter in great numbers. Many of them are fleeing this exact violence in their home countries.

In my psychotherapeutic approach in the refugee camps, I see many women seeking asylum for gender reasons, many of them traumatized in their home countries or during the flight from home. However, the men also often have terrible traumas and are even exposed to violence in Germany from right-wing people and are not at all safe.

Therefore, I am very much interested in papers presented here from the remarkable COWAP Conference held in Washington in 2016, and I am very grateful to COWAP North America for having chosen this subject.

Opening words by the sponsors of the conference "The Courage to Fight Violence Against Women"

Alexandra Billinghurst, Jack Rasmussen, Peter Starr, and Cecile Bassen

The conference at which the papers that comprise this book were presented began with words of introductory welcome from its several sponsors, and we felt that as the book was made possible by the conference, those words should be included here, since they are equally apposite to this volume.

Alexandra Billinghurst, of the International Psychoanalytical Association, welcomed the participants with the following comments.

"COWAP is one of the most productive committees of the IPA, engaging the psychoanalytic community in addressing gender-related topics, through scientific meetings and constructive dialogue.

"The focus here is on violence against women, which, unfortunately, remains a universal and seemingly intractable challenge. As a representative of the IPA, I insist that it is important that we as an organization stand up for the equal value of every individual, fighting oppression and the fear of "the other" in all its shapes and forms. We must never cease working to understand underlying causes of violence, both from an individual and a societal perspective.

"As vice president of the IPA, I am responsible for the International New Groups committee, which supports individuals and groups working to form psychoanalytic societies in places where none yet exists. We are currently putting a substantial focus on organizational issues, helping to foster democratic organizations and to understand group dynamics. However, democracy is not a given: it is not enough to put in place the constitutional framework, it is something you have always to have your eyes on and strive for—just as you have to keep the ethical thinking alive. Living the equal rights for all, both on a governmental level and in our daily life as individuals, is of central importance.

"I once read about an experiment conducted in an elevator, where abuse against a woman was staged by a young man. It began with ordinary quarrelling, escalating to verbal and then physical abuse, which only one bystander acted to stop. I was shocked by this result. We must not only deal with the abusers, but also understand the mechanisms behind people turning away when they witness a violent confrontation.

"A prominent psychoanalyst in my mother society, Sweden, the late Ludvig Igra (2001), wrote of 'the thin membrane between care and cruelty', in which he points to the schizo–paranoid and the depressive position, which he chose to call the distinguishing and integrative positions. As we know, for babies, the dependence on the caregiver is a matter of life and death, making it crucial to be able to distinguish the hostile and dangerous from the enriching and good.

"Igra posited that an ethical stance is born in the integrative position, which can be seen as the wellspring of ethics. That is, the ethical stance within us is formed in the striving for caring for—and taking responsibility for—'the other'. This striving has no other aim than respect for this 'other' and her inviolability and integrity.

"He writes that the thin membrane is a border region where man's psychic creation continuously takes place. You can see it as a door in the area between the destructive and the life promoting within us. Depending on the situation, it may be opened in different directions. We have to keep being aware, to be reminded of the issues, to remain empathic and ethical. In the schizo–paranoid position, the world is divided into good and bad, bringing a sense of security in that evil is placed in 'the other' because it is not bearable within the individual. When anxiety becomes unbearable, any of us can enter the position where the world is divided and, thus, easy to understand.

"Brutality aimed at women and children can be seen from an individual as well as group and societal perspective. I want to stress the importance of the latter, and the responsibility of the individual to react and counteract destructive, paranoid, and vengeful tendencies. Society and its institutions can have the role of containing these primitive tendencies in individuals as well as groups, but it can also have the opposite effect. As psychoanalysts and psychoanalytic psychotherapists, I believe we have a responsibility to guard, understand, and spotlight tendencies in society, just as we, in our best moments in the consulting room, help the individual to become aware of, and withdraw, his projections.

"Violence towards women and children is not new, but the societal climate we are living in at the moment seems again to turn to schizo-paranoid splitting in a new 'wave', spurred by an economic philosophy of individual primacy that pushes solidarity with those in need to the back of the queue.

"The need to define oneself as part of a group is a universal drive. The greater the strain on the group—or the individual—the greater becomes the need to define clear borders around the group.

"Bion (1970) spoke of containment in relationships with both groups and individuals. A way to define this at the individual level is the ability (or lack thereof) to take in and give meaning to that which is contained.

"With new technologies bringing ever-faster delivery of news from around the globe, we are virtually forced to take in more information about topics over which we have no power of control. It might well be that this stream of information puts more strain on the individual's ability to contain, increasing the need to build conceptual walls around the group or nation and inflaming the tendency to find fault in 'the other'.

"Igra (2001) did not see sexual violence by men as a product of uninhibited male sexuality, writing that

> Male *genital* expressions are not characterised by more violence than those of females. It is not a *phallic* element in male sexuality that in itself is disastrous. As I see it the problem is not that the genitally based male love possesses powerful and penetrating qualities . . . An interesting aspect of sexualized violence seems to me rather to be that male genital sexuality in our culture, more easily than the female, lets itself be imbued with anal–sadistic forms of expression. The reason for this surely has to do with the fact that men have long dominated societally sanctioned violence. For a long time, men have practically been

in sole possession of the roles of warrior, judge, and police. The code of power has literally incorporated images of male genitalia. This means that male genitalia have been woven into the symbolic world of violence and power, not the other way around. It is, therefore, not strange that the penis, under those circumstances, has come to be used to exercise power, instill fear, and desecrate. (pp. 150–151, translated for this edition)

"When fear and violence, wall-building and oppression dominate our daily reality to such a large extent, acts by individuals and groups that show and inspire empathy and compassion can, in and of themselves, be understood as active containment in the Bionian meaning.

"This Conference [and the book], the contributions within it, and the examples of projects which, in different ways, deal with the abuse and violations of women, is in itself part of a necessary movement to keep aware and alive."

Jack Rasmussen, of the American University Katzen Center for the Arts, offered these welcoming words.

"While we were hosting your important and powerful conference, 'The courage to fight violence against women', we asked the participants to take an hour (well, fifty minutes) to walk through the museum and experience the fifty women artists who were exhibiting then in the American University Museum. The artists ranged in age from twenty-nine to ninety-nine; they were African-American, Asian-American, Latin American, Hispanic American, and European American. While the artists have strong individual voices, I believe I could feel the crackle and hum of psychic energy coming off of all those voices lifted together. There was struggle depicted in the museum . . . and great courage and great beauty. There was superstition (to which we all subscribe to varying degrees) and emotional intelligence (to which we all aspire). The museum offered a very positive experience—one you could take home with you when your fifty minutes are up. Our exhibition was perfectly complemented by your gathering of the psychoanalytic community from across the world doing the hard work of healing!"

Peter Starr, of the American University, then made the following contribution.

"On behalf of my American University colleagues, welcome to the 'The courage to fight violence against women' conference. We at

American University take particular pride in contributing to debate on the great issues of our time, both domestic and international.

"This topic resonates for me personally in a number of ways. As a scholar, I have written for decades on the cultural afterlife of traumatic events and have thought long and hard about the potential of psychoanalysis to empower women. As a husband, I have watched proudly as my wife founded the Blue Campaign against human trafficking, at the Department of Homeland Security just across the street. As a dean, I have long admired my colleagues' commitment to telling the untold stories of women subject to violence, beginning with the work of the AU Museum, a partner to the conference. At a moment in American history, however, when a presidential candidate [now the President of the USA] can insinuate that a respected journalist and debate moderator asked hard questions of him simply because she was menstruating, the commitment to fight violence against women should—indeed, must—resonate for us all.

"Many thanks and congratulations to Paula Ellman and Nancy Goodman for their stellar leadership in organizing conference and to you all for your many contributions to it!"

This was followed by the contribution of **Cecile Bassen**, of the Committee of Women and Psychoanalysis of the IPA.

"I'm delighted to be part of COWAP, the Committee on Women and Psychoanalysis, which was established by the IPA in 1998. Our mandate is to provide a framework for the exploration of issues of concern to women and to men, including exploration of the relationship between men and women. COWAP encourages and supports local, national, and international study groups, organizes theoretical and clinical conferences on issues of social relevance, and fosters the publication of psychoanalytic papers related to gender. This conference is an excellent example of what COWAP was designed to do, to bring together interdisciplinary colleagues from around the world to explore the issue of violence against women.

"I especially want to thank Paula Ellman, who serves on COWAP with me, and who, with Nancy Goodman, initiated the planning for the book [of the conference] and made sure it came together every step of the way.

"The results of the most recent World Values Survey were released in 2015, based on polls conducted from 2010–2014 (see www.world-valuessurvey.org/wvs.jsp). At least one third of men in thirty-one of sixty countries surveyed said that it is sometimes acceptable for a husband to beat his wife, and at least one third of women in twenty countries agreed with them. Approximately two thirds of women in South Africa endorsed this point of view, along with 96% of Rwandan women, one third of women in India, one out of five women in Germany, and one out of ten women in the United States! Yet, the same survey also found that women's attitudes in some countries have changed dramatically over the past ten years, with a marked decrease in the number of women seeing spousal abuse as justified in Nigeria, Benin, and Haiti. Conferences like this one are critical to improving our understanding of the beliefs that underlie these findings, and our understanding of what we can do to facilitate intrapsychic and cultural change.

A common theme that emerges is the critical importance of speaking out about violence against women in all of its different manifestations, in the face of widespread reluctance to recognize the seriousness of this issue. I am prompted to reflect on our innate tendency to resist being aware of disturbing information, and this inspired me to write a blog post titled "Why don't we speak up about sexual assault?" for the American Psychoanalytic Association website (www.apsa.org/content/blog-why-don't-we-speak-about-sexual-assault).

"As I noted in this post, awareness allows us to focus on decreasing the frequency of assault, protecting potential victims, supporting those who have been assaulted, and helping them heal. However, we often need to fight our reluctance to know in order to become aware of disturbing information. I hope that this conference [and the book that will follow] will inspire all of us to join the contributors in confronting our own barriers to awareness of violence against women."

References

Bion, W. R. (1970). *Attention and Interpretation.* London: Tavistock.
Igra, L. (2001). *Den tunna hinnan mellan omsorg och grymhet.* Stockholm: Natur och Kultur.

INTRODUCTION

The courage to fight violence against women

Paula L. Ellman and Nancy R. Goodman

The International Psychoanalytical Association Committee on Women and Psychoanalysis co-sponsored a Conference, "The courage to fight violence against women" March 3–4, 2016 at the American University Katzen Center for the Arts and sponsors a book series with Karnac Books, the publisher of this COWAP Book. When Paula Ellman was invited by the North American Co-Chair, Cecile Bassen, to join the IPA Committee on Women and Psychoanalysis as a North American member, she understood the expectation of a COWAP Committee Member is to plan a conference and to write on topics relevant to women and gender issues. She invited her colleague, Dr. Nancy Goodman, to join her to carry forward a vision bringing psychoanalysis into an exchange with other disciplines[1]: social policy, human rights, humanitarian work, medicine, law, history and the arts: film, poetry, theatre, sculpture and painting. Together we embarked into the area of "the courage to fight violence against women" that painfully continues as a major global problem. The multiple disciplines have much to offer each other in exploration and understanding, and in moving forward our efforts to effect a change in this problem.

All contributors to this book also presented at our March 2016 Conference and demonstrate the courage to fight violence against women as they craft their thoughts and reflections from their courageous work. Facing this topic demands courage. Contributors write chapters that are disturbing as their traumatic stories are transmitted. Opening our eyes and minds to violence in its many forms pushes through customary ways of denial and disavowal that protect us from knowing troubling truths. Only with knowing does effecting change become possible. Only with seeing and knowing, can we admit the existence of the problem and begin to find a way to make a difference. We encourage you, the reader, to find the courage to open yourselves to be immersed in the varied topics of our contributors and be inspired by them.

* * *

Painful traumatic events concerning violence against women around the world served as the catalyst for this edited volume addressing the global problem of victimization of women. Horrific national and international events captured our attention, leading us to develop a volume of multi-disciplinary and globally represented chapter contributors. Our collaborative effort brings together a rich array of courageous contributors with a wide range of foci on the terrible truths of violence.

Throughout this book there is an interweaving of psychoanalytic thinking with chapters involving activism at home and abroad, in which scholars, psychoanalysts, artists, and medical doctors gather information, intervene, and represent the traumatic information about violence against women. Authors are from Argentina, Germany, Mexico, Peru, Sweden, the UK, and the East and West Coasts of the USA and together address the many aspects of the courage to know violence against women on the world stage.

It is almost impossible to listen to stories of traumatic violence taking place for individual women and communities of women in our contemporary world. Psychoanalytic concepts about identification with the aggressor, trauma, shame, witnessing, and resilience help to open space for the courage to represent, and symbolize, the existence of rape, trafficking, femicide, and all heinous hate crimes against women. Unconscious fantasies about the dangers of the female body and envy of the procreative power of women, when mixed with phallocentric societies, can potentiate violence against women. Psychoanalysis helps to identify the power of the unconscious and interrupt the influence of unconscious scripts (Ellman & Goodman, 2017). Here, we understand how to create resilience and an internal witness to begin healing and to break cycles of repetition. The presence of active witnesses, such as the authors in this book, counters the silent force of passive bystanders harboring disregard for acts of violence against women.

Since the initiation of this collaborative effort, discussions of violence against women has moved to the center of the political scene in the USA as two presidential candidates starkly represented the issue. One candidate [now the President of the USA] has exposed his history of using language suggestive of sexual aggressions against women; the second was the first woman presidential candidate in the history of the United States. Crucial now is the consideration for the courage to fight violence against women that is necessary to steer towards a future of human dignity and respect. We observe in the discussions and activism today, as in the international Women's March the day following the US presidential inauguration (1/20/2017), that there is public recognition of violence against women and the need for attention to women's rights.

The effort to bring attention and understanding to this rampant problem is moved forward with the diverse voices in this book. This book includes presentations on sex trafficking, sexual assaults on college campuses, and the rampant rape of incarcerated women. Vivian Pender, in her chapter on sex trafficking, presents the statistics and prevalence both nationally and internationally and describes the depth of pain experienced by victims whom she has interviewed. Margarita Cereijido writes a commentary on Pender's chapter on sex trafficking and provides a psychoanalytic and developmental commentary on it in her own chapter. Annie Clark describes the development of EROC ("End Rape On Campus") in response to female coeds feeling there was no way to receive recognition of the violence of rapes taking place at universities. In her commentary on this chapter, Joy Kassett focuses on the making of the film, *The Hunting Ground*, by Annie Clark and Andrea Pino, in which they speak of their courage in receiving rape stories from others and in organizing support and activism on university campuses. Identifications with the perpetrators are broken through containment and alliances.

Paula Ellman introduces Brenda Smith's powerful depiction of the nature of abuse of women in custody in our prisons. Smith makes a compelling corollary to the history of women slaves on plantations and describes her legal research on the rape of women prisoners. Chapters by physicians address their medical work with refugees in camps and with asylum seekers who were victims of violence, including sex trafficking, rape, and genital mutilation.

Maureen Meyer, an activist and policy-maker, reports on her work in combatting rampant femicide in Mexico. She describes the particular terror, helplessness, and rage at having these young women disappear through the deliberate killing of women. Hope Ferdowsian, in her international work providing medical care to underserved areas, describes the violence against women in areas of conflict and unrest. Katalin Roth writes about her medical examinations of women seeking asylum. Here, she frequently evaluates instances of rape, genital mutilation, and forced sexual submission. Louis Goodman comments on the chapters of Meyer, Ferdowsian and Roth, stressing their courage in addressing global situations of violence, and offers analysis of societal influences.

Paula Ellman writes on the importance that unconscious fantasy brings to understanding and fighting violence against women. Psychoanalytic insight facilitates the containment of horrors and trauma, understands ways to interrupt identification with the aggressor, and works to transform shame into courage.

Nancy Goodman discusses the process of witnessing that recognizes the traumatic and brings about resilience. She speaks of the horrific impact of physical rape and of "psychic rape" when there are passive bystanders; that is, when no one acknowledges or cares about the violence of body and mind taking place.

Psychoanalysis and community work come together in a variety of projects in underserved communities. On the Yucatan Peninsula, Raquel Berman and colleagues work with young professionals traumatized through their ongoing interventions with adolescent and latency-aged female victims of rape, childhood marriage, early pregnancies, and abuse. Her chapter presents the utility of applying psychoanalytic understanding to promoting growth of young women who were victimized in Quintano-Roo.

A powerful effort at promoting a process of healing by symbolizing trauma is demonstrated in the chapter by Rachel Cohen and Ana Maria Ramirez. Women victims are invited to weave story-cloths, bringing community bonding, narrative, and symbolization to processing unnamed trauma. Cohen's research demonstrates the lessening of clinical symptomatology from the participation in sewing circles where symbolization and trust are actualized.

Carla Neely offers a commentary on the chapters by Raquel Berman, and Rachel Cohen and Ana Maria Ramirez, using ideas about human development and culture.

Janice Lieberman delves into the way paintings and sculpture, both classical and contemporary, provide representations of violence against women. Moisés Lemlij shows the sensuality and sexuality of women appearing in pre-Colombian Andean ceramics. Both chapters bring about a deepening understanding of how art mirrors cultural phenomena and psychology, both currently and historically.

Filmmakers, poets, and a playwright's musical docudrama provide further artistic exploration, demonstrating courage to represent, know, and fight violence against women. In the film, *Nina Quebrada* (Broken Girl), an adolescent girl is betrayed by her boyfriend, imprisoned in a brothel, and comes close to being defeated by shame and helplessness. Transforming shame into courage, she breaks out and reunites with her family. Psychoanalytic understanding of ruptured object relations and reparation is dramatically demonstrated. The film-maker, Diana Romero, writes of her intent to bring the reality of sex trafficking to awareness as a demonstration of her own courage to fight violence against women.

E. Ethelbert Miller's poems are introduced by Louis Goodman and present raw depiction of violence. Myra Sklarew, introduced by Nancy Goodman, faces directly the violation of rape. Poetry brings closeness to affect and experience with courage. Robin Dean introduces and comments on the chapter by Gail Humphries Mardirosian. Mardirosian writes about her musical docudrama of the resilience of three women Holocaust survivors who courageously persisted in creating art. She presents descriptions of the lyrics and script along with results from her study of audience responses to the theatrical portrayal of "Traces in the wind".

Donald Campbell's chapter examines the background of psychoanalytic understanding of child development, separations from mother, and thoughts about sadomasochism. In this chapter, Campbell presents the psychoanalytic treatment of a man showing "ruthless rage" toward women. Fortunately, this man was frightened by his own rage and the analytic work demonstrates the process of finding early experience and its vicissitudes. Justine Kalas Reeves contributes a commentary on Campbell's chapter.

Rosine Perelberg also writes a clinical chapter on the presence of a terrifying "maternal imago" that appears in this analysis of a woman by a woman analyst. Psychoanalysts consider the place of unconscious fantasy in the traumatized mind. In her commentary, Arlene Kramer Richards writes of the unconscious fantasies in men and women about the all-powerful mother, and fears of needing mother and feeling shame at the experience of the infantile.

This book, with its immense creativity, brings together both internal psychic realities with harsh external realities. The editors want psychoanalysis to meet the traumas of violence in scholarship, activism, and the arts, and to highlight the courage it takes to know, confront, and fight the horror of violence. We also want scholarship in other fields of study to inform psychoanalytic efforts to understand human motivation for destructiveness and motivations for courage.

Note

1. We formed collaboration amongst the three DC-based IPA affiliated Psychoanalytic Societies (The Contemporary Freudian Society, The Baltimore Washington Center for Psychotherapy and Psychoanalysis and The Washington Center for Psychoanalysis) along with COWAP and The American University's Katzen Arts Center.

Reference

Ellman, P., & Goodman, N. (2017). *Finding Unconscious Fantasy in Narrative, Trauma and Body Pain: A Clinical Guide*. London: Routledge.

CHAPTER ONE

Unconscious fantasy and the courage to fight violence against women

Paula L. Ellman

The discourse of this book among psychoanalysts, scholars, artists, and activists locates us at a border territory where consideration of unconscious fantasy *and* conscious realities are both essential. Launching this effort, our Book and original Conference on "The Courage to Fight Violence against Women" is one of the rare opportunities for psychoanalysis to move beyond the consulting room and into an exchange with an array of relevant disciplines of thought and professions. We aim for positions of both receptivity and generativity. We wish to bring our areas of expertise to the fore, and at the same time to welcome perspectives that are initially unfamiliar to us. This exchange offers us ways to enrich our knowledge and our work in this effort to find courage to fight violence against women. The challenge is how to bring the resources of psychoanalysis into our effort to understand an area where reality has gone awry. I begin by relating an experience that illuminates the challenge of bridging attention to the realities of destructive violence with attention to unconscious psychic processes. Attending a recent scientific meeting, where I presented on aspects of sadomasochism in the psychoanalytic treatment process, was an early career psychology postdoctoral student from a university counseling center. At the conclusion of the program, she approached me to tell me about her work facilitating a group of female college students at her counseling center *all* of whom had been sexually assaulted on campus. She expressed her struggle to integrate the content of that day's scientific program with her work with this group of students. She wished to work with her group on the place of the unconscious in their minds, but feared the group experiencing her as possibly "blaming the victim" and effecting an enactment of shutting down their coming to know the place of assault in their minds. Her dilemma underscores the need to clarify that the process of working to understand the unconscious does not involve the imagined blaming of the victim. Conversely, efforts to bring light to unconscious processes enable understanding the meaning of assault so as to protect from repetition compulsion and open possibilities to turn passive hurt into active healing.

Understanding the mind becomes the utmost challenge when horrors occur. We are drawn to want to take action in response to action. When in a position of helplessness, taking action can often appear to be the way to find freedom from paralysis and to feel empowered to effect change. We search for ways to link with others for the purpose of empowerment so that we may inform and act with the hope of creating and constructing the means to fight violence. Also, examining the mind in times of violence is crucial. Active reflection must accompany taking action. In reflection, we come close to our personal troubling affective experiences. In our efforts to understand the psyche, there might be temptations to blame the victim in order to disavow the violence and even repeat the trauma as a perverse attempt at mastery (Ellman & Goodman, 2012). Instead, bringing an understanding to the victim's compulsion to repeat trauma, often their attempt at mastery, can interrupt the repetitive trauma-filled cycle. Efforts to understand unconscious processes serve to open pathways to knowing the nature of trauma repetition. The process of knowing can be the turning into active what has previously been experienced as painfully helplessly passive.

This healing and transformative work requires a witness. Creating a witnessing community serves as a foundation for the working through of trauma. Psychoanalysis informs that bearing witness to the narrative of the traumatized victim supports mastery (Goodman, 2012). The witnessing process both affirms the horror and accompanies in the aloneness of victimization, supporting the development of courage and resilience as an antidote to prior helplessness. In witnessing violence against women, psychoanalysts and activists vicariously experience the horror of both victim and perpetrator. Because of our own unconscious fantasies, witnessing brings vulnerability to identifying with either victim or perpetrator and fending off the alternative identifications. Crucial to our working with victim or perpetrator is retaining the understanding that sadomasochistic fantasies carry both sides of the sadomasochistic relationship, even though one side is expressed and the other side is repressed, disavowed and/or projected (Basseches et al., 2013). The excruciating challenge of serving as a witness to the perpetrator's experience is that here the sadomasochism, fueled by a fantasy of omnipotence and conquest, transforms internal fantasy into the actual assault. Violations of boundaries become a liability. The courage to witness and examine the mind allows for opportunities to differentiate fantasy from reality, to heal psychic helplessness, to interrupt repetition compulsions and destructive identifications with aggressors, and to ameliorate the constriction of denial, making space for the possibilities of complex thinking and creative growth (Ellman & Goodman, 2017).

This volume is an opportunity to create bridges between those who inform and take action, and those who work to understand the forces in the psyche. Both forms of addressing the horror of violence against women are crucial, and opening communication between these two very different modes of work furthers understanding and efforts to bring change. Central to both forms of addressing the horror is the place of the witness. Whether in the form of a community outreach project in countries where women are abused, or working with incarcerated women who have suffered sexual abuse, or organizing activists on college campuses where college students have been raped, whether it is medically evaluating women for female genital mutilation (FGM) or domestic abuse, or assessing circumstance of cultural femicide in Mexico, whether it is clinical work with patients in our offices that are sex-trafficked, or those that are perpetrators of violence, all forms of work demand the position of serving as witness. One must endure the empathic identifications of the pain. The trial identifications that are often with the victim are excruciating. Yet, the witnessing process enables the victim to find or create their internal identifications of strength that offer a way forward from helplessness and aloneness.

Psychoanalytic understanding of violent abuse informs that the roles of victim and perpetrator are not necessarily fixed positions and can be fluid. The perpetrator has been a victim, or can become a victim, and the victim may have been or can become the perpetrator in order to find empowerment and revenge. When there is an early history of abuse where control of pain is taken away and pain becomes too much to bear, attachment to the perpetrator of pain is a liability, even a likelihood (Bach, 2002). Unconscious fantasy life incorporates the early attachments to objects of pain into scenarios, into narratives, that become psychic scripts.

> "... Unconscious fantasy compromises ... coalesce around internal representations of a relationship where someone is hurting and dominating the other with the correlate of someone being hurt and dominated—a coupling that can easily reverse ..." (Basseches et al., 2013, p. 22).

I am reminded of a female patient, Ms. M., who suffered horrific psychological and physical abuse in her early life family. Her adult body is constantly in a state of rupture; her experience of a self is a body that is racked with pain and has no way out of the torture. The unconscious psychic narrative of abuser and abused pervades the analytic relationship, capturing me—the analyst—in an interminable cycle, moving between the position of feeling beaten down and the tortuous place of being an abuser. Ms. M. cannot depart from her early attachments to pain with me or any other.

Freud (1905d) states, "A sadist is always at the same time a masochist" (p. 159). However, the *fantasy* of painful relatedness that is embedded in the early life attachment does not necessarily have to translate into actually dehumanizing the object and robbing the ownership of one's body. Both the male *and* the female internally carry the early relationship in the form of unconscious fantasy. The attachment to the mother of pain (the "mother of pain" being the earliest of relationships that are carried in the unconscious mind) is embedded in the psyche. The mother who hates herself, was hated by her mother, is hateful of her mother, conveys to her child an attachment in the unconscious fantasy of acceptance of the attack on the female. When early attachments include pain, or there is pain in the attachment to the self-hating or hateful mother or father, the unconscious script involves identifying with the hated or hating person and pain is libidinized. ". . . [T]he sadomasochistic object relationship . . . [is] . . . in the service of maintaining the tie to the early mother . . ." (Basseches et al., 2013, p. 29). The presence of the unconscious fantasy of painful attachment in the male or female, victim or perpetrator position, makes for the ongoing potentiality of breakdown in the fantasy becoming realized and enacted (Ellman & Goodman, 2012).

While the early life relationship of pain might be one source for development of the unconscious fantasy of violence against women, the woman as creator, with the power to give or withhold life, can stir terror in the son and daughter (Chasseguet-Smirgel, 1993; Lax, 1997; Notman, 2003; Richards, 2015). The woman as a sexual being capable of sexual pleasure can be frightening, such that female genital mutilation (FGM) or rape become ways to subdue the frightful unconscious fantasy (Richards, this volume). Childhood marriages, rape, and sex trafficking invite participation from both men and women as perpetrators where the unconscious fantasy of dominating and degrading the powerful terrifying maternal object is enacted (Perelberg, this volume). In this way, movement from the place of powerless helplessness transitions into a position of violent destructive omnipotence.

Klein's emphasis is on the relationship between the infant and the maternal body in her exploration of hateful destructive envy of the mother. She describes the little girl's earliest anxiety of "having the inside of her body robbed and destroyed", as she believes her mother's body contains everything that is desirable, including the father's penis (1930, 1932). As a consequence, the little girl is filled with hatred towards her mother, and enviously wishes to attack and rob the inside of her body. As unconscious fantasy rooted in hateful early attachments can lead to enactments of violence against women, it is incumbent on us as psychoanalysts to bring our understanding of the place of unconscious fantasy in the psyche to effect change (Joseph, 1985).

We can appreciate that the psyche that has been traumatized often looks to master the trauma with unconscious motivations to repeat trauma. Also, an important unconscious effort the psyche makes to overcome the traumatized place of helplessness and humiliation is often by developing unconscious fantasies of identifying with and becoming the perpetrator, and aggressing against the self or the other. Unconscious fantasies can include pleasure in the mastery of the pain.

Crucial to addressing the problem of violence against women is to allow this idea, without judgment, and, at the same time, to carry the conviction that robbing anyone of the authority over their body integrity is profoundly unacceptable. Psychoanalysis affords us the understanding of unconscious fantasy (Arlow, 1969; Ellman & Goodman, 2017; Freud, 1896; Isaacs, 1938; Klein, 1930, 1932; Laplanche & Pontalis, 1973). Freud (1916) wrote "If hysterics refer their symptoms to imaginary traumas, then this new fact signifies that they create such scenes in their phantasies, and hence psychic reality deserves to be given a place next to actual reality" (p. 414). In our consulting rooms our attention is on the psychic realities of our patients. This is the arena for the work of psychoanalysis. We want to promote the development of internal strengths that can displace the fantasies heightening a woman's vulnerability to perpetrators of all kinds. We want to curtail the unconscious fantasies in the perpetrator that can lead to attacks on the degraded object. Psychoanalysis grants us the perspective to understand the traumatic impact on the victim of violence and the vulnerabilities to becoming a perpetrator of violence. Through the psychoanalytic process of finding unconscious fantasy, the reverberations of unconscious fantasy in the mind, we initiate the therapeutic action of creating new, more adaptive, life-giving internal scripts (Ellman & Goodman, 2017; Richards, 2017). Above all, we must represent our stalwart belief in human rights, the right of every human being for their body to be their own and for their mind to be understood and embraced.

This edited book is an exchange of many diverse approaches to the problem of finding courage to fight violence against women: art, poetry, dramatic representations, and psychoanalysis and humanitarian work. There is the courage of women who talk about their abuse, and the courage of women and men who listen to the stories of abuse and tolerate the vicarious experience of both victim and perpetrator in order to help. There is also the courage demanded of our readers to know the stories. Courage is warranted in these many dimensions. We must recognize the reverberations of violence in victim, perpetrator, helper, and witness through the medium of unconscious fantasy.

References

Arlow, J. (1969). Fantasy, memory and reality testing. *Psychoanalytic Quarterly*, *38*: 28–51.

Bach, S. (2002). Sadomasochism in clinical practice and everyday life. *Journal of Clinical Psychoanalysis*, *11*: 225–235.

Basseches, H. B., Ellman, P. L., & Goodman, N. R. (2013). *Battling the Life and Death Forces of Sadomasochism: Clinical Perspectives*. London: Karnac.

Chasseguet-Smirgel, J. (1993). Women's social status as a reflection of the internal relationship to mother and father in both sexes. *International Forum of Psychoanalysis*, *2*: 24–29.

Ellman, P., & Goodman, N. (2012). Enactment: opportunity for symbolizing trauma. In: A. Frosch (Ed.), *Absolute Truth and Unbearable Psychic Pain: Psychoanalytic Perspectives on Concrete Experience* (pp. 57–72). London: Karnac.

Ellman, P., & Goodman, N. (Eds.) (2017). *Finding Unconscious Fantasy in Narrative, Trauma and Body Pain: A Clinical Guide*. London: Routledge.

Freud, S. (1896). Further remarks on the neuro-psychoses of defense. *S. E.*, *3*: 159–224. London: Hogarth.

Freud, S. (1905d). *Three Essays on the Theory of Sexuality. S. E.*, *7*: 133–246. London: Hogarth.

Freud, S. (1916). The history of the psychoanalytic movement. *Psychoanalytic Review*, *3*: 406–454.

Goodman, N. R. (2012). The power of witnessing. In: N. R. Goodman & M. Meyers (Eds.), *The Power of Witnessing: Reflections, Reverberations, and Traces of the Holocaust—Trauma, Psychoanalysis, and the Living Mind* (pp. 3–26). New York: Routledge.

Isaacs, S. (1938). The nature and function of phantasy. *International Journal Psychoanalysis*, *29*: 72–97.

Joseph, B. (1985). Transference: the total situation. *International Journal of Psychoanalysis*, *66*: 447–454.

Klein, M. (1930). The importance of symbol formation in the development of the ego. *International Journal of Psychoanalysis*, *11*: 24–39.

Klein, M. (1932). *The Psycho-analysis of Children. The International Psycho-Analytical Library*, *22*: 1–397.

Laplanche, J., & Pontalis, J.-B. (1973). *The Language of Psycho-Analysis*, D. Nicolson-Smith (Trans.). London: Hogarth Press and the Institute of Psycho-Analysis.

Lax, R. (1997). Boys' envy of mother and the consequences of this narcissistic mortification. *Psychoanalytic Study of the Child*, 52: 188–139.
Notman, M. (2003). The female body and its meanings. *Psychoanalytic Inquiry*, 23: 572–591.
Richards, A. K. (2015). *Myths of Mighty Women: Their Application for Psychoanalytic Psychotherapy*. London: Karnac.
Richards, A. K. (2017). Discussion of unconscious fantasy. In: P. Ellman & N. Goodman (Eds.), *Finding Unconscious Fantasy in Narrative, Trauma and Body Pain: A Clinical Guide* (pp. 227–229). London: Routledge.

CHAPTER TWO

Witnessing and resilience: commentary on being involved in "The courage to fight violence against women"

Nancy R. Goodman

For the title of this book, we emphasize *courage*, not being a victim. As psychoanalysts, we know the ravages and despair that violence brings to individuals, families, and communities when women are denigrated and abused. Acts of violence invade the psyche, creating helplessness and fear. We also know the courage it takes to speak of trauma in order to find one's resilience and help others turn shame into pride. This is what takes place in psychoanalytic treatments and this is what we bring to others through the courageous chapters in this book. Receptiveness to the terror of survivors of incidents of violence described here helps titrate loneliness through the formation of a bond between all of us.

Witnessing

The worst wounding, when there is violence, is when no one recognizes it or calls it what it is. An extra layer of damage takes root when no one says, "This is wrong, you do not have to feel ashamed and alone. I see what has happened. I recognize it and will fight so it will not happen again." Active witnessing and the development of resilience go together. It is the power of witnessing that begins to bring light to the darkness of unrecognized trauma (Goodman, 2012). Sometimes, the leader is the brave woman who wants others to know and she speaks out. She creates the secondary witness, widening a pathway for resilience. It is often the second witness, the one saying, "I want to know," who opens the possibility of feeling human once again. The scholars, psychoanalysts, activists, and artists writing in this book instill a healing process with their determination, creativity, and interventions. Once telling and receiving all of the forms of unbearable traumas of violence, the capacity to speak and fight against violence expands. Courage gets into the soul alongside of terror and fear and births more courage and resilience. Being believed and heard helps individuals regain agency and know that what happened to them matters—that the reality is true and their psychic reality of internal pain is worthy of acknowledgment.

Witnessing can be thought of as having layers, as does psychic life. There is the event, there are associations and feelings about the event, and there are relationships with external and internal objects who receive or deny the experience. There is the original witness of the horror and the acts that hurt so much; there is the second level of witnesses who hear the story for the first time, and then there are those who take what is known and transform it into research, or teaching, or documenting, or making art to bring to others. Similarly, witnessing is present in depth psychotherapies where whatever is in the mind, whatever was experienced and is experienced is conveyed, received, and talked about in order to allow creativity to take place. It takes courage to speak of what one fears and it helps when there are two, a speaker and a receiver, each helping to contain the trauma as they resonate with each other. It is in these micro-communications that trauma is transformed into meaning. The chapters in this volume, individually and together, offer creation of meaning in the revelations of trauma and courage.

The importance of rape and of psychic rape

Rape, unfortunately, is an act we hear about, read about, and continue to have difficulty comprehending—the violence and destruction, the body intrusion, ripping of tissue, destruction of a sense of being whole and intact, and the terror. I use the term "psychic rape" to describe the violent invasion of the psyche that takes place when individual rights and respect are overridden by rageful attacks, dominance, and disregard. All of the violent acts described in the book (rape, femicide, genital mutilation, enslavement, use of pregnancy to control, denial of legal rights) are forms of "psychic rape" for the victim and for our human community. If the crime is not regarded as such, and is implicitly condoned and hidden by society, all women and men suffer from despair and helpless rage that women are not treated with love and respect. Scars spread across generations until there is speaking out against such violence, introducing the courage to fight violence against women. We all share the psychic helplessness when there is no recognition of the violence and no support or intervention. We all help the development of resilience when receiving stories of violence and making room to perceive and to think together.

As a therapist and supervisor of clinical cases, I have heard many stories of rape, and each is unique. All are more complex than just an incident of rape, unwanted genital penetration. Each story involves betrayal, humiliation, forcing, physical attack and threats, and often being drugged. One patient said that she was repeatedly told she would be killed. As she spoke, she was concerned that she would frighten me and she listened carefully to see what I could tolerate knowing. She was determined to not rape my mind. Another woman had a knife held to her throat. Another was talked to in vulgar, intrusive ways about parts of her body. Another was terrified when she realized no one was around to hear her scream. For many, the most terrible time is when they bring their story to others—the police, parents, friends, authorities in the army, in governments, and at universities—and no one does anything, often revealing that they view the woman as the "instigator", the one who did something wrong.

In the film, *The Hunting Ground*, Annie Clark and Andrea Pino present how the responses of denial from family and university personnel cause the most wounding to victims of rape, inducing the terrible sense that no one would ever again see the victim as a whole, trustworthy person. Annie Clark (Chapter 12) describes how they came to create an organization to End Rape On Campus (EROC), which was highlighted in *The Hunting Ground*. The determined witnessing of Annie Clark and Andrea Pino brings resilience to those who suffered such violence. They demonstrate a fighting spirit to help others and then others identify with them. While the pain of being hurt remains, there is profound reparation and renewal when offered a way to join a movement to honor the truth, to fight denial, and to develop safe environments for others. They researched to find the relevance of Title IX—a way to bring law to campuses to develop safety for women on an equal footing with safety for men.

Pairing violence and courage

With the pairing of stories of violence and stories of courage, we are able to speak of atrocities and recognize the enormous efforts scholars are making to witness, actively to gather information, and to create effective interventions. With pairing of psychoanalysis and scholarship and of research and activism, an environment is developed enabling knowledge to accrue and be communicated, bringing about meaningful interventions. Paula Ellman (Chapter One) writes about the importance of bringing the unconscious mind to the realities of violence in order to understand tendencies to internalize the atrocity and identify with sadomasochistic dynamics. Pairing psychic mechanisms with the realities of traumatic violence helps form a foundation for resilience, reflection, and development of active bystanders. The chapter by Rachel Cohen and Ana Ramirez (Chapter Seven) describe transformations that take place as victimized women in refugee communities become more resilient when part of sewing circles. The sewing panels show the representations that these courageous women are able to make as they sit with other traumatized women in the sewing circles. Maureen Meyer (Chapter Fifteen), of the Washington Office on Latin America, gathers information about femicide in Mexico, making efforts to have the knowledge recognized by authorities. As a medical doctor, Katalin Roth (Chapter Seventeen) conducts asylum interviews and listens to brave women tell of brutalizations. She is being witness to the wounds of the body and psyche. She considers these women to be remarkably courageous and is courageous herself in her presence for their stories.

Brenda Smith (Chapter Thirteen) is Professor at the American University Washington College of Law. She documents the way rape of women (and men) in the prison system bears similarity to subjugation techniques in slavery. Her research and writings on this topic leave no stone unturned, so that ignoring the problems in the prisons is no longer possible. Hope Ferdowsian (Chapter Sixteen) is a human rights physician and knows of the violence and sexual abuse sustained by women around the world. These women, too, have gained a witness. The creativity of artists to symbolically represent pain and suffering is present in this book. Janice Lieberman (Chapter Twenty) writes of the making of art about violence by women artists, for example, Kiki Smith (see photos in Lieberman's chapter). Moisés Lemlij (Chapter Twenty-one), in contrast, writes about cultures of the Andes in which women are depicted as sensual and powerful (see photos). This was a culture experiencing the pleasures of plenty and the mother was not feared, but revered. Gail Humphries Mardirosian (Chapter Twenty-five) contributes her description of her staged musical docudrama, *Traces in the Wind*, about three women survivors of the Holocaust who persisted in developing their art forms throughout their lives. Each of these chapter topics is concerned with overwhelming destructiveness to women and each is well researched. They represent activism, directly and indirectly, and the creative endeavor of writing the chapter and producing art—much like the three female artist survivors of the Holocaust.

Another pairing of oppression and courage is evidenced in the report of the activism of three women psychoanalysts, written by Raquel Berman (Chapter Six), who developed a program to support women running groups for underserved and abused teens in Quintana Roo in the Yucatan. Their psychodynamic interventions change the way young women think about themselves and lessens their vulnerability to early pregnancies and childhood marriage. In clinical treatments, Rosine Perelberg (Chapter Twenty-two) and Donald Campbell (Chapter Ten) illustrate changes that were possible when violence against self or others was present in psychoanalytic treatment. Unconscious fantasies became available for understanding, especially in the transferences. Arlene Kramer Richards (Chapter Twenty-three) speaks to universal presence of fears about the power of women, the early mother, which enter analytic understanding. She writes of the ways that primitive unconscious fantasies affect thinking until they become more consciously accessible.

The horrors of trafficking are found in these chapters, particularly in the accounts of Vivian Pender (Chapter Three), a psychoanalyst, and the filmmaker, Diana Romero (Chapter Four), who produced

Nina Quebrada ("Broken Girl"). These two chapters complement each other, placing together the basic statistics and stories written about by Pender's work at the United Nations and the personal portrayal of a teenager being trafficked in the film. In the last scene in the film, a good father welcomes his daughter's return and there is a rare offering of reconciliation after trauma. The emotions of the poetry written by E. Ethelbert Miller (Chapter Nineteen) and Myra Sklarew (Chapter Nine) beautifully bring together scenes of raw violence and poetic voice, conveying feeling.

The readers of these chapters receive this mix of trauma and wonder. There is a sense of joining a community of vigilant witnesses. Psychoanalysts recognize the value of communications of shame and rage, and of creating narrative from the terrible "toomuchness" of trauma. In its entirety, *The Courage to Fight Violence Against Women* is a book providing hope and offering resilience.

A personal note about involvement with "The courage to fight violence against women"

I feel fortunate to be part of "The courage to fight violence against women". It began with the planning of a conference on this topic when Paula Ellman invited me to be the Associate Chair for its development. We came to share a vision for the conference and for this book. We were continually inspired by all of the women who speak to their experience of being victims of violence.

When we started our project, there was continuous news reporting, with video, of a woman who was hit, knocked out, pushed, shoved, hated—she ended up on the floor of an elevator and he, her NFL (National Football League) husband, stepped over her and picked her up like a piece of laundry. The video from the elevator played over and over on television news feed. It was as if the elevator had a psyche of its own, showing how repetition of trauma becomes a psychic necessity when one is overwhelmed and cannot make sense out of what is happening. The scene takes on a perverse fetishism as if it were exciting rather than devastating. This particular news brought us to the need to recognize the global news about women being captive, tortured, raped, and murdered and the constant repetitiveness of these awful events. We wanted to break though the numbing repetitions.

This is how trauma works, it gets in, it fragments, it murders the soul, and it stays in the mind, replaying itself. It creates havoc with one's feelings and then there is vulnerability, and knowing and not knowing the now terrible internal landscape. We were stirred to collect together writers from a far reach of scholarship and to focus on the courage it takes to witness violence and to intervene.

We were determined to have a book demonstrating life forces, not only destruction and death. Something new and energizing for us was to reach out to other disciplines. In this way, we could honor our psychoanalytic clinical knowledge of trauma and psychic helplessness, and also honor artists, poets, and activists who were representing and chronicling violent events against women in venues around the world and were developing interventions. At times, we were attentive to details of putting together this volume and, at times, we were overwhelmed and stunned by the stories of violence we were collecting. It was comforting to discover so many individuals who wanted to contribute and help make *The Courage to Fight Violence Against Women*. It seemed that each day there was something else in the media about violence against women calling for our attention. Late in the Presidential campaign in the USA, violence against women and how to define it became a central theme of discussion. News articles highlighted how women and men were speaking out to define the importance of recognizing what is abusive, bullying, and assaultive of women. We knew then that our book was a collection of work worthy of its title. I carry with me the courage of all of the topics in this book and the courage of all who fight violence against women through their work.

Reference

Goodman, N. R. (2012). The power of witnessing. In: N. R. Goodman & M. Meyers (Eds.), *The Power of Witnessing: Reflections, Reverberations, and Traces of the Holocaust—Trauma, Psychoanalysis, and the Living Mind* (pp. 3–26). New York: Routledge.

CHAPTER THREE

Human sex trafficking: extreme violence against women and children

Vivian B. Pender

Definition

Human sex trafficking is defined as the use of force, fraud, or coercion for the procurement of commercial sexual services. This need not be proven in minors, since sex with minors is considered *de facto* forced, coerced, or fraudulent. This internationally agreed definition of trafficking is in the United Nations Protocol to Prevent, Suppress and Punish Trafficking in Persons, Especially Women and Children.

Article 3, paragraph (a) of the Protocol

> ... defines Trafficking in Persons as the recruitment, transportation, transfer, harbouring or receipt of persons, by means of the threat or use of force or other forms of coercion, of abduction, of fraud, of deception, of the abuse of power or of a position of vulnerability or of the giving or receiving of payments or benefits to achieve the consent of a person having control over another person, for the purpose of exploitation. Exploitation shall include, at a minimum, the exploitation of the prostitution of others or other forms of sexual exploitation, forced labour or services, slavery or practices similar to slavery, servitude or the removal of organs. (UN Office of Drugs and Crime, 2016; UN Office of the Commissioner for Human Rights, 2015)

Scope of trafficking

In the USA, the statistics are striking. The 2014 Annual Homeless Assessment Report to Congress by the Department of Urban Housing (HUD) found that on a given night in January there were 578,424 total number of homeless persons, of which 135,701 were children under the age of eighteen, and of those children, one third were unaccompanied by an adult (US Department of Housing, 2014). Furthermore, the US Office of Justice Programs estimates that 300,000 children are at risk for sexual exploitation each year (Office of Justice Programs Fact Sheet, 2011).

Internationally, the situation is grim. It is estimated that millions of humans, especially poor, uneducated, or migrating, mostly traumatized women and children, are trafficked for sexual servitude. To add to the problem, prostitution, brothel ownership and pimping are fully legal in forty-nine countries, including the USA, where brothels are legal in eleven counties in the state of Nevada. Countries in which it is illegal have flourishing sex trades nevertheless (ProCon.org, 2016). The USA is thought to be second only to Germany as a trafficking market destination. Many countries have employed sexual servitude to address the sexual needs of soldiers in the military. In addition, state-sponsored rape has been used as a military tactic and a means of genocide.

The World Health Organization (2013) reported on global and regional prevalence of violence against women and its health effects. Developed in collaboration with the London School of Hygiene and Tropical Medicine and the South African Medical Research Council, the report classified two types of violence against women. One was sexual violence by an intimate known partner and the other by an unknown non-partner. They found that 35% of women worldwide have experienced either or both forms of violence, but predominantly intimate partner sexual violence. Worldwide, almost 40% of murders of women are committed by an intimate partner. When there is sexual abuse by known partners, there are increased health problems such as depression and low birth-weight babies, and sexually transmitted diseases such as HIV. When violence is committed by a non-partner, anxiety and alcohol use disorders are common.

Human sex trafficking is an extreme distortion of sexuality where sex and violence are split and operate independently. Although sex with a trafficked victim is dehumanized and violent, it can still be considered sex: that is, the buyer experiences desire and orgasm. Although most victims are women and girls, and most buyers are men, traffickers are almost equally split between men and women. Victims, buyers, and traffickers suffer with difficulties in their mental functioning.

These three critical and necessary elements will be discussed in turn: the victim who is exploited, the trafficker who profits, and the buyer who consumes.

The victim

Youth are particularly vulnerable to recruitment by traffickers, and multiple studies indicate that among younger women involved in the sex trade, the average age of entry was 12–16 years (Salisbury et al., 2015; Silverman et al., 2006).

Most are women and girls who have psychological vulnerabilities that make them susceptible. Early childhood sexual and emotional abuse, neglect, and addictive disorders have contributed to diminished ego strength. Once in captivity, or in "the life", victims present some common signs: emotional instability, low self-esteem, anxiety, anger, depression, suicidal thoughts, cognitive disabilities, identity diffusion, and other signs of personality disorders related to abuse.

A composite example is instructive.

A thirty-year-old woman from a mid-Western American town was asked, "Why didn't you run away from your pimp?" She said, "I didn't have anywhere to go. I couldn't go home." She had grown up in an abusive, neglectful family and was passively wishing she could run away. Her stepfather, uncles, and neighbors had sexually molested her repeatedly. By the time she was fourteen years old, she wished she could be somewhere else and someone else. She felt invisible. Although she was desperate for affection, she did not go out and look for a pimp. However, it was easy for him to spot her. She was the one looking down, hanging back from her group of friends at the Mall. She looked older than her friends because of her make-up and dress. He approached her and said "Nice shoes", or "Nice bag." She could not remember which. She did not look up or say "thank you". That is when he knew that he had a young teenager who did not have the self-esteem or self-confidence that would allow her ever to leave him. All he had to do was manipulate her psychologically, something easily accomplished with one so vulnerable.

The pimp, posing as her boyfriend, initially spent a good deal of time with her. He promised her a place to stay, new clothes, manicures, and spending money. He offered her love and affection. He jealously guarded her daily movements. It all changed suddenly after about two weeks of yearned for attention when he suddenly and brutally beat and raped her. He knew she would not leave after that. There might have been another young woman there at the time, already "in the life". This woman comforted her afterwards. To convince her of her new life, he did it a few more times. She was deeply ashamed and would never tell anyone for twenty years. She felt silenced and isolated. He forced her to post escort services on Backpage.com. Her pimp became her boyfriend: he chose her clothes, when and how much she would eat, sleep, and have sex. Her mother and stepfather never tried to find her. She was tattooed on the inside of her lower lip with the word "Daddy". She had two children with her pimp. She found a way to survive and imagine that he loved her, otherwise, "how could these babies be so beautiful?" She said she felt for the first time empowered and in control when she had sex with buyers. It was a business transaction. She knew what it was going to be and did not ever hope that the buyer would care for her. She knew when and where and that she would be paid. She did not care that her pimp would take all of the money. In her mind, by maintaining her pimp as a constant object, she could dismiss the role of the buyer.

By the age of thirty, she had been trafficked from state to state and sold from one pimp to another. At one Super Bowl, she was forced to have sex with fifty men a day for two weeks. She slept two or three hours each day and used cocaine to stay awake. She no longer knew where she was or to whom she belonged. She eventually became addicted to heroin and her children were removed by social services. It is hard to know how she survived and how she eventually escaped "the life". As fraught as it was, the connection she had with her children and the intervention by social services helped her to become a survivor.

After she left she suffered from complex trauma. Ten years later, she still has nightmares, numbness, depression, avoidance, and lives an inhibited life. When she is stressed, she dissociates psychologically.

Complex trauma applies to the victim both during and after she is out of "the life". It derives from chronic and multiple traumatic events, resulting in long-term and wide-ranging consequences. The particularly invasive and personal nature of the trauma results in deep shame. She might blame and hate herself, leading to self-injury. This kind of trauma disrupts the sense of self and there is fragmentation. The victim is subsumed by a new identity as "a prostitute". There is no cohesive life narrative. Attachments are insecure and based on threats of violence and isolation. Complex trauma affects her physiology, her immune system, her thinking and learning, her concentration and impulse control.

Even the legal sex worker can be found to have a childhood history that is rife with abuse for adult sexual enjoyment. The sex worker might seek to rationalize their abuse to legitimize identity as an experience. It is as if the sex worker is thinking: "Abuse happened to me for a reason. I was vulnerable but now I can be the one in control, use sex as a caring activity, identify with the vulnerability of the buyer and care for the buyer as a [self-representation]." One example is the sex worker who provides sexual services for the disabled homebound person and thinks of his work as a profession for the "greater good". Such sex workers, a small but vocal group, formed the International Union of Sex Workers, a legally recognized organization, based in the UK.

The trafficker

While victims are mostly women and buyers mostly men, traffickers are split almost equally between men and women. The trafficker is, perhaps, the most severely psychologically impaired. Traffickers can be sociopaths and, indeed, have no guilt, remorse, or regard for human life. They conduct a lucrative business, more profitable than selling drugs or guns. Unlike these latter commodities, women and children can be reused and resold for many years. They encourage use of the term Daddy to exploit the victim. The trafficker might even have the fantasy that he is one step removed from a homosexual relationship with many men. That is, when he has sex with his prostitute, he could vicariously fantasize that he is having sex with hundreds of men.

Traffickers may be family members, acquaintances, or strangers to the victim. Frequently, the trafficker acts as if he were a boyfriend. In a recent Wisconsin study, the most common traffickers were parents or other caregivers selling sex with their children for money or drugs, and minors trading sex for a place to stay or to meet basic needs (Wisconsin Department of Justice, 2016).

There is a chilling assuredness in the way they talk about their "girls", or "stable". One pimp made this distinction: the prostitute gets paid and the whore gives it away. He was quite sure that getting paid was undoubtedly preferable. He owned limousines and a house. He had so much money he could not spend it fast enough and, anyway, did not have time to take a vacation. He worked too much of the time. His policy was not to physically abuse his prostitutes because they would not be able to get customers if they were bruised or scarred. He supplied them with drugs and said they were happy to be doing what they were doing. He told them they could leave but, to his surprise, they never did. He decided that he has good, mutually rewarding relationships. He found them at a bar or online by talking to them. He tested them by asking them to do something for him that was extraordinary. One example was to ask her for the keys to her car after speaking for fifteen minutes. If she did this without question and little reassurance, he took this as a clue that she would do other things for him. He thought it worked most of the time. He enjoyed going to the Player's Ball, a regular event in the USA that awards the "pimp of the year" with a trophy-like Player's Cup (*Tricked: The Documentary*, 2013).

Most commonly, the woman trafficker has been prostituted but is now older. It is not uncommon for younger prostitutes to recruit other young women, or for female brothel owners to buy young women for their stable. The woman trafficker is not well studied. She is frequently a former victim herself, sometimes of incest. Economic factors play a large role for both victim and trafficker. If she had other opportunities for employment, she would not choose to continue in the life. However, most are unskilled or have an untreated psychiatric disorder, but have learned that violence against sexual bodies can be used as a means of employment. Some are well known public figures, such as Heidi Fleiss. Most have been incarcerated. Many are famous because of their high profile clients: for example, governors, professional athletes, bankers, and so on (Knufken, 2010).

The buyer

The buyers of sex are in a different category. Economic factors also apply here in that they must have money (or drugs) with which to pay. They may delude themselves that they are being kind or providing pleasure, but it is not the reality. While they might have suffered significant physical, psychological, or sexual abuse, economic factors do not play a role. Rather, they are more likely to have an addictive disorder (not alcohol) that might be involved with their sexual needs and performance.

Some examples of buyers can be found in a report of interviews with men who paid for sex (Rohrer, 2008). This report indicated that ten percent of men regularly used prostitutes.

One said he had been monogamous all his life and, after meeting someone in a sauna, experimented and had fun. He said he felt closer to his wife, although she did not know. He said he could demand oral sex from the prostituted woman that his wife refused to do. He found the internet a convenient place to order sex. Most of these men thought they were not hurting anyone and that the sex was basically consensual. These are the men who think that they have found good relationships: "I see us as adults. I want to pay and someone wants to sell. They seem to enjoy my company, several have moved onto more of a friendship." In *Tricked: The Documentary*, another interviewed man said, "I don't have to be charming. I don't have to get involved. I can pick and choose whom I'll have sex with tonight. I love the variety."

Most buyers are not pedophiles, although there is an emphasis on the victim who has a young, innocent, vulnerable appeal. Purity, like virginity, seems to be an attraction for some. This aspect might allude to the denial of maternal sexuality. The buyer, in a vertical splitting of his state of mind, envisions that the woman (or child) is enjoying having sex with them. The buyer believes that he is wanted, admired, and sexually attractive in a frequently surreal setting. That said, it is especially the symbolically de-headed body that is frequently valued. There is much literature on the psychoanalytic meaning and semiotics of the female body, but the literature is lacking in the study of buyers of sex and compulsive users of pornography. There has been a mainstreaming of pornography so that it is now more open. Many involved in the pornography industry are also involved with prostitution. It is difficult to study the chronic users of strip clubs, phone sex, and erotic masseuses except in the clinical setting with individuals. Some of the frequent buyers are addicted to cocaine that they buy from their prostitute. They might share it and have sex. Sometimes, these are the only women with whom the buyers have sex. Many are single or divorced, but some are still married and have not had sex with their wives for many years.

The fantasy life of buyers might require real, tangible props so that they can perform sexually. Some men, physically and sexually abused in their childhood, had no words for their trauma. They could not use their symbolizing function and needed to act out. Many individuals use fantasy to mitigate behavior and polymorphous perverse fantasy can be considered within the normative range. However, some of the buyers of sex could have perverse and violent fantasies that could not be translated into action with a known intimate partner. Beheadings, amputations, devouring, demolishing, and devastating a female body are likely linked to the buyer's relationship with his mother. It is the violent hatred of her that is perpetuated and acted out with the prostitute. Not uncommonly, fathers or uncles initiate teenage boys to have sex with a prostitute.

Discussion

Despite the statistics, human sex trafficking is effectively invisible. Many say they know nothing or very little about sex trafficking. However, it can only exist in an atmosphere of indifference and implicit approval. Acceptance, either explicit or implicit, of this widespread social phenomenon is a projection of generally prevalent attitudes towards sexuality. Sex and violence are institutionalized. Just as prostitution, pornography, and sexual abuse of children are not uncommon, the same can be said of human sex trafficking. They are, rather, entrenched activities in our society and communities and are tacitly accepted. Child pornography, while illegal, is easily obtained on the internet by manipulating a child with flattery and/or threats into taking her own pictures with a cell phone or computer and emailing them (National Center for Missing and Exploited Children, 2016). Social acceptance, combined with the underground criminal nature, inevitably results in poor detection and very low rates of intervention.

It is not difficult to understand how vulnerable, weaker, and disenfranchised humans are exploited. Economic factors play a large role for both victim and trafficker. If they had other opportunities for employment, some would not choose to continue in "the life". Many victims are unskilled but have learned that they can use their sexual bodies as a means of employment. However, they deny the potential that they will be the objects of repeated violence.

There are many forms of violence towards women and children—for example, domestic violence and intimate partner violence can be preludes to trafficking. There is a historical subordination of women and children, socially, economically, politically, and psychologically, that contribute to this. Even though sexual harassment, gender discrimination, and other forms of sexual violence have become illegal in some areas of the world, attitudes persist that extend to the semiotic symbol of women as depersonalized objects to be adorned, bought, and sold. Misogyny and hatred of the female must play a major role, because at least one in three girls is at risk of sexual violence. This is concordant with the long history of acceptance of prostitution and pornography. These attitudes reflect that sex and the individual need for sex have always been difficult for society to grapple with. In such circumstances, religious belief, legal authority, and cultural mores have become the arbiters of sexual behavior (Pender, 2016).

Many healthcare providers may be encountering trafficking victims without realizing it. Victims will not be able to offer a coherent complaint or history. For example, they might not be able to verbalize that they have foot pain (plantar fasciitis) from walking and standing in very high-heeled shoes for long periods of time. Thus, providers are often not prepared to respond to victims, survivors, and those at risk (Beck, 2015; Cronholm, 2014). This occurs far more often than is commonly believed. How often do we ask a patient about whether they use prostitutes to buy drugs or sex? Yet, sex trafficking is the second largest grossing illegal business in the USA.

In addition to healthcare providers, other groups may witness human sex trafficking: for example, lawyers, police, prosecutors, and media. Secondary trauma to witnesses (including the reader of this article) is not to be underestimated as an important factor in the denial of human sex trafficking. Unconscious vicarious interest in prostitution and pornography represents a projection of the wish for freedom and abundance of fulfillment of desire. Sexual interest is also related to the forbidden resources of the maternal representation (Pender, 2016).

In ideal conditions, ordinary adult sexual activity itself alludes to a regressed and infantile need. The nudity, skin-to-skin contact, orifices involved, sensory systems dominant, and the rewarding oceanic experience of orgasm contain remnants of the state of the infant child. The neurotransmitter dopaminergic reward system of the brain is activated. Unconditional loving erotic emotions usually predominate over hostile aggressive feelings. For most individuals, sexual activity is predominantly and significantly involved with a relationship. However, the opposite is true in human sex trafficking, where the sexual object and aim are effectively dehumanized, that is, dissociated and distorted from loving associations. Humans can adapt to repeated experiences of violence and the effect degrades over time, whereas the experience of sexual arousal does not diminish over time. This might account for escalating forms of violence in modern culture but acceptance of the sexual status quo. It seems that sexual violence has long been tolerated and accepted.

It is only recently that some of the terminology has changed. The prostitute is now referred to as an individual who is prostituted. Nevertheless, there has been a transformative experience in the individual. The surreal quality of the experience is encapsulated in the phrase of the victim that she is now "in the life," or "on the track," as if to confirm that she is living in an alternative universe. The surreal quality of human sex trafficking and the minds of the victim, buyer, and trafficker can only be related to an understanding of the uncanny (Freud, 1919c).

Conclusion

It should be clear that persons who are prostituted are trafficked persons.

There is hope that the Nordic Model can be embraced in the USA. In this model, the victim is not arrested, but, rather, offered safe haven, housing, and treatment. Buyers and pimps are arrested instead (Aslanian, 2016). It is unknown if the model would substantially decrease trafficking if widely adopted and vigorously implemented. However revolutionary in its concept, the model does not address a qualitative understanding of what individuals do with their sexual needs and neither does it help to guide the sexual development of children nor remedy cultural attitudes. It does not increase understanding of a sexual drive that overrides attachment to a person who otherwise seems to have meaningful attachments in their lives.

Furthermore, the Nordic Model ignores the difference between the sexual behavior of men and women. It remains unclear why women generally tend towards attachment and preserving a relationship, sometimes over their own needs and survival. Once the bond of attachment is repeatedly betrayed, the result can sometimes be so devastating that the self, the personality, and the psychic structure are more or less permanently damaged.

References

Aslanian, S. (2016). Victims, not criminals: rebranding sex trafficking. www.americanradioworks.org/segments/victims-teen-sex-trafficking/.

Beck, M. (2015). Medical providers' understanding of sex trafficking and their experience with at-risk patients. *Pediatrics*, *135*(4): 895–902.

Cronholm, P. F. (2014). Trends in violence education in family medicine residency curricula. *Family Medicine*, *46*(8): 620–625.

Freud, S. (1919c). The "uncanny". *S. E.*, *17*: 219–256. London: Hogarth.

Knufken, D. (2010). Business pundit. www.businesspundit.com/americas-most-notorious-pimps-and-madams/. Accessed June 2016.

National Center for Missing and Exploited Children (2016). http://blog.missingkids.com/post/146409058295/sextortion-a-growing-crime-in-the-digital-world. Accessed June.

Office of Justice Programs Fact Sheet (2011). http://ojp.gov/newsroom/factsheets/ojpfs_humantrafficking.html. Accessed June 2016.

Pender, V. (Ed.) (2016). *The Status of Women: Violence, Identity and Activism*. London: Karnac.

ProCon.org (2016). 100 countries and their prostitution policies. http://prostitution.procon.org/view.resource.php?resourceID=000772. Accessed June 2016.

Rohrer, F. (2008). *BBC News Magazine*. The men who sleep with prostitutes. news.bbc.co.uk/2/hi/7257623.stm. Accessed June 2016.

Salisbury, E. J., Dabney, J. D., & Russell, K. (2015). Diverting victims of commercial sexual exploitation from juvenile detention: development of the InterCSECt screening protocol. *Journal of Interpersonal Violence*, *30*(7): 1247–1276.

Silverman, J. G., Decker, M. R., Gupta, J., Maheshwari, A., Patel, V., & Raj, A. (2006). HIV prevalence and predictors among rescued sex-trafficked women and girls in Mumbai, India. *Journal of Acquired Immune Deficiency Syndrome, 43*(5): 588–593.

Tricked: The Documentary (2013). www.imdb.com/title/tt2246924/. Accessed June, 2016.

United Nations Human Rights: Office of the High Commissioner (2015). Optional Protocol to the Convention on the Rights of the Child on Sale of Children, Child Prostitution and Child Pornography. www.ohchr.org/EN/ProfessionalInterest/Pages/OPSCCRC.aspx. Accessed June 2016.

United Nations Office on Drugs and Crime (2016). www.unodc.org/unodc/en/human-trafficking/. Accessed June 2016.

United States Department of Urban Housing (2014). www.hudexchange.info/resources/documents/2014-AHAR-Part1.pdf. Accessed June 2016.

Wisconsin Department of Justice (2016). www.doj.state.wi.us/ocvs/human-trafficking. Accessed June.

World Health Organization (2013). Global and regional estimates of violence against women: prevalence and health effects of intimate partner violence and non-partner sexual violence. www.who.int/reproductivehealth. Accessed June 2016.

CHAPTER FOUR

How art imitates life

Diana Romero

As a filmmaker, I strive to bring true stories to life and raise awareness to the different horrors happening in our world. Prior to becoming a filmmaker, I was a social worker. The stories I encountered while working with people, combined with my wish to bring awareness via a narrative film format, is paramount to my growth as an artist. My company, dreamFILM supports and works with artists from under-represented communities to achieve their goals of making films.

Fresh out of college, I got my first job as an outreach worker in the streets of the world-famous boulevards, Sunset, Santa Monica, and Hollywood, in Los Angeles. Naïve, innocent, and very young, I was thrust into the seedy worlds of runaway, drug-addicted teenagers, pimps, and prostitutes (both male and female). I was so naïve that my work partner (a 350lbs. 6´5 gentle giant) had to explain to me the breakdown of the boulevards: Hollywood Boulevard was where the runaway teens spent their time on the streets or in squats (abandoned/condemned buildings where they would set up camps), Sunset Boulevard was where "johns" would approach female prostitutes, and Santa Monica Boulevard was where "johns" found the male prostitutes. Wait, I said, you mean "janes" not "johns", right? No, he explained, *men* pick up young boys, often underage and Latino on Santa Monica. Yes, I had a lot to learn.

This was the mid-1990s. And I did learn a lot. One could argue that I grew up very sheltered, but, truth be told, by the time I was a college graduate I had lived in three different countries; I was raised by a psychoanalyst and an early childhood educator and so was quite knowledgeable in the ways of humanity on either extreme, the very rich and the very poor. But nothing had prepared me to experience the inhumanity and extreme violence the people I reached out to had to endure on a daily basis.

Along with my love for human beings and my wish to help, I also began to explore my creative side. I had always loved to perform (putting together intricate shows for my parents and directing my sister), play music, and write. So, in the mornings I would audition for acting gigs and go to an internship at a film production company while working in the seedy boulevards at night as an outreach worker. I slowly began to realize, though, that I could not make much of a difference as a social worker. I could make a difference to one or two people, but I could not create awareness or a movement to end the unfair treatment of humans. After much consideration, I decided to leave my career as a social worker and begin a new career in the creative arts as a filmmaker. Throughout that adventure, I discovered that I wanted to make films that would emotionally impact others and bring awareness to subject matters too difficult to deal with.

I clearly remember being five years old and going to see an Alfred Hitchcock film in Colombia. My dad was, and continues to be, a film buff. I do not think he or my mom realized the impact a film like that would make on a five-year-old. If a film could make someone feel so many emotions, then surely it was a world I wanted to be a part of. Of course, in those days, our parents were lawyers and doctors, teachers and accountants, etc. No one was a filmmaker, or at least no one I knew was. So, following that mentality, I forgot my creative wishes. A joy of living in Los Angeles is that it is impossible to ignore the film industry and I was bitten by the "bug" that seems to bite everyone here. So, armed with resolve and passion, I went back to school for film (behind the camera) and ultimately went further in my schooling to receive a Masters in Fine Arts from the prestigious American Film Institute (AFI). And there, my career truly began to shape up.

I considered AFI a boot camp—a two-year boot camp and probably the hardest route I ever took. The end of my marriage was not that hard, nor was my diagnosis of MS in 2003. This filmmaking business is a tough one, a soul breaker if one lets it be, and includes a life full of rejection. When asked to talk to students at my *alma maters*, I always suggest that filmmaking and telling stories has to be in your blood, because if it is not and you are not committed for life, then you will not have the thick skin it takes to survive in this business—or in the city I call the "City of Broken Dreams".

In order to graduate from the American Film Institute, we had to complete a thesis film, so I set out to write a script. In previous years, I had written about prostitution and vindication. I wanted to produce a short film based on that script and so I began to read up on prostitution. My research took me to the hidden, dark secret that is sex trafficking in the USA. What?? Sex trafficking in the USA? I could not believe that this even existed in my own backyard. Apparently, neither does a huge majority of Americans. So I wrote a story based on sex trafficking in the USA using true stories as inspiration.

Let me make a side note here. Our task for our thesis films (in order to graduate) was to submit short film scripts. AFI staff would then select the scripts to be made that year and we would form a team around those projects. AFI is discipline specific, which meant that anyone could write a script, but if you were there as a producing MFA candidate (like me), you could only produce, the same with directing, cinematography, editing, etc.

So I wrote *Niña Quebrada* (Broken Girl), the story of a sixteen-year-old girl who is coerced into running away to Los Angeles from Mexico with the love of her life. Sadly, her nightmare begins when she finds out she was drugged, raped, and sold to a sex slavery ring. The script was one of the few chosen from a large number of submissions and now the real task began. I had to get a director, cinematographer, and editor to team up with me to make this film. Three students, one from each discipline, chose this project. But since the task for this chapter is to focus on the courage to fight violence against women and not the sweat, blood, and tears it took to make this film, I will highlight some of the lessons I took from the making of this work and the treatment of women.

Media and entertainment have always played a key role in raising awareness to many real life subject matters, from drama to comedy, each story reflects society in some way or another, from the animated WALL-E, a lonely robot who yearns for companionship, to Batman, who, after witnessing the murder of his parents, swears revenge on criminals, an oath tempered by a sense of justice. These films have one thing in common, they are fiction, but fiction is based on reality and, thus, the choice to give a robot humanistic feelings and needs is a way to reflect loneliness in society and giving a fictional superhero human qualities is a tool for audiences to relate to the superhero and also experience his journey as he accomplishes humanly impossible feats in the name of humanity. Themes such as love, fear, happiness, sadness, laughter, and anger are all emotions that can be found in every film ever made.

When writing *Niña Quebrada*, there were some specific themes I wanted to explore, but, as the writing began, I found that this short film would not only explore every theme mentioned above, but also other themes of betrayal, violence, abuse, and complete inhumane treatment of humans by other humans. I used juxtaposition to explore the horrific treatment a teenager endures as a sex slave while also portraying the inhumane treatment of roosters in cockfights.

The first hurdle the team needed to overcome came from AFI's acting dean. While giving me a snide grin, and somewhat mockingly, he stated, "What I would really like to see is how you will re-create a cockfight. I'd like to see if *you* can pull that off." This was a comment he made to me privately and away from the rest of the team. I was shocked. This is a man who had committed to serve the AFI community, meaning to support students and their "lofty" ideas, not to make a mockery of a difficult task. But little did I know that this was going to be the start of a tough and sometimes defeating plight. Armed with the knowledge that re-creating a cockfight was not going to be easy, we set out to raise funding for the making of this film.

The funding was to be raised by the four of us through family, friends, and any other creative and legal means. We first turned to women's groups and support groups for trafficked persons. *None* of these groups had enough funding to carry through their mission, much less fund someone else's mission, even if on a par with theirs. *But* we did find some money through a grant . . . from the Humane Society. Because we were portraying the horrific act of a cockfight and focusing on the friendship between our trafficked protagonist and a rooster, we were awarded close to $10,000 for our film. The surprising factor here is that there was money from an animal protection agency, but none from women's groups. This was the first message I encountered that animals have become more important than other humans. And, although I love animals, it was beyond my comprehension that people were more inclined to support animal rights groups but not women's protection groups.

There was no shortage of actors to audition for the film. Even underage actors were a-plenty to play the roles of young, trafficked girls. However, when we tried to "cast" animal actors, we faced extreme scrutiny. This was to be expected, because even though we never intended to hurt the animals and we were going to recreate a violent scene by the use of film magic, animal rental companies were very hesitant to work with us because of recent acts by Los Angeles County to take down real cockfighting rings. The companies were concerned that LA County would target them for illegal cockfighting. This was understood but, with the Humane Society's support, we were able to sway one company to work with us.

As a comparison to animal protection *vs.* the protection of underage female actresses, this is what we had to deal with: in order to use the "No Animals Were Injured in the Making of this Movie" trademark, we needed permission from the Humane Society to include that text in the credits part of the film. In order to get this permission, we needed to provide the following.

- Storyboards (illustrations) of each scene where we were going to have roosters in a cockfighting ring. The illustrations had to be specific and detail how we would keep the animals from hurting each other and had to implement rules such as how many hours the animals could be on set (under lights) and how many feet they had to be apart from each other.
- When filming, there would be at least two Humane Society representatives on set making sure we were following all rules with the live animals. This included taking pictures of the "blades" that were affixed to the roosters (made of cardboard and aluminum foil). The pictures had to show someone from the crew bending the "blade" to certify that it was not a real blade.
- We had one animatronic rooster (a taxidermied rooster that had been converted into an animatronic rooster controlled by a remote control). In order to use this animatronic in the film, we

had to provide the Humane Society with paperwork from the prop company stating that the rooster had not been killed for the purposes of making this film.

Now, allow me to create a juxtaposition here: roosters *vs.* underage actresses. The following is what we needed in order to employ underage actresses to play victims of sex trafficking.

- Limited hours on set depending on age.
- Parental permission.
- Studio teacher on set for the children's welfare and for school, etc.
- No restrictions on clothing, except for nudity.

And for the girls, that was it. When mothers began to complain of a "sketchy" male studio teacher with whom they did not feel comfortable, we asked him not to return to set the next day. But that was it; that was the extent of the protection for the girls. Luckily, we ran a decent and very protective set and therefore there were no issues with the actors, but this is not a guarantee for other film sets, especially those that pay a lot of money, have children whose stage mothers will do anything to get their kids on film or on a set. We have heard the nightmare stories—Bill Cosby comes to mind.

During the preproduction of this film and the actual production of it, we were reminded time and time again that animals are more important than humans and this was a hard reality to accept. Everything went without a hitch in making this film, and the cockfight scene was very realistic and, to this day, people are amazed that "no animals were harmed . . .". In addition, the film is very well made and brings a lot of awareness to a practice that is not discussed much in American society. The desensitization of violence towards women has become just as large as the awareness and fight to protect animals. It was evident in the making of this film, as well as in our society. When there are funds from animal protection groups to issue grants for the portrayal of animals in a film but there are no funds from women's groups to raise awareness on violence against women, I realized there is a huge disconnect in our society.

When asked why I did not choose to do a documentary on this subject and instead chose a fictional character and storyline, my response has always been that with a documentary, although you are interviewing people who have lived through those experiences, you would never be able to bring a camera and film a sex trafficking victim while she is being raped, beaten up, or mistreated in any way. This is an example of where fictionalizing characters and recreating scenes allows a filmmaker to portray these violent acts in the most realistic way possible. When an audience watches the horrors that can happen to humans and animals, even if recreated, it brings knowledge of acts that would not be seen in a documentary.

Future works for me include a film based on a true story about Stockholm Syndrome and the downward spiral a young woman takes from being a track star with big college plans to becoming a drug addicted prostitute who commits murder to protect herself and her child. She is now in prison for the rest of her life, without the death penalty because she has AIDS. Her abusive pimp is still walking the streets free. Again, I believe that creating a documentary regarding this story would not do her experience justice. The audience has to go through the protagonist's journey of abuse, drug addiction, and murder in order to understand the severity of these acts and in order to understand how a bright, smart, and successful track star can go from one extreme to an extreme act of desperation.

As a storyteller, I strive to find stories that reflect life. Pursuing the notion that art imitates life, we can see that artists have always recreated life, whether it is through paintings, poetry, film, theatre, or any other type of art. Artists find a way to incorporate their stories using real life scenarios, but through the use of creative tools such as colors, words, or visual effects, artists can cast a creative and different perspective on real life scenarios. So, for example, a painting that shows vibrant colors for a sunset reflects the sunset in real life, but the artist's rendition of the colors, which could be deeper and brighter than those seen by the naked eye, portrays the artist's experience with that real life occurrence. As a storyteller, I can tell real stories based on real life, but my task is to create complex characters and stories that will immerse my audiences in those worlds, which, although imaginary by design, are based on true stories.

> Sex trafficking involves some form of forced or coerced sexual exploitation that is not limited to prostitution, and has become a significant and growing problem in both the United States and the larger global community. The costs to society include the degradation

of human and women's rights, poor public health, disrupted communities, and diminished social development. Victims of sex trafficking acquire adverse physical and psychological health conditions and social disadvantages. Thus, sex trafficking is a critical health issue with broader social implications that requires both medical and legal attention. Healthcare professionals can work to improve the screening, identification, and assistance of victims of sex trafficking in a clinical setting and help these women and girls access legal and social services. (The National Center for Biotechnology Information, 2013)

In order to bring about public awareness, an audience has to believe your story. There were many elements I had to analyze as I wrote *Niña Quebrada*. For example, I had to stay true to the acts of human trafficking and, most specifically, sex trafficking. My research led me to the discovery that there are four main ways to recruit a young woman unknowingly into a sex trafficking ring. In smaller, third world countries, girls living in poverty are sold by their parents. The "sale" can consist of selling the underage girls' virginity or selling the girls outright to go to live with the traffickers. Kidnapping is another frequent practice, although somewhat harder to achieve in larger, first world countries. The most common recruiting techniques are *via* promises of a better life in another country (typically the USA) and good jobs, namely nanny jobs, modelling, and acting. For this film, I chose the tactic that is extremely common, which is the psychological mind games played by the traffickers with young girls and adult women. This devious technique is that these men pretend to fall in love with a vulnerable, more than likely a survivor of previous abuse, and financially unstable girl. With gifts, affection, and promises of a much better life, these men are able to brainwash these girls into leaving their families and, more often than not, leaving the country as well. Once in a different country, the girls find themselves trapped in the horrific nightmare of sexual exploitation. Their passports are confiscated and they are forced to work as sex slaves in order to "pay back" all money that was spent to transport them to the new country, and on their sleeping quarters and food. These "debts" are impossible to pay back and, facing horrific acts of abuse, neglect, and death threats to them and to their families, these women find themselves unable to escape or find help.

> The global sex trade is the fastest growing form of commerce, worth $32 billion annually. In fact, human trafficking is the fastest growing

area of organized crime and the third largest income revenue for organized crime after narcotics and arms sales. What makes this business unique is that women and girls sold into sex trafficking earn profits for their pimps and traffickers over a great number of years, unlike the profits earned from drugs and narcotics that are sold and used only once. (The National Center for Biotechnology Information, 2013)

Human traffickers have been quoted as stating that humans are more profitable than drugs. One can sell a woman, man, or child over and over again, recouping money time and time again, while when one sells drugs, that drug is not resalable.

In the case of *Niña Quebrada*, these practices are clearly noted. When Lucena (the protagonist) tells the Madame, Melinda, that her father can buy her back, Melinda deliberately brings up her little sister, implying that her family is in grave danger, forcing Lucena to stop trying to talk reason to her captor. Melinda also tells Lucena that all debt must be repaid before she can be freed. This is obviously a fake statement, as there is no way Lucena will be able to "work off" the debt.

The challenge in writing this story was to tell a story based on true facts and to combine the many personal stories I had read. But it was also important to create compelling cinema that would allow audiences to go through the emotional rollercoaster that Lucena experiences in those few days as a sex slave. In order to create a compelling story we had to fall in love with Lucena. This was accomplished by casting an actress that brought innocence and vulnerability to the screen while also revealing her inner strength and backstory. As a teenager growing up in a poor country (Mexico) and wishing for a better life, we discover that Lucena's father was potentially unfaithful to his wife and daughters and also abandoned them for a period of time. Lucena, as a rebellious and angry teenager, falls into the claws of a human trafficker who is able to psychologically seduce her and promise her a better life *via* affection and displays of love and concern. Once he has been able to get Lucena properly "primed", he gives her a fake passport and transports her across the border to the USA, where she quickly finds out she has been drugged, raped, and sold. Enduring the horrors of being trafficked, Lucena finds a way to escape the ring and find help. Not many girls are so lucky; attempts at escape are met with physical and mental abuse and even death. Lucena's courage is multiplied when she decides that she wants to also save a twelve-year-old girl who is also a sex slave. Stockholm syndrome and brainwashing themes are portrayed here when Susana refuses to go with Lucena, claiming that this is their family now. Much to Lucena's heartbreak, she realizes she has to leave alone or risk her own death at the hands of Melinda. Lucena is able to escape and find help. One could argue that not all (in fact, a very low number) of sex slavery cases end well. But this was an effort on my part to show girls who might see this film that anything is possible and that there is help for them. The film ends with Lucena telling her story to the police and leaving the audience with the hope that her captors and traffickers will be caught and justly punished.

> The US Department of State estimates that anywhere from 600,000 to 800,000 people are trafficked worldwide annually. Victims tend to be recruited mostly from Mexico and East Asia, followed by the former Soviet Union, Africa, Eastern Europe, and, finally, Latin America. Typically, the countries from which many of the victims originate have unstable political climates and are economically disadvantaged. This facilitates trafficking, as it is easier to recruit and transport women, bribe officials, and forge passports and other travel documents. The United States is one of the top destinations for sex trafficking, and many children from the United States are trafficked to other industrialized nations, including the Netherlands, Germany, and Japan. (Dovydaitis, 2010; see also Hodge, 2008)

In the years since this film premiered (2008), I have been shocked at how little the USA and other countries have pursued the growing disease of sex trafficking and I am equally surprised at the emotions people display after having seen this film, claiming that they had no idea this was happening in our own backyards. The film itself has won many awards from numerous film festivals and continues to be screened at conferences and universities throughout the USA and the world.

The fact that this film still brings shock and a desire to do something to its audiences clearly proves that art can make a difference in bringing awareness to our society on many different topics.

In order for art to permeate into the collective mentality of audience members, the artist must find relevant themes with which people as a whole can empathize. For example, it was important for me to portray the horrors of sex slavery in a short film that audiences would embrace and be willing to join the protagonist in her journey. The protagonist had to be lovable and had to exude the innocence and vulnerability of a teenager (emotions we can all relate to) and I had to shock the audience with the harsh realities of this horrific act. One of the best compliments I ever received was from a gentleman who came to me after a screening, shaking. As he introduced himself to me, he also explained that he has a daughter and that, watching this film, all he could think was about his daughter and how this film brought the reality of human trafficking to light. His parting statement was, "You did not spare your audience at all!" But how could I? What I did do was that I protected the film from being exploitative and also gratuitous: for example, I made it clear that it was important to not show the rape, but I found that it was more effective to hear the screams and the struggle while visually showing the window that foreshadowed her future escape.

The scene where she reunites with her father at the police station was a tough scene to write. No dialogue worked for that scene. What words can be said at a moment like this? So, the creative decision was made to have no dialogue in that scene. It is probably the best scene in the film. Not only because of the emotional aspect of it, but also because it brings a reality to the screen. What happens during the calm after the storm? How does a human being recover from such a traumatic experience and how do those who love her and care for her support the psychological needs this woman will now have? The answer is that you do not. There are no words and no actions that will return things to what was normal in the past.

I recently took a poll asking people to name the one film that brought awareness of some subject to them. The top two films mentioned were *The Color Purple* and *The Burning Bed*. Both films clearly depict the types of horrific violence women have had to endure for so many years. The creative forces behind both films do an excellent job of portraying the violence these women experience, while staying away from gratuitous sex scenes, exploitative emotional scenes, and unrealistic scenarios. Certainly, this is why these two films were nominated and won so many awards when they premiered.

Filmmakers can tell stories that bring about public awareness of societal ills, but, in doing so, they must be able to combine storytelling with facts. And they must really focus on creating something so compelling that their audience will want to stay through the journey and is willing to partake in the emotional rollercoaster required in order for the story to make a difference in the world.

As *Niña Quebrada* finished its round of film festivals, I was pleased to learn that there was a huge interest in screening this film in universities and conferences around the world. Since 2008, the film has screened at schools such as the University of Washington, Women's Studies Department; Department of Religion and Women's Studies at Cal Poly San Luis Obispo, CA; Hermanas Unidas De Cal Poly Pomona, Cal Poly Pomona, CA; and The Courage to Fight Violence Against Women (IPA Committee on Women and Psychoanalysis COWAP Conference), American University, Washington, DC. Additionally, I was approached by the FBI to use the film as a training tool for its agents.

Upcoming screenings include: IPA Congress, the International Psychoanalytical Association Congress, Buenos Aires, Argentina, and a three-year training program at the Wuhan Hospital for Psychotherapy, China.

References

Dovydaitis, T. (2010). Human trafficking: the role of the health care provider. *Journal of Midwifery & Women's Health, 55*: 462–467.

Hodge, D. R. (2008). Sexual trafficking in the United States: a domestic problem with transnational dimensions. *Social Work, 53*: 143–152.

The National Center for Biotechnology Information (2013). *Sex Trafficking of Women and Girls*, Nawal M Nour, MD, MPH, Department of Obstetrics & Gynecology, Brigham and Women's Hospital, and Harvard Medical School, Boston, MA. MedReviews®, LLC.

CHAPTER FIVE

Sex trafficking: commentary on Chapters Three and Four

Margarita Cereijido

Human sex trafficking is the use of force, fraud or coercion for the procurement of commercial sexual services. According to a UN report from 2012, 2.4 million people are victims of human trafficking at any given moment. The victims tend to be poor women, who are socially and psychologically vulnerable.

Two views of sexual trafficking have been presented in Chapters Three and Four: Chapter Three by Vivian Pender, who is a psychoanalyst, and Chapter Four by Diana Romero, who is a filmmaker. Vivian Pender has worked extensively against sex trafficking through her research, her clinical work, and her advocacy work. She is the author of many books and articles on the issue, she trains health workers to identify and rescue victims, and she is the chair of the Committee on Mental Health at the United Nations. Her chapter is both comprehensive and insightful. First, it explains how sex trafficking works, and it gives statistics and references the laws and regulations that attempt to eradicate trafficking. Second, it provides a socio-economic understanding, pointing out that the victims tend to be poor women who come from the poorest countries in the world, and the buyers from the richest. Mainly, though, it talks about the psychological characteristics of the persons involved, pointing out that traffickers, buyers, and victims all share a dehumanized attitude toward sex.

Diana Romero is a filmmaker. She wrote and produced *Niña Quebrada* (Broken Girl), about a girl who is abducted to work in a brothel. Her chapter, "How art imitates life," tells how she, as a social worker in Hollywood, witnessed the inhuman experience endured by female prostitutes and society's tolerance of violence against women. This prompted her to become a creative witness to violence against women.

Presenting these works jointly engages the reader in complementary ways, both rational and emotional. While Pender's chapter is academic, Romero's tells her own personal story. Whereas Pender's chapter is data-rich and analytical, the intimate nature of Romero's chapter promotes empathy and identification. Their combination informs us about sexual trafficking and compels us to combat it.

Discussion

Sexual trafficking is supported by a culture of indifference and implicit tolerance of women subordination (Pender, in this volume). Both men and women share conscious and unconscious legitimating beliefs that men are superior to women. These conceptions of gender dynamics are hegemonic; they are perceived as "normal". However, they are the result of social constructions of gender identity related to conscious and unconscious identifications, and to the history of the place women and men have occupied within their families and society.

Exploring some sources of violence against women from a psychoanalytic perspective

Biology

A biological source of men's dominance of women is that men are bigger and stronger, enabling them to physically dominate women. That might have been particularly relevant when more labor activities were physical.

Intense dependency

According to Chasseguet-Smirgel (1964), infants' long and intense dependency on the mother might foster angry, vengeful feelings and fantasies of dominating women, particularly if the mother is unable to mitigate and contain the child's intense anxieties.

The sadistic instinct

According to Freud, it is active during the anal phase and is involved in mastery: for example, sphincter control. It is also active later, during the genital phase, in dominating the sexual object, only as much as is needed to execute the sexual act (Freud, 1920g). Nevertheless, the sadistic instinct can become eroticized. If the child suffers intense anxieties, instead of becoming mitigated and fused during the genital phase, the sadism can extend into other areas and aggression becomes associated with sexual gratification.

Gender stereotyping

Psychoanalytic work shows that the subjective sadist/masochist positions can be incarnated by either men or women. Nevertheless, masochism is identified as a feminine quality, even if it is incarnated by a man. This further suggests that, in our culture, aggression and activity are associated with masculinity (Glocer Fiorini, 2015).

Once the infant is born, it is assigned a masculine or feminine gender, and receives the projection of all the ideals and values that parents, family, and culture have about gender stereotypes. The child gradually understands who she is, and what is expected from her. Thirty years ago, a relevant study on gender stereotypes was conducted with a newborn baby in a nursery. First, the baby was displayed dressed in light blue, and both men and women observers said it looked "strong and wise". Then the same baby was displayed dressed in pink, and the observers said it looked "pretty and delicate". Clearly, gender stereotypes are perpetuated by both genders.

The Oedipus complex

The Oedipus complex conception maintains that the mother establishes a symbiotic relationship with the child and the father is the only one who can liberate him from maternal engulfment. That can exacerbate pressure on males to be aggressive and independent.

Cultural change

Finally, according to Sluzky (2016), physical violence against women has been exacerbated by the disruption of unconscious structures stemming from cultural change in the dynamic between men and women. Men feel disempowered and respond by becoming physically aggressive, therefore "reaffirming" their masculinity.

Psychoanalysts' prejudice

Psychoanalysis should challenge current constructions of gender dynamics and tolerance of violence against women by questioning and understanding each patient's conscious and unconscious gender identification, their sense of their role as partners, parents, and members of society.

As members of society, we psychoanalysts tend to identify with society's values. We need to be aware of our own prejudices about gender stereotypes and dynamics, since that will affect how we understand and give meaning to our patients' material.

Instead of assuming that our conception is shared by our patients, we should be able to question each patient's conscious and unconscious beliefs. A patient might make a remark about gender dynamics which she assumes is a "universal truth" that is shared with the analyst. If the analyst agrees with the statement, it will not be examined. On the other hand, if, instead of taking it as an unquestionable premise, the analyst is able to question it, analyst and patient will be able to explore it, analyze it, and challenge it. Moreover, the analyst will be able to distinguish between the popular stereotype and the patient's personal beliefs and anxieties related to it (Blanck-Cereijido, 2014).

If we, as analysts, are blind to our own prejudices, we are at risk of perpetuating misogynous perceptions.

References

Blanck-Cereijido, F. (2014). *El Siglo del Prejuicio Confrontado*. Mexico: Paradiso Editores.

Chasseguet-Smirgel, J. (1964). *Sexualidad Femenina*. Barcelona: Editorial Lara.
Freud, S. (1920g). *Beyond The Pleasure Principle*. S. E., *18*: 1–64. London: Hogarth.
Glocer Fiorini, L. (2015). *La Diferencia Sexual en Debate, Cuerpos Deseos y Ficciones*. Buenos Aires: Editorial Lugar.
Sluzky, C. (2016). Personal communication, Washington, DC.

CHAPTER SIX

Girls at risk: paths to safety, interventions with female adolescents at sexual risk in Quintana Roo, Mexico[1]

Raquel Berman

Introduction of the Quintana Roo project

This chapter describes how psychoanalytically informed interventions contributed to an ongoing, three-year long multidisciplinary approach to helping girls in Quintana Roo, Mexico. There were 1,031 girls (aged from thirteen to nineteen years old) who attended fifty-one female youth councils (outside of school hours) in five municipalities, attached to eight vocational schools of Conalep (National Council for Technical Education (SEP), a branch of the National Ministry of Education (SEP), that teach technical skills to adolescents of both genders. These councils were coordinated by nineteen female school psychologists of Conalep who, in turn, participated in a monthly, three-hour "emotional accompaniment group" in Cancun led by three women psychoanalysts. The initial purpose was to provide the psychologists with an emotional space in which they could ventilate their feelings, unburden their stress, and share their problems and achievements in their leadership role of the Councils. The idea of female youth councils was originated exclusively in Quintana Roo by Clara Scherer, who is a pedagogue, journalist, and female rights leader. She developed the programs with the cooperation of

Cecilia Loria, head of Conalep in Quintana Roo. The original objective of the councils outlined by Clara was to prepare the girls to assume equal rights, now extended to both genders by the Mexican Constitution. The necessity for the program was due to the enormous gap between female legal rights and their fulfillment in reality. The interventions included providing stimulating readings, developing group dynamics and group discussions among the girls about their female experience, and encouraging economic and political autonomy. Traditionally, Mexican "macho culture" enhances obedience to authority figures while downgrading personal autonomy in general. Girls are usually discouraged from, or even punished for, having autonomous strivings. On the other hand, the government sends contradictory messages. It proclaims democratic laws, including gender equality, while its judiciary branch obstructs their implementation and also influences the unbalanced distribution of wealth, systemic corruption, and criminal impunity. However, with increasing criticism from civil society, the growing number of NGOs, feminist politicians, and feminine rights leaders, there are attempts to confront and to counteract the above anomalies by making demands for effective implementation of human rights, including women's rights. This project is one of such attempts.

Description of councils and their functions

Each council is made up of twenty girls and a female coordinator. They meet weekly for two hours, with the girls' commitment to stay for four semesters. The coordinators are provided with manuals about autonomy topics and guidelines on how to transmit them.

In the area of sexuality, the girls are given written information about female sexuality, gender, gender diversity, adolescent pregnancy, sexual harassment and coercion, how to say *no* under these circumstances, and how to demand sexual security by use of contraceptives in consensual sexual relations. They are asked to dramatize such situations, which are then followed by discussions and reflections among them. They also write stories about different difficult situations that are shared and discussed, voicing their anxieties, doubts, and their aspirations to change these circumstances and create new ways to engage.

Some of the participants were pregnant and some were adolescent mothers, and, inevitably, their own experiences with early pregnancies emerged as well as their difficulties with the adolescent maternal role and the restrictions that it imposes. Other girls reported that listening to all of this helped them to avoid the same pitfalls. They narrated traumatic memories about childhood incest with fathers or grandfathers. In one instance a girl started screaming and weeping about childhood incest with her father never revealed before; the girls rushed towards her holding her within a tight circle and soothing her with kind words. Another dramatic instance involved a fourteen-year-old girl who repeatedly opened and closed the door of the room in which the group assembled, and finally told her story of incest with a paternal uncle. The coordinator understood that the repeated opening and closing of the door referred to her inner conflict about loyalty to the family by keeping silent *vs.* her need to cry out about her suffering. Cases of cutting, bulimia, and anorexia appeared and produced stress. There was keen interest and empathy expressed by the coordinators, with some cases needing specialized attention. Female adolescent lesbian inclinations also appeared and were treated with empathy. Thus, the councils served also as centers of early detection of adolescent problems that required specialized attention outside of the group.

The group participants talked about fathers' desertions, family violence, fears of diseases and death, as well as unfairness in their families: for example, excessive pressure to do family housework from which male siblings were exempt and having to ask permission for each outing outside the home, while male siblings do not.

Those who come to study from rural communities, and are without their families, considered the youth council as a refuge, without which "they could not have survived emotionally". They also talked about family and partner pressures to abandon their schooling. They were asked to write letters to a friend who asks for personal help about one of the above concerns. They learned to associate to significant words such as: prejudice, equality, sex/gender, sexual identity, sexual diversity, reponsibility, confidentiality, pregnancy, motherhood, guilt, contraception, and to discuss their different meanings for each of them.

There was a shift from the girls' initial obsessive talk about "clothes, shoes, and boys" to showing an interest in themselves and the female group they were now part of. They became particularly interested in thinking about their ambitions, different life options, career planning, friendships, and cultural interests. The Cinderella phantasy of the rescuing prince and the idealization of motherhood receded and other ego ideals and personal aspirations emerged.

The emotional accompaniment group: the excitement of developing the program

The establishment of the emotional accompaniment group for the school psychologists/coordinators of the councils was the result of an encounter in 2013 between Clara Scherer and Raquel Berman in which Clara first spoke to Raquel about the councils just founded. She mentioned the frequency of early adolescent pregnancies in Quitana Roo. Raquel Berman agreed that adolescent group intervention was perhaps the best way to provide youngsters with "the second opportunity" to undo childhood stalemates of the separation–individuation process, given their preference for peer groups and learning from each other. She also pointed out that effective learning about autonomy topics necessarily implies emotional involvement, and that these subjects will inevitably bring to the surface the girls' memories of narsistic injuries and traumatic events and may touch on parallel vulnerabilities in the coordinators. Also, mental health workers who intervene professionally for a prolonged time with fragile, helpless, and traumatized persons are challenged in their emotional balance and require an ongoing support system.

The emotional accompaniment group for the nineteen coordinators of the youth councils took place monthly in Cancun for three hours headed by three female psychoanalysts: Berman, Fontanot de Rhoades, and Torres Torrijo de Bolio, who are long-time colleagues from the same IPA psychoanalytic organization, MAPPTR (Mexican Association for Psychoanalytic Practice, Training and Research). One is also a group psychoanalyst and all three have experience heading organizations. Two of them commuted monthly to Cancun. Some of the coordinators travelled for as long as five hours to attend the group sessions, with covered expenses. Between the monthly sessions, they maintained frequent contact with each other through the internet.

The main objectives for the coordinators' group were stimulating group constancy, cohesion, and solidarity through containment, empathic listening to each other, validation, mentalization, witnessing, and learning from each other's successes and difficulties in managing the councils and sharing of their reactions to the girls' traumas and emotional needs. The emphasis was on the group as a whole, recognizing predominant group anxieties and defenses as well as unconscious resistances to the above consciously shared objectives. Individual symptoms and behaviour concerns were viewed as ingredients of the potential presence of the same in others, though to different degrees and in different modalities.

Outside resistances to the project

The project was almost aborted during the first year, due to the change of three heads of Quintana Roo Conalep. Cecilia Loria, head of Conalep at the inception of the project was removed abruptly to fill another position. The following two showed interest in the project but abruptly left their job in order to advance their political careers. The persistence and constancy of Clara and the three psychoanalysts to pursue their objectives during that uncertain period, in spite of these disruptive factors, contributed to the project's survival at that time, as did the reassignment later of Cecilia Loria as head of Quitana Roo Conalep.

Another obstacle from outside reality were conscious and unconscious sabotaging actions by the principals of the schools, some of whom considered the councils a waste of time in their pursuit of "concrete educational aims and statistical results". They used the psychologists in all kinds of school emergency situations, including as transitory replacement for an absent school janitor, demanding their presence at any time and scheduling their participation in other school activities at the same time as the emotional accompaniment group. In the beginning, the coordinators colluded with these unstructured demands because of deficient professional identity and self-esteem, lack of self-limits about their tasks, submission to the authority figure, and fear of losing their jobs.

At first, the councils were ridiculed by male students as a place for pregnant girls, for *mujeres jodidas*—fucked-up women—or crazies.

Later on, male youngsters expressed demands for their own male youth councils, as an aggressive manifestation of being unequally treated, denying, however, the reality of female gender inequalities as well as their own problems. Clara was requested to organize male groups but she insisted that they have to be male motivated and led by a male. One female coordinator wanted to lead a male group with the aim of "teaching males to treat women well", related to her personal history of severe mistreatment by her father. Male adolescent groups were later established, led by male coordinators.

Group process and resistances in the emotional accompaniment group

At the beginning, there was chaotic application of the frame of the monthly gatherings, irregular attendance, late arrivals, subgroup conversations, and prolonging eating periods (buffet food was provided, as many arrived from distant places). The leaders attributed obstacles in the project exclusively to school authorities, quoting their cynical and dismissive remarks about it. Some felt victimized, some identified with the aggressor, or expressed messianic and dependent expectations, demands for individual therapeutic attention and disbelief in the continuity and constancy of the project. However, presently, after three years, most express pride in belonging to an "elite and pioneering group".

The most striking resistance during the first year was denial about women's real status in Mexican society and families by proclaiming that, at present, there were constitutionally instituted equal rights for both genders. This involved denying the discrepancies between this official message and what they themselves were experiencing in their daily life. This was an eloquent example of receptivity to government "brainwashing" due to daily government propaganda on television. They were convinced that they should be in a mixed gender group. This attitude reflects the common female gender determined primacy of the desire of the other and the early abdication of female desire. This was expressed through manipulative and appeasing reactions to the negative male responses toward the female councils. The underlying anxieties were of losing the male's love, fear of his retaliation, being branded as a "feminist male hater" (someone who was waging war against men in order to grab their power), anxieties about ceasing to be "a good woman", that is, unconditionally obedient, self-sacrificial, and appeasing. In turn, these ways of thinking uncovered a modified version of the Stockholm syndrome, "love of the aggressor", as a masochistic female survival mechanism in a macho society. The psychoanalysts became aware that these reactions in the coordinators' emotional accompaniment group were parallel to the girls' responses in the female youth councils. The girls' stories were narrated by the coordinators in their own group session, creating confusion as to whether they were talking about themselves or about the girls.

Gradual awareness of the status quo in their schools, with their dysfunctional, even sociopathic, features, enabled some of the coordinators to finally distance themselves emotionally from their school setting, realizing that their paranoid or depressive reactions led nowhere. They accepted that they are working in "hostile territory" and in a dysfunctional school system, in spite of its positive objectives. They also realized that this could not be modified quickly and that they must rely on their own strengths and creative endeavours to further the aims of the councils as well as their own. They acquired better negotiating skills in their dealings with the principals and most were attending the group sessions in spite of some principals' demands that they participate in coinciding school activities.

The appearance of parallel experiences of the coordinators to those revealed by the girls in the councils was striking. Denial and trivialization of sexual traumas was initially prominent. At that time, a wave of femicides were happening in Quintana Roo. Initially, this subject was met with silence, or it was brushed off as unimportant to them as it only occurred in Cancun. They rationalized that the problem in Cancun was due to it being an international tourist center, having an international prostitution trafficking industry, including pederasty, and producing pornographic videos for local and international markets. They were denying that femicides were occurring in non-tourist places as well. These denials were defensive to the daily peril of sexual violence that young women face in Quintana Roo and other places in Mexico. One coordinator who was invited to talk on a Mexico City radio station, when asked to comment on the Quintana Roo femicides, reacted with confusion and inhibition. These reactions paralleled that of the silence of the Quintana Roo press about the femicides, which were reported in the capital's press.

Issues around sexual violence happening to the girls of the councils as well as those pertaining to the coordinators usually appeared in discussion half an hour before the end of the coordinators' group session, as if there was a generalized prohibition against airing these painful matters. Personal experiences of attempted or actual rape and sexual harassment were expressed by the group participants. One coordinator reported a rape attempt on a female Conalep student by a taxi driver who was taking her to school. She threw herself to the pavement, reached school on foot, told the psychologist about it, who then immediately reported it to the male director of the school. He personally took her to legally report the attempted rape, not waiting for the parents' approval, because he said it is illegal to be an accomplice in not reporting this crime, which is punishable with eight to thirty years in prison. This principal's behavior was exceptional in his support of the coordinators and councils in his school, which contrasts with the negligence and indifference of others towards female human rights. Most girls of fifteen years or less do not denounce sexual violence and neither do their parents. In spite of the law mentioned above, it is very rarely implemented.

A coordinator cried in a session when she spoke about her experience with attempted or real rape (this was unclear) by a doctor in a hospital where she had previously worked. Another coordinator spoke about her unfortunate experience in a Conalep school where a teacher attempted to rape her; she reported it to the principal and, as a result, was removed from her job and sent to another Conalep school while the perpetrating teacher stayed on. Another telling instance was when one of the coordinators, who was usually an active participant, literally lost her voice during a group session in response to her being told by a colleague, while travelling to the group encounter, that a man in her neighborhood raped his four-year-old daughter. This coordinator had a daughter of the same age whom she left with her husband in order to go to work. The most painful effect on those who narrated these stories was not the trauma event *per se*, but the family's disbelief about it and lack of empathic reactions or punishment from school authorities after they denounced these events. The shattering disillusionment with those who were supposed to contain and protect was more traumatizing than the actions of the aggressors, creating a devastating sense of rejection, abandonment, and heightened annihilation anxiety.

Another preoccupation voiced from the beginning by the coordinators referred to the limits of their professional role. They narrated instances of giving money to a malnourished girl, or taking girls to Starbucks for the first time in their lives, thus over-identifying with the victim. Another modality was assuming a superior benefactor's role by "doing good deeds" for the deprived girl. They worried about assuming an advocate role with a girl's family and being sucked into negative family dynamics that they could not handle. All these behaviors were explained as referring to the savior role that some mental health workers adopt unconsciously as a defense against their own feelings of helplessness, vulnerabilities, and psychic pain, which, by projective identification, they locate in the victim and deny in themselves, thereby assuming an omnipotent and controlling role over the victim.

Henry Krystal, who worked with survivors of the Nazi Holocaust, observed the therapists' impulse "to play God" towards these patients. Some of these actions are rationalized on the basis of the patient's desperate need to be rescued. Some analysts distinguish the savior role from the therapist's auxiliary ego support, which is beneficial to the patient. We all know that the most efficient therapy for the traumatized individual is to provide help in teaching and restoring relative control of one's life. Also important is enhancing his or her emotional resources and skills, avoiding pathologizing their weaknesses.

Transferences

As the emotional accompaniment group consolidated, paranoid, depressive, and idealizing transferences were pointed out. These were predominantly to authority figures, including the two founders of the project, the three psychoanalysts (age-wise, the coordinators were of the same age as their daughters), as well as to school authorities. They dealt mostly with reactivated daughter–mother tensions, female and male authoritarianism, narcissistic, or self-sacrificing styles of leadership, as well as abdication of the leadership role. Also present were reactions of submissiveness, idealization, and anger towards school authorities, as well as conflicts with girls' teachers, reflecting rivalrous relations on both parts. Being able to fantasize about possible conflict solutions revealed their innovative and creative approaches to the teachers in order to gain their cooperation with the councils. A few outside the group acted out rivalry and envy towards coordinators who were particularly successful in their work with the councils. However, within the group, they were usually tamed by the majority's task-oriented reactions of cooperation.

A telling transference moment was the emotionally charged narrative of one psychologist who, during a Youth Councils Choir festival in which 1000 girls participated, witnessed two women in red dresses refusing to tip a Mayan woman in charge of the public sanitary services because water was unavailable at that moment. She denounced them to the group as discriminatory and unempathic to poverty and race. During that session, two analysts wore red garments. One of them pointed out to the group that perhaps this narrative was also referring to the analysts as being equally unempathic to them. A discussion followed about the psychoanalysts' motivations to lead the coordinators' groups as well as their own motives in working with the girls. The outcome was that both coordinators and psychoanalysts found common ground about the emotional and professional enrichment that mental health workers found in this kind of work,

The main obstacle to group cohesion and horizontality were intermittent tendencies to hierarchical or symbiotic attachments between some members of the group. That is, one coordinator placed another one in a superior position to her own, or clung to another coordinator. Some of these arrangements changed when one domineering coordinator dropped out of the group, or when another became more autonomous.

The accompaniment group permitted the detection of coordinators unfit to work with the girls. Two dropped out because of narcissistic features such as exaggerated power strivings and control over others, disinterest in becoming involved with the girls, and using the councils as a platform for too many invitations to outside lecturers as a way of self- aggrandizement and avoiding their coordinator role.

The coordinators were repeatedly surprised that their messages had positive resonance among the girls and that the girls were discussing openly topics that they themselves felt uncomfortable with. This inner contradiction, on the one hand, doing well with the girls and, on the other hand, lack of self recognition and low self-esteem can be attributed to a harsh female superego, representing the inner absence of approving and praising parents—especially as female work is traditionally unappreciated. Frequent expressions were "Not only did the girls change, but I have changed with them"; "My life is different"; "I feel more humane and humble". Coordinating the youth councils and the accompaniment group "were the most important learning experiences, which opened my eyes to what was really happening around me and inside me and was affecting me personally". Some stopped being submissive to marital mistreatment and divorced in "order to be congruent with themselves", while others improved their couple relationships due to increased self-esteem and their newfound ability to negotiate greater couple equality. Many expressed the utmost personal importance of their participation for the first time in a non-hierarchical women's group and the support they found in their colleagues. Modification of self-sacrificial attitudes in their personal and professional life was manifested in expressing their right to have time for themselves and to pay more attention to their partner, as well as voicing their professional aspirations beyond Conalep. They showed positive changes towards their own mothers by being more supportive to them and encouraging them towards greater personal autonomy. In the presence of their mothers, some were assertively able to express their own views about female sexuality and equal rights with males in marriage and work, thus questioning the traditional, maternal self-sacrificial, idealized role.

Aversion to politics and to participation in the political process remained unmodified during the three years' process. The coordinators perceived Mexican politics correctly as authoritarian, abusive, corrupt, and against the "common good". They were equally suspicious of the same motives in women politicians and refuted the possibility of becoming personally involved in politics in the future. This reflected the introjected traditional view that politics are for men only and, most importantly, expressed the coordinators' fatalistic view of any future social and political change. This was reinforced by a series of disappointments with local female politicians who were submissive to male politicians. Some of them, after being elected, resigned their local congress seats in order that their male substitutes could occupy their places. Others did not deliver on time their anti-resolution document against discriminatory gender measures in the local Congress and lost their chance of opposing them. The official support of the President for 50–50 gender parity in federal and local congresses was opposed on local levels by male followers in his own party.

The above mentioned female reactions indicate self-sabotaging deeds to female power which should never be manifested in outer reality because it threatens female submissiveness to males, tied unconsciously to being the only way to obtain their love.

Results obtained in the girls

At present, Clara and Cecilia consider the councils a surprising success due to three results.

1. Decreased number of female school desertions.
2. Decrease in the number of adolescent pregnancies.
3. Decrease in the girls' obsessive interest in boys, and manic heterosexual sexual actings out.

This is due to how increased confidence in their own abilities has settled into their egos and how their ego ideals have expanded beyond the traditional roles for women, such as spouse, mother, and caretaker of aging parents, towards a variety of professional aspirations.

Another significant result is a change in strategy in dealing with adolescent girls in the eight Conalep Quitana Roo schools. Before the implantation of the project, the school psychologists dealt with each girl's troubles by intervening with her parents and expecting the parents to deal with her. This ceased with the realization of the parents' severe emotional disabilities impeding their positive parenting and, instead, the psychologists concentrated on the direct approach with the girls through their participation in the youth councils. The separation–individuation process in the girls advanced, but without breaking up the connection with parents, except in very toxic cases. There is strong parental approval of the councils manifested in growing demands to increase the number of councils to which they desire to send also their younger daughters. The emotional accompaniment group for the coordinators is presently considered a decisive and indispensable ingredient contributing to the success of the female youth councils project.

From time to time, one of the psychoanalysts explained to the two founders of the project and to school authorities the characteristics of the emotional processes that operate in groups. These included expectable progressions and regressions, and diverse outside and inside triggers provoking them, the transference phenomenon, the benefits of talking about problems instead of acting them out, the importance of problem solving within an empathic group, and many other issues. Non-governmental organizations that have international financial support showed interest in evaluating the project, the local and the capital's press have written positively about it, and authorities in the National Education Ministry showed interest in extending female youth councils and coordinators' emotional accompaniment groups in all Conalep schools in the country.

However, at present, the future of the youth councils in Quintana Roo is uncertain because they are not yet integrated legally in the federal by-laws of Conalep. Their financing depends partially on continued local government support, which is uncertain. Also, extension of the Quintana Roo youth councils' model to other states requires more trained school psychologists and more psychoanalysts/ psychotherapists willing to participate.

I chose to participate in the pilot project for the following reasons.

1. There is a long-standing tradition in psychoanalysis to reach the "wider social strata" (Danto, 2016) by attempting to apply psychoanalytic information (especially the importance of the unconscious) to human groups excluded from that knowledge.
2. My other objective was to attempt to build bridges between contemporary psychoanalysis, especially pertaining to female development, and Mexican feminism and female human rights movement (at odds with Freud's phallocentric theory of female development), which, through this project, I feel proud to have initiated. The three years' experience has heightened my admiration for, and empathy towards, that segment of Mexican women who, though intrapsychically still conflicted about their gender, struggle to obtain their internal and external autonomies.

Note

1. The Quintana Roo/Cancun Project is in its 4th year and has been extended into the city of Toluca, State of Mexico. Principals of schools, school psychologists, and the young women students are being helped by psychoanalytic guidance with the traumas of femicides and victimization in these areas.

Recommended reading

Balsam, R. M. (2012). *Women's Bodies in Psychoanalysis.* London: Routledge.
Benyakar, M., & Lezica, A. (2006). *Lo Traumatico, Clinica y Paradoja.* Buenos Aires: Biblos.
Berman, R. (1993). La mujer, cómplice inconsciente del machismo. *Imagen Psicoanalitica, 3*: 117–133.
Berman, R. (2003a). Solo hija de su padre en la huella del padre en el desarrollo de la hija. Publicaciones AMPIEP, Octubre, Mexico City.
Berman, R. (2003b). La explotación sexual de la transferencia erotica. In: A. Araceli Gómez & G. A. Pace (Eds.), *Etica En El Diván* (pp. 183–206). Buenos Aires: Lumen.
Bernstein, D., Freedman, N., & Distler, B. (1993). *Female Identity Conflict in Clinical Practice.* Northvale, NJ: Jason Aronson.
Bion, W. R. (1961). *Experiences in Groups, and Other Papers.* London: Tavistock.
Blos, P. (1962). *On Adolescence.* New York: Free Press.
Breen, D. (1993). *The Gender Conundrum: Contemporary Psychoanalytic Perspectives on Femininity and Masculinity.* London: Routledge.
Cacho, L. (2005). *Los Demonios del Eden.* Mexico City: Penguin Random House.
Cacho, L. (2010). *Esclavas Del Poder: Un Viaje Al Corazón De La Trata Sexual De Mujeres Y Niñas En El Mundo.* Mexico City: Grijalbo.
Chodorow, N. (1978). *The Reproduction of Mothering: Psychoanalysis and the Sociology of Gender.* Berkeley, CA: University of California Press.
Erikson, E. H. (1964). *Childhood and Society.* New York: Norton.
Freud, S. (1912–1913). Totem and Taboo. *S. E., 13*: 1–161. London: Hogarth Press.
Freud, S. (1921). Group Psychology and the Analysis of the Ego. *S. E., 18*: 67–143. London: Hogarth Press.
Freud, S. (1930a). Civilization and its Discontents. *S. E., 21*: 59–145. London: Hogarth Press.
Herman, J. (1981). *Father–Daughter Incest.* Cambridge, MA: Harvard University Press.
Herman, J. L. (1997). *Trauma and Recovery: The Aftermath of Violence, from Domestic Abuse to Political Terror.* New York: Basic Books.
Hoffman Baruch, E. (1991). *Women, Love and Power.* New York: New York University Press.
Kardiner, A. (1941). *The Traumatic Neuroses of War.* Washington, DC: Hoeber.

Kernberg, O. (1998). *Ideology, Conflict, and Leadership in Groups and Organizations*. New Haven, NJ: Yale University Press.
Mahler, M., Pine, F., & Bergman, A. (1975). *The Psychological Birth of the Human Infant: Symbiosis and Individuation*. New York: Basic Books.
Mead, M. (1949). *Male and Female: A Study of the Sexes in a Changing World*. New York: William Morrow.
Roth Walsh, M. (1987). *The Psychology of Women: Ongoing Debate*s, New Haven, NJ: Yale University Press.
Rozenfeld, A. (2012). *La Resiliencia. Esa Posicion Subjetiva ante la Adversidad*. Buenos Aires: Letra Viva.
Weinberg, K. S. (1955). *Incest Behavior*. New York: Citadel Press.
Welldon, E. V. (1992). *Mother, Madonna, Whore: The Idealization and Denigration of Motherhood*. New York: Guilford Press.
Young-Bruehl, E. (2008). *Anna Freud: A Biography*. New Haven, CT: Yale University Press.
Zukerfeld, R., & Zonis Zukerfeld, R. (2005). *Procesos Terciarios, de la Vulnerabilidad a la Resiliencia*. Buenos Aires: Lugar Editorial.

Reference

Danto, E. A. (2016). *Freud's Free Clinics: Psychoanalysis & Social Justice*. New York: Columbia University Press.

CHAPTER SEVEN

Sew to speak: story cloth healing with survivors of sexual violence

Rachel A. Cohen and Ana Maria Ramirez

When her village was attacked, seventeen-year-old Surita (pseudonym) was gang raped by soldiers as she fled her home. Alone and afraid, she fell into the hands of traffickers who promised her safety, but sold her into sexual slavery. Months later, she escaped and found her way to a women's shelter, but, when asked questions, she was unable to speak about what had happened to her, not only because of the fear of retaliation, or the way that survivors are stigmatized, or the taboos of her culture, but also because of the complex consequences of trauma, in which verbal channels may become inaccessible— these experiences often become unspeakable.

Women like Surita deserve a safe and effective way to break their silence and to make their journey to recovery in solidarity with other survivors.

Gender-based violence (GBV) in post-conflict regions

Gender-based violence (GBV) is a global problem that disproportionately impacts women. According to an estimate by the United Nations

Population Fund (UNFPA, 2016), one in three women will experience either physical or sexual violence due to her gender during her lifetime. Gender-based violence is a serious health problem because it has impacts on reproductive health, places women at risk for STIs and HIV, and causes emotional and psychological harm; it is a social problem because it further undermines the power and equality of women in society and it is a human rights problem because it strips women of their autonomy, safety, and even their lives. In post-war situations, where displacement of populations is common, gender-based violence is especially pervasive.

As of 2014, there are an estimated 59.5 million people globally who were forcibly displaced and projections for the end of 2015 are expected surpass 60 million people (UNHCR, 2015). Of the total number of displaced people, 15.1 million are refugees, the highest number of refugees in the past twenty years. The startling growth in refugees and displaced persons can be linked to violent conflict in countries such as Syria, Afghanistan, Somalia, South Sudan, Burundi, Democratic Republic of the Congo (DRC), and Mali. Syria has the largest number of refugees, upwards of 3.5 million people, seeking asylum in European and middle-eastern countries such as Turkey, Jordan, and Lebanon. In 2015 alone, there were more than 839,000 displaced people across international borders, a large number coming from sub-Saharan African countries such as Burundi and South Sudan. While current conflict is responsible for an increase in refugees, there are also those who remain in asylum from previous civil war and conflict such as Rwanda and Burundi.

Displacement of populations, the lack of security, failure of the legal system, economic hardship, and the breakdown of community structures all heighten the rates of gender-based violence against women and girls in the long aftermath of war. For example, in the Central African Republic among the 600,000 internally displaced people living in camps, close to 40% of women and girls reported being raped, making it the most common violence experienced by women and girls (International Rescue Committee, 2014). Further harm can be done in situations of armed conflict and displacement because individuals are torn from those mechanisms that would promote their recovery and resilience, such as support networks, access to health care, community institutions, cultural traditions, and family relationships. Particularly in the absence of these countervailing factors, victims suffer enduring and debilitating psychological consequences. In a dialogue for women coordinated by the United Nations High Commissioner for Refugees (2013), two of the main findings were the similarities in shared experiences of sexual and gender-based violence, and the lack of support in the aftermath for women across cultures and contexts. Gender-based violence is a common experience among displaced women and girls, and is a growing problem as the number of refugees and displaced persons increases around the world.

Response initiatives—where they do exist—focus on the immediate medical and security needs of women who have endured violence. However, in the long term, these women are left to suffer silently, the trauma often speaking through somatic symptoms. Frequently, they must also contend with being ostracized by shame and stigma in communities that have turned their backs on them. Creative and effective solutions are urgently needed.

Rationale for using story cloths as an access point

We would do well to take our inspiration from what has worked for women in diverse cultures across the centuries: Women who face atrocities have often come together to share their stories, to support one another, and, especially, to sew their stories into cloth. Exploration of this ancient and widespread cultural practice can help develop new recovery methods based on old practice.

One example of these sewn stories comes from Chile in the form of *arpilleras*, images created by pieces of material sewn on burlap flour sacks that depict the experiences of Chilean people during military dictatorship (Moya-Raggio, 1998). During the Pinochet dictatorship, 1973–1990, Chilean women gathered in secret workshops to tell their stories of brutality, disappeared family and friends, and hardships experienced, through the expression of *arpilleras. Arpilleras* were not only a form of active social commentary and economic participation on the part of Chilean women, but also a form of communal therapy (Cohen, 2013). The images range from illustrations of family life at home when the water supply has been cut off to more violent illustrations of passages through torture camps depicted through simple human figures being hung by the wrists and ankles, stretched across electric grates, and tightly confined in wooden boxes with bound hands and feet. Sometimes, the cloth used for these images were even pieces of clothing that belonged to disappeared family members. Although the *arpilleras* originally set out to describe the experiences of Chilean people as a form of political participation, women also found therapeutic value in textile making:

> The *arpilleras* were a beautiful kind of therapy for me. The first one I made showed the disappearance of my son; it took me a month because every doll I made had something so desiring about it. I lived alone, coming back to my home to sew and weep, which caused me great suffering. To relieve my anguish I made *arpilleras*. (Maria Eugenia, in Agosin, 2007)

Another example of a well-known tradition of story cloths is seen in the Hmong people describing atrocities perpetrated on their people and their experience as refugees in Laos. Colorfully sewn illustrations of Hmong people in traditional clothing show how they, as refugees, have faced physical and human rights abuses by soldiers and government officials in Laos. Examples of images in story cloths include the Hmong people escaping bombings from Laotian soldiers by floating down the Mekong river on hand-made bamboo rafts, fleeing their villages to escape in the mountains, and dead family members along the path of their escape. Other images depict the physical violence the Hmong people experienced, such as women being raped by Laotian soldiers. The story cloths that beautifully illustrate the trauma and violence of their escape serve as a powerful tool of expression and remembrance for the Hmong women.

Four decades after her escape from the Nazis during the Second World War, Esther Weisenthal Krinitz stitched the details of her history in thirty-six intricately embroidered large textiles (www.artandremembrance.org). Spending the last ten years of her life on this monumental project, she documented the death of her loved ones and recounted her story of survival in these story cloths. "The Nazis beat up my father" (Figure 7.1) depicts one of her memories.

In another example of documenting unspeakable history through personal story cloths, the Amazwi Abesifazane (Voices of Women) project in South Africa invited women to stitch the stories of their experiences under apartheid. More than 3000 of these story cloths are held in a small museum in Durban, SA (http://www.amazwi-voicesofwomen.com/) (Figure 7.2).

SEW TO SPEAK: STORY CLOTH HEALING 67

Figure 7.1. Esther Weisenthal Krinitz: "The Nazis beat up my father."

The powerful artwork the women have produced on cloth speaks to us not only of their pain, but also of resilience and strength (for examples of story cloths in diverse cultures, view video: https://vimeo.com/84129707). Through it, they find a way to speak to one another and to the world about their experiences and activate their capacity for coping with what has happened to them. These organic healing practices have much to teach us about effective recovery.

Figure 7.2. Amazwi Abesifazane (Voices of Women) project in South Africa—experiences under apartheid.

Indeed, discoveries in neuroscience validate the therapeutic value of this ancient practice. Research on how the brain responds to traumatic events demonstrates that at moments of mortal threat, in order to allow an individual to act quickly in self-protection, the verbal language centers in the left pre-frontal cortex deactivate, while the visual cortex increases activation, for scanning the environment and searching for ways of escape (Van der Kolk, 2014). Thus, traumatic memory is likely to be encoded in visual images, and in body-based sensations, more than in verbal forms. For example, survivors often develop somatic symptoms that express embodied pain (Ogden, 2006). In order to gain access to these experiences for therapeutic purposes, non-verbal modalities may prove most effective (Rothschild, 2000). Survivors of sexual violence might find that a conversation in images provides an access route to healing. The capacity to put words to these experiences becomes a step in the integrative process of trauma recovery.

Therapeutic aspects of hand sewing groups

Another key element of these sewing circles is the healing power of the group itself. Pioneer in therapeutic work with survivors of violence against women, Judith Herman, said this in 1992:

> The solidarity of a group provides the strongest protection against terror and despair, and the strongest antidote to traumatic experience. Trauma isolates, the group recreates a sense of belonging. Trauma

shames and stigmatizes; the group bears witness and affirms. ... Trauma dehumanizes the victim, the group restores her humanity. (Herman, 1992, p. 214)

One of the key elements of the small sewing circles is the ability to reconnect with others. Women discover that they are not alone, and are provided the opportunity to offer understanding and support for others' suffering. One reason that the small hand sewing circles allow this connection is that eye contact is not required. This allows for verbal discussion of the experiences as the person feels ready to do so without the intimate eye contact. This creates a private space for the individual within the group, but allows for interaction when individuals wish to engage with others. Women find it much easier in this setting to talk freely and allow feelings to surface. Sewing is, by nature, a slow process, gradually allowing relationships of trust to develop where more can be shared over time. This connection with others has a profoundly healing effect.

Just as women are given the space to verbally share when they feel comfortable, the creation process of story cloths provides an opportunity for piecing together a narrative at the comfort of one's own pace and initiative. Sewing is also a common practice in many cultures, allowing women to practice something that feels safe and familiar. It has positive, reparative associations for many people (linked to a nurturing figure—often grandmother or mother). This provides an optimal context for processing material that has people feeling at their most vulnerable. The story cloth functions as a transitional object for women who have experienced massive losses.

A second key element to hand sewing is that it is a profoundly self-soothing activity. Stitching is a very natural way to calm a nervous system that has been functioning in the "high alert" mode of post-trauma vigilance. Engaging in a repetitive, rhythmic motion promotes the regulation of neurophysiological arousal. The use of the hands in coordinated activity such as sewing aids in the reorganization of the somatosensory cortex and enhances interhemispheric integration (McCormack, 2014).

A third key element is reclaiming some sense of agency in the world. To undertake a concrete project and bring it to completion supports a sense of efficacy so badly needed for women who have been rendered helpless. Story quilts have exposed torture, rape, and genocide where regimes have attempted to silence their victims. Part of the healing process of sewing narratives is that it can begin a process of developing a voice and narrative of the experienced violence. Creating something of beauty out of a horrific experience promotes mastery and agency that has often been lost.

It is clear that there are numerous elements of hand sewing circles that are beneficial for the individual and the collective. It is also clear that there is a need for different responses to the psychological harm done to those who have experienced gender-based violence, specifically among displaced populations in post-war settings. The lessons learned from the benefits and the cultural relevance of sewing circles are key to informing the work of Common Threads.

The Common Threads approach

Inspired by this tradition, we created a comprehensive intervention called Common Threads (CT) that integrates story cloth making with a variety of other practices from art therapy, psycho-education about trauma and its consequences, symptom management, and body work (breathing, muscle relaxation, guided imagery). We train local practitioners to adapt the program for context and to lead the women's circles during an intensive eighty-hour training course.

In the non-stigmatizing and supportive setting of traditional sewing groups, CT participants create narrative textiles to serve as the basis for processing traumatic experiences. The sewing circle is conducive to quiet contemplation, sharing of stories, building of trusting relationships, and lasting bonds. Here, the women are available for specific psychotherapeutic activities that enhance coping skills for healing and resilience (Figure 7.3).

Common Threads is a three-phase program: During Phase I, participants meet in weekly 4.5-hour workshops for fourteen weeks. They master techniques to manage intense emotions and maintain stability, practice art therapy techniques for self-expression, and develop basic sewing skills to design and complete their narrative textiles. With the help of facilitators, they are encouraged to share these stories with one another. As they consider these narratives, they work to reduce stigma, guilt, self-blame, to process loss, grief, and traumatic memory, to reclaim hope and a sense of future.

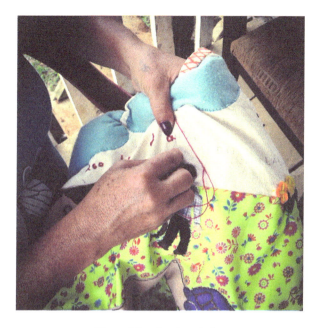

Figure 7.3. Sewing circle.

Phase II of Common Threads accompanies survivors for six more months of sessions as they consolidate gains, internalize strategies, continue to process the narratives in a new way, and progress towards recovery, thriving, and empowerment.

By Phase III, those who have completed Phases I and II are ready to establish their own self-led support group. They have taken turns in leading activities with the support of facilitators in Phase II. They have internalized the techniques of coping, which they can continue to practice as a group in Phase III.

Common Threads has been implementing and studying this approach over the past several years. Our first pilot took place in refugee communities in Ecuador in 2012. In 2014, we launched a project in Nepal, training sixteen facilitators and initially serving seventy-five women in Nepal's refugee communities. New rounds of these women's circles are launching in Kathmandu and several other districts of Nepal. In 2015, CT established its program in Bosnia-Herzegovina, where the women's circles are currently running. We are exploring future project sites in the Democratic Republic of Congo, and in refugee communities in the US.

72   THE COURAGE TO FIGHT VIOLENCE AGAINST WOMEN

Expressing trauma narratives

After a few weeks of stabilization work to create a safe foundation for the exploration of traumatic memories, the CT circle facilitators present a selection of five prompts to evoke material for the individual story cloths. They allow time for the participants to silently consider the images that surface internally in response to the prompts, and then draw them on paper. The story cloths they create based on these designs become an opportunity for disclosure and access, opening the door for continued trauma work.

The following section presents the phrases Common Threads offers as prompts, followed by an example of a story cloth that was created in response to that phrase.

"This is a moment I will never forget"

Maria depicts the day her village was attacked and her life destroyed (Figure 7.4). She remembers how the family's livestock was killed and the scene of chaos that ensued. She herself escaped on a small boat, but others in her family were left behind. The images of that day haunted

Figure 7.4.   "This is a moment I will never forget." Maria depicts the day her village was attacked and her life destroyed.

her. During the many weeks Maria spent sewing this scene, she continued to process and heal from the horrific event and its aftermath. Others in the group helped her to overcome fears that remained from the violence and a sense of loss about the death of family members, the destruction of her village, and her displacement. Her frequent nightmares ceased and she began to form new trusting relationships.

"This is what I cannot say"

Pilar remembers how her brother threatened to kill her with a machete because she had witnessed his paramilitary activities in Colombia. She "knew too much" he said. In this scene (Figure 7.5), she is forced to flee for her life, and she has no chance even to say goodbye to her beloved father (foreground) whom she will never see again. It is this loss that she addressed during the therapeutic process. She worked to forgive herself for doing what she needed to do to survive.

"This is what I need you to know"

Rosa sewed the scene of her children being shot at on the river in front of their home. Notice also that she portrayed her husband holding a

Figure 7.5. "This is what I cannot say." Pilar is forced to flee for her life and has no chance to say goodbye to her father.

bottle in his hand (Figure 7.6). What Rosa needed us to know is that amid the violence surrounding the family, it was the domestic violence that was of most concern to her. Caught in a civil war, she felt especially vulnerable, and desperately sought to protect her children from attackers. But her husband was usually too drunk to notice, or to help defend them. During the course of the program, she revealed years of abuse by her husband, and her exit from this relationship became the focus of her therapeutic work.

"This is what the cloth is trying to say"

Often it is too difficult to own the painful story. For this reason, CT offers an opportunity to ascribe the motive to the cloth itself. When she joined the CT circle, Blanca was severely depressed and non-communicative. Although she said almost nothing in the group discussions, she was able to express deep emotions in her story cloth. In it, the cloth spoke of the trauma that held her in its grip: in the scene, her daughter is being raped and murdered by soldiers one night over a year earlier (Figure 7.7). As she listened to the other women, and

Figure 7.6. "This is what I need you to know." Rosa sewed the scene of her children being shot at on the river in front of their home, her husband holding a bottle of alcohol in his hand.

SEW TO SPEAK: STORY CLOTH HEALING   75

Figure 7.7. "This is what the cloth is trying to say." Blanca's daughter is being raped and murdered by soldiers.

witnessed their discussions, Blanca seemed to do a lot of healing work internally. Her mood was lifting, and she began to be less withdrawn. As the end of the program approached, she added two colorful elements to her cloth. When other women in the circle asked Blanca about the rosebush in the foreground, she said, "This is my daughter's soul." The yellow bird, she said, sings with her daughter's voice. Now that she had a safe place to grieve, she could hear her daughter's voice again.

"This is what I hope for the future"

We offer this prompt for those who choose not to look back. But, of course, the buried material may still find a way to surface as the individual is ready to process it. Carla created a vision of her future—grandchildren playing in her garden, bright colors, a house, and the pastoral scene of a peaceful life (Figure 7.8). When she shares her textile with the circle, a peer says, "Tell us about the tree?" Quite out of character, Carla bursts into tears: "The mango tree is actually from my parents garden—not from my future! What is it doing there? That

Figure 7.8. "This is what I hope for the future." Carla created a vision of her future—grandchildren playing in her garden, bright colors, a house, and the pastoral scene of a peaceful life; the mango tree is where she hid when her father came to beat her.

is where I hid when my father came to beat me!" This opened the door for the first time to exploration of childhood abuse buried for more than fifty years. Ultimately, she renamed the textile: *This Is what the Cloth Is Trying to Say!* to indicate that the non-verbal process had led her to significant new insights. The stories behind the stories seem to take the healing where it needs to go.

Outcomes of Common Threads projects

Evaluations of the Common Threads approach used a mixed method approach that collected both quantitative and qualitative outcome measures. Qualitative methods include interviews with participants and facilitators, while quantitative methods used the Hopkins Symptom Checklist (HSCL-25) (Derogatis et al., 1974), the PTSD checklist (PLC-M for *DSM-IV*) (Weathers et al., 1994), and an abbreviated version of COPE (Carver et al., 1989) to measure changes in depression, anxiety, and trauma-related stress.

There are limitations to the study design that are notable and should be taken into consideration for implementation and evaluation of future Common Threads programs. First, the sample sizes were small ($N = 72$, with only fifty-four completing the study during the post earthquake period) which decreases the statistical power of the quantitative results and weakens the generalizability of findings. Additionally, the instruments were self-reported, allowing room for social desirability bias from participants to report what they think researchers might want to hear. There was also no control or comparison group to measure results against. In addition to limitations in design, there was a poor collection of data, where much of the desired data are missing; some of this is due to attrition at post-Phase II data collection. Last, the quantitative measures used do not capture the changes in aspects of important constructs of agency, voice, empowerment, reintegration, social coherence, and "meaning-making". To capture these constructs, qualitative data was collected and analyzed.

Overall quantitative outcomes show a significant decrease in depression, anxiety, and trauma-related stress from baseline to post-intervention. The percentage of respondents meeting criteria for a diagnosis of depression decreased from 80% pre-intervention to 40% post-intervention. Anxiety measures decreased from 58% pre-intervention to 38% post-intervention, and PTSD measures decreased from 52% pre-intervention to 22% post-intervention. All of these measures were taken over the course of six months. Complementary qualitative results also show a reduction of mental health symptoms, improvements in functioning, outlook, coping, self-confidence, self-assertion, and connection with others (Figure 7.9).

Thematic analysis of the interviews was done to illustrate the impact of the intervention from the perspective of participants. A key reason for adapting the sewing circles for the Common Threads approach also emerged in the themes of connecting with others and solidarity. Connecting with others was expressed by one participant, who said, "They listened to us, they understood us. I know they cannot do anything but even if someone listens to you that is a great thing." One participant expressed solidarity as, "It's only after we came to the program that we knew that it's not just us who are having such problems. Everyone had it." The group aspect of the sewing circles elicited a sense of community for women in circumstances where sense of community and belonging had been torn apart.

Quantitative findings (Nepal)

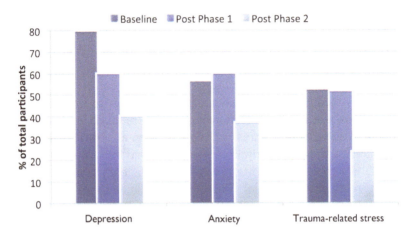

Figure 7.9. Graph of research results.

During the aftermath of the 2014 earthquakes in Nepal, many of the women from CT circles found themselves living outside with their neighbors in Kathmandu. They began spontaneously to teach friends and neighbors relaxation and breathing exercises to help their community deal with the stress of the crisis. They had clearly internalized these practices, and were motivated to help others as well. This anecdotal data spoke eloquently of their connection with others, and the integration of coping skills they had learned in CT.

One theme that emerged from the data was that of self-regulation, where women talked about how the use of sewing and the ability to express themselves helped with anger and emotional issues they faced in their lives. One participant said, "I used to get angry at the smallest things and would beat my daughters in frustration. Even though I used to feel guilty about it, I could not control myself . . . my anger's in check now, I don't fight with my husband and I don't beat my daughters." This woman attributed this change in behavior to the impact of the program on her emotional stability. This is another demonstration of the bigger impact of the Common Threads approach outside of the sewing circles.

Symptom reduction was described by many participants who expressed lowered levels of stress and less emotional and psychological weight. One participant said, "I was feeling terrible, heavy, desperate, disoriented. I didn't have strength for anything, in my home and at my work. What I used to do was to cry. I feel like a new person. I feel lighter, with more strength to work and to have my own business." This quote also demonstrates the positive long-term impact of symptom reduction in the lives of these women.

The interviews also demonstrated that that self-expression was a domain of change for participants. Women felt that they could finally start to share their difficult and painful stories with others through the expression of sewing. One woman said, "It's here that we share what we keep hidden." Another woman said, "I used to be disturbed while recalling my past incidents. I always thought about it. But this made us express our stories into one textile and now I don't feel very disturbed when I express those things. We expressed it in a piece of cloth." One woman expressed the importance of the story cloths as a vehicle of expression, "This was a unique thing, that the story that we cannot speak about we could express in pictures." This theme illustrates the power of story cloths and their use as an outlet of expression for the difficult memories that could not be expressed with words.

Similarly, the theme of personal empowerment was emphasized by participants. Personal empowerment was expressed by one woman as, "We used to be scared. But now we don't feel scared, we can speak and are confident of doing something." Another participant said, "I thought that I can't do anything but now I feel I can do something."

In Ecuador, we discovered that the women continued their process of healing beyond our planned three-month program. They requested more meetings with facilitators, which ultimately became Phases II and III of CT. During this time, many focused on healing from abuse they had suffered in childhood (including a number of cases of incest) that preceded the trauma of war-related sexual violence and displacement.

* * *

More than a year after CT participants in Ecuador had begun the women's circles, their process of healing led them towards a collective project. They began to channel their anger about the injustices they had suffered towards working for change in the larger community. As Judith Herman proposed in her pioneering work (Herman 1992), the final phase of their healing involved engaging in activism: The women who had been silenced victims initiated a public exhibition of their work in the capital city to commemorate the Global 16 Days of Activism against gender-based violence. They made speeches at this event, promoting women's rights in Ecuador. Their exhibit later came to the UN headquarters in Geneva (*The Fabric of Healing*, 2014).

One test of whether the women in CT groups have internalized what they learn in the program is how they weather subsequent major stressors. In Nepal, unfortunately, we had a prime example of a community stressor when the country experienced a series of major earthquakes and aftershocks in 2014. During this period, many of the women from CT circles found themselves living outside with their neighbors in Kathmandu. We heard reports from the community that spontaneously they had begun to teach friends and neighbors relaxation and breathing exercises to help their community deal with the stress of the crisis. They had clearly internalized these practices, and were motivated to help others as well. This anecdotal data spoke eloquently of their connection with others, and the integration of coping skills they had learned in CT.

Conclusions

The pilot projects of Common Threads in Nepal and Ecuador have shown quite promising results. Our current project in Bosnia adds rigor to the research design (i.e., a control group is also being studied), data collection, and data analysis to address weaknesses of the prior research. This will allow us to refine and scale up the intervention for future project sites, and to understand more about the mechanisms of change that fuel Common Threads.

The women's circles in Nepal and Ecuador have taught us a great deal about how women help each other in the process of healing. As we work in these contexts, we are also learning to think in new ways about trauma. The purely medical model of trauma for survivors of mass violence has proved inadequate: symptom reduction is only one aspect, providing a solid foundation for other changes that need to develop. As we listen to the women carefully, we understand that they are engaged in a transformational personal and collective process. Survivors have taught us that their larger healing process involves reclaiming a sense of purpose, meaning, agency, re-establishing trust in others, and a shift in their attitudes about gender norms. In its ideal form, this journey becomes one of meaning-making, post-traumatic growth, and empowerment. The recovery strategies we develop need to support this process. Having achieved their own recovery, these women can become the strongest advocates for prevention of gender-based violence. This is what is needed to address the challenge of violence against women.

References

Agosin, M. (2007). *Tapestries of Hope, Threads of Love: The Arpillera Movement in Chile*. Lanham: Roman and Littlefield.

Carver, C. S., Scheier, M. F., & Weintraub, J. K. (1989). Assessing coping strategies: a theoretically based approach. *Journal of Personality and Social Psychology*, *56*: 267–283.

Cohen, R. (2013). Common threads: a recovery programme for survivors of gender based violence. *Intervention: Journal of Mental Health and Psychological Support in Conflict Affected Areas*, *2*(2): 157–168.

Derogatis, L. R., Lipman, R. S., Rickels, K., Uhlenhuth, E. H., & Covi, L. (1974). The Hopkins Symptom Checklist (HSCL): a self-report symptom inventory. *Behavioral Science*, *19*: 1–15.

Herman, J. (1992). *Trauma and Recovery*. New York: Basic Books.

International Rescue Committee (IRC) (2014). Bearing the brunt of violence: women & girls in the Central African Republic. Accessed at: www.rescue.org/sites/default/files/resource-file/CAR%20advocacy%20sheet%20on%20women%20and%20girls_26March2014_0.pdf on April 15, 2016.

McCormack, G. L. (2014). The significance of somatosensory stimulation to the hand: implications for occupational therapy practice. *Open Journal of Occupational Therapy*, *4*: 1–25.

Moya-Raggio, E. (1998). Arpierras: Chilean culture of resistance. *Feminist Studies*, *10*(2): 277–290.

Ogden, P. (2006). *Trauma and the body: A Sensorimotor Approach to Psychotherapy*. New York: W. W. Norton.

Rothschild, B. (2000). *The Body Remembers: The Psychophysiology of Trauma and Trauma Treatment*. New York: W. W. Norton.

The Fabric of Healing (2014). Public exhibit at UN Palais, Geneva, July.

UNFPA (2016). Gender-based violence webpage. Accessed at: www.unfpa.org/gender-based-violence on April 27.

UNHCR (2013, 14 February). UHCR's dialogue with refugee women. Accessed at: www.refworld.org/docid/5231b1214.html on April 15, 2016.

UNHCR (2015). Mid-year trends 2015. Accessed at: www.unhcr.org/56701b969.html on April 15, 2016.

Van der Kolk, B. (2014) *The Body Keeps the Score: Brain, Mind and Body in the Healing of Trauma*. New York: Viking.

Weathers, F. W., Litz, B. T., Herman, D. S., Huska, J. A., & Keane, T. M. (1994). The PTSD checklist (PCL): reliability, validity, and diagnostic utility. National Center for PTSD, Behavioral Science Division.

CHAPTER EIGHT

Commentary on "Girls at risk" and "Sew to speak"

Carla Neely

The two preceding chapters, "Girls at risk: paths to safety" by Dr. Raquel Berman, and "Sew to speak: story cloth healing with survivors of sexual violence" by Rachel A. Cohen and Ana Maria Ramirez, are examples of community outreach underpinned by psychoanalytic ideas. The application of psychoanalytic thought to groups of traumatized girls and women in Quintana Roo, Mexico can result in creative ways to provide opportunities for resilience in the face of acute and ongoing traumatic experience. Common Threads is a model program whose purpose is to aid in the repair of sexual and other trauma resulting from war and subsequent displacement perpetrated on females. These females live with a power base inferior to the male population in their cultures.

Dr. Cohen offers a vivid pictorial and verbal description of the assault on the female psyche and the repair that can occur through the establishment of group sewing circles, including the production of story cloths that tell without words of the trauma endured and survived.

Dr. Berman's work addresses female adolescent development and the trauma that ensues from young girls' relative lack of power in the culture of Quintana Roo, Mexico. Inevitably, trauma is found in the lives of these young women. In Mexico, unlike the war-torn countries cited by Dr. Cohen in Common Threads, the public face of the political system is one of democratic gender equality. Yet, young girls are failed in a system that does not follow its own rule of law.

In Dr. Cohen's project, the rule of law has not only been fractured, but has not included gender equality as a part of the culture prior to the trauma of war and its aftermath. In her cohort, we see that there is no pretence, no conscious intent in the structures of the culture to grant equal power and protection to all citizens. In Dr. Berman's report, we can see that, despite a public structure of equal rights for all, the implicit bias against female equality is deeply embedded in the culture. Implicit bias has a pernicious hold on the minds of adolescent females as well as on those of the male population.

Dr. Berman's presentation of a psychoanalytically informed intervention in a three-year multi-disciplinary approach to adolescent girls involves the construction of female youth councils, groups of young girls led by school psychologists who are supported by psychoanalysts. The groups have an educational focus with the goal of preparing young girls to assume the equal gender rights afforded by the Mexican Constitution. They are discussion-based, with readings, awareness of group dynamics, and wide ranging group participation. These methods help to make clear the contradictions between the public and implicit ideas about gendered capacities and behaviors.

Having grown up in a contradictory culture, adolescent girls in Quintana Roo are just as subject to such cultural biases as "machismo" as are young boys. The group experience over time allows such contradictions to be confronted, giving girls the opportunity to expand their hopes and beliefs about their capacity to create a future for themselves, rather than one proscribed by cultural limitation.

As Dr. Cohen tells us, the use of story cloths as an access point to a traumatized psyche has an ancient and widespread history in cultures that might otherwise differ from each other in many ways. Across varied cultures, Common Threads addresses, from a neuroscience perspective, the silencing of the self that trauma can create. Dr. Cohen explains the rationale for sewing circles as a means of giving voice to the trauma of violence through the non-verbal medium of art. What the brain has shut down, here the mind finds other means of expression. Her study also provides a remarkable picture of the ways that group experience and the concrete representation of trauma can produce resilience and strength. The shared experience of the group as its individuals create their story cloths gives rise to the restitution of verbal capacity that had been diminished in the face of trauma. Each woman is enabled by this process to develop her own narrative, thus reclaiming a sense of agency that extreme traumatic events have taken away. Regaining a sense of agency is crucial to the capacity to cope with overwhelming trauma.

The therapeutic value of sewing circles is multi-determined, outlined in detail by Dr. Cohen. The "common" aspect of Common Threads relates not only to the concrete pictorial representations created by each group member, but also to the idea of a "common" experience of war that each woman gives witness to in the others. The sharing of experience, both concretely in the story cloths and, eventually, in verbal communication, does a great deal to ameliorate the extreme isolating effects that trauma produces.

Cultural bias denying gender equality, conscious and unconscious, has a profound effect on the continuation of perpetrated trauma. The programs described in this chapter go a long way to providing females with an understanding of what must be confronted in the culture to create change. Hopelessness produced by violent trauma is survived creatively when traumatic experience is given voice by the violated and understood by the group.

CHAPTER NINE

Violation: a poem

Myra Sklarew

Introduction by Nancy R. Goodman

Myra Sklarew is a courageous witness to violence and atrocity. She is willing to face the horrors and to find in her soul a way to write and bring it to others in poetic form. Her poem "Violation" captures the sense of violence and the courage to feel and represent that is the central focus of this book. Myra's use of language unveils the ravages of rape. She presents her poem here with comments about her desire and determination to write this poem. The anthology in which the poem appears is *Veils, Halos & Shackles* (Fishman & Sahay, 2016).

Her current work centers on trauma and memory: Her interviews in Lithuania have led to her new book: *A Survivor Named Trauma: Holocaust and the Construction of Memory—The Impact of Trauma on the Encoding and Retrieval of Memory: Conversations with Survivors, Witnesses, Rescuers and Collaborators* (forthcoming from SUNY Press), and she has a number of other publications to her credit.

Myra Sklarew is Professor Emerita in the Department of Literature at American University in Washington, DC and former president of Yaddo Artist's Community. Her writing shows her special capacity to be a witness to individual experience of trauma: she listens, she waits, she creates. She wrote a chapter, "Leiser's song" in *The Power of Witnessing: Reflections, Reverberations, and Traces of the Holocaust* (Goodman & Meyers, 2012) about conversations with her cousin Leiser over nine years from his home in Switzerland. He called her at all times of the night and day to reveal and live with his own poignant evolving rememberings of the horrors of the Holocaust in Lithuania.

* * *

Violation

> I thought sorrow would drown me, but then my sorrow learned to swim.
>
> Tranquilino Castaneda

> Even the mourning dove stands guard
> over its dying mate at the traffic circle;
> no matter the crush of oncoming cars.
>
> Even the male frog refuses to abandon
> its young, making a home in its vocal pouch
> for its tadpoles until they hatch.
>
> What does it mean for a man
> to use what perpetuates life
> to destroy life? To inflict a wound
>
> so deep into the body of a woman?
> Does he try to erase the mother
> who bore him? Or obliterate himself?
>
> It is not love he brings to this meal.

I have thought for a long time about what it means to violate a woman, to use that means to express rage and aggression. Many have written on the subject. But to destroy that most sacred process, the progenerative function that renews and ensures the continuance of life, seems to me a form of suicide, a wish for the obliteration of the perpetrator. The epigraph to this poem was spoken by Tranquilino

Castaneda on public radio. He was one whose wife and children were raped and killed and whose last remaining small son was taken by one of the military and raised, never knowing who his real family was until he grew up.

The massacre happened in a Guatemalan town, Dos Erres, during the civil war there in the 1980s. Over 600 villages were destroyed; over 180,000 people were killed or "disappeared." The government denied this but, eventually, in this particular town, bodies were found. The one surviving son of Tranquilino Castaneda was Oscar Ramirez, who learned only at age thirty-one, through DNA testing, that Tranquilino, then seventy, was his real father. He was three when taken from his original family and had no memory of them. One can read/hear the transcript on *This American Life*.

However, Tranquilino's story is not what initiated the poem: my eternal work on Lithuania, Holocaust, and memory, and my belief in the natural world as our teacher, are what did. But I happened to hear a portion of this radio program and it seemed appropriate to the poem.

References

Fishman, C., & Sahay, S. (Eds.) (2016). *Veils, Halos & Shackles: International Poetry on the Oppression and Empowerment of Women*. Alfei Menashe, Israel: Kasva Press.

Goodman, N. R., & Meyers, M. B. (2012). *The Power of Witnessing: Reflections, Reverberations, and Traces of the Holocaust*. New York: Routledge.

CHAPTER TEN

Anatomy of a man's assault on a woman

Donald Campbell

The self-preservative function of the ego

I view aggression as an instinct that is available to the ego in the pursuit of its primary function—the preservation of the self. This view of aggression and its relation to the ego is based on Freud's remarks in "Instincts and their vicissitudes" (1915c). When considering hate, he wrote, ". . . the true prototypes of the relation of hate are derived . . . from the ego's struggle to preserve and maintain itself" (Freud, 1915c, p. 138).

When I view the ego's primary function as the preservation of the self, I am referring to anything that constitutes a threat to physical or psychological homeostasis. This includes narcissistic equilibrium, that is, good enough feelings about oneself, appropriate self-esteem, and psychological integrity. The aim is to maintain a dynamic balance, a steady state of physical health and psychological wellbeing at optimum levels.

The ego's task is to solve problems that threaten to destabilize us. Therefore, the "best" solution negotiated by the ego is that which creates and maintains a feeling of physical safety and psychological wellbeing. A violent act, a neurotic or psychotic state, a symptom, or a character trait, a defence mechanism or a perversion, however maladapted in the outside world, might be the "best" solution the ego can negotiate given the external circumstances and the ego's internal resources (Sandler & Sandler, 1992).

Ruthless aggression

Following Glasser (1998), I distinguish between two types of aggression: first, ruthless aggression, which is primary, and second, sadistic aggression, which is the result of a modification of ruthless aggression. Bio-physiologists such as Cannon (1939) have shown that the body has an elaborate reflexive reaction pattern that prepares it for fight or flight in the presence of danger. This reflexive fight/flight mechanism, which we share with all living organisms, is our most primitive defence and serves the ego's self-preservative instincts. The fight mechanism is a primary aggression, which I will refer to as ruthless aggression. In the psychic sphere, all aggression is self-preservative. All of us, as infants and adults, are capable of self-preservative aggression. When ruthless aggression is enacted in relation to an object, it becomes ruthless violence.

Ruthless violence is a fundamental, immediate, and substantial response to any threat to the self with the aim of negating this source of danger. Here is an example: If you suddenly found yourself being stalked by a lion in the African bush and unable to run, you would normally react with self-preservative aggression with the aim of getting rid of the lion. Self-preservative aggression has a single-minded, narrow-vision quality like a laser beam, which focuses on the dangerousness of the object rather than the object itself. If a person's look is experienced as threatening through accusation, it is the eyes that are attacked; if what is being said is intolerable, the mouth is punched, and so on (Glasser, 1998, p. 888).

During a moment of self-preservative aggression or violence, the object holds no personal significance other than his/her dangerousness: an attack is carried out in the interest of self-preservation and any other considerations are not relevant. The response of the object in any other respect is of no interest (Glasser, 1998, p. 891). When the mother fails to contain her child's ruthless aggression, the child "can only hide a ruthless self and give it life in a state of dissociation" (Winnicott, 1958, p. 154) or psychosis.

Threats to the infant's psyche and/or physical survival (the infant cannot be expected to know the difference between them) normally mobilize ruthless aggression directed towards the object that is perceived as dangerous. The threat might be experienced as a direct assault, engulfment, smothering, or abandonment to starve. As I explained earlier, the aim of ruthless aggression is to negate the threat.

However, when the object that is perceived as threatening the child's survival is the same object upon which it depends for its survival (the mother), the exercise of ruthless aggression poses a dilemma for the child. How is the child to survive if it cannot afford to get rid of its mother? Children fashion an ingenious solution by fusing their love for their mother with their aggression to create sadism. Sadomasochism, which all mothers and babies employ, becomes a primary way of dealing with anxieties about loss and separation. The games of peek-a-boo, or hide and seek and mild teasing are common examples of this. Mothers and children teasing each other are examples of the fusion of their aggression with their love for each other. In this way, the child changes the aim of its ruthless aggression from eliminating mother to controlling her in a libidinally gratifying way. Ruthless aggression is, thereby, converted into sadism, where gratification is derived from inflicting anxiety, fear, discomfort, or pain upon another. As you can see, sadism, like the primary, ruthless aggression it is based on, is motivated by self-preservation.

The role of sadism

In a ruthless attack where the aim is, by fight or flight, to eliminate the threat to one's survival, the impact upon the object is irrelevant beyond the achievement of this aim. However, in a sadistic attack, the relationship to the object must be preserved, not eliminated. By radically altering the relationship to the threatening object to ensure that both self and object survive, sadism now offers the child a second line of defence.

Subtly modulated mild sadomasochism emerges now as a libidinal component of the good enough bond between mother and child. However, when the mother's sadism is not tempered by reparation or extends beyond the child's capacity to recover a nurturing image, or when mother's narcissism makes it impossible for her to be aware of her infant's needs and respond appropriately, the child might rely on more frequent and more intense sadomasochistic exchanges to control a not good enough mother.

When the line of development from self-preservative aggression to the libidinalization of aggression progresses to the intensification of sadism, the psychic groundwork is laid for the use of sadism as a solution to neurotic or psychotic conflicts. When the mother's sadism fails to defend her against what she experiences as her child's persecution, she is at risk of relying upon ruthless aggression or its psychic equivalent. The child's wellbeing is then no longer relevant to the mother. The mother's only concern is negating or eliminating any aspect of the child that poses a threat to her survival. At this point, the child's development, and, in extreme cases, its survival, is at risk.

Initially, the child responds to what is experienced as an accelerating risk to its survival by intensifying its sadistic control of any increasingly dangerous parent. Yet, what recourse does the child have available if its sadism fails to satisfactorily control a frightening parent? In such cases, the child, and, later, the adolescent and adult, is likely to abandon its sadomasochistic relationship with the object and regress to reliance upon ruthless aggression with the aim of eliminating a too painful reality by psychotic withdrawal from, or destruction of, the object.

I have found that when the child persistently, over time, has to rely upon sadomasochism to defend against anxieties associated with engulfment and abandonment, sadomasochism permeates fantasies, masturbation fantasies, and the way his body is used in relationships, the foundations are laid for perverse sexual development, and/or the eroticism of aggression and, in some cases, the repetition of violence to generate sexual gratification.

Violence rarely occurs in pure form as simply ruthless or sadistic attacks. More often, the violence is mixed, or begins as a sadistic exchange that breaks down and, thereby, increases the perpetrator's anxiety and his or her reliance upon ruthless violence.

An account of a violent assault

To illustrate my views about the ruthless and sadistic nature of aggression, I will report Mr. Giles's account of an assault on his girlfriend, Sylvia, which he described as follows: He and Sylvia were having dinner with an "older woman" at her flat. He found himself being irritated by the older woman, who said "ridiculous things". Mr. Giles took Sylvia back to his flat and made sure that there were no neighbors around because he "didn't want the police alerted". He then tried to force Sylvia to admit that the woman had said ridiculous things but Sylvia denied that this was so. He escalated his threats and attacks from slapping to punching as Sylvia repeatedly refused to agree. Eventually, he found himself kneeling over Sylvia on the bed with his fingers in her eyes trying to gouge them out. At this point, he suddenly realized what he was doing and backed away. Afterwards, he felt shame and guilt about having made Sylvia feel "so worthless". Sylvia, who was, in fact, badly bruised around the head and eyes, left him. This was not the first time he had been violent, but I think it was the first time he caught himself about to inflict permanent damage on his victim, and this is what alarmed him and led him to seek help with his violence.

The anatomy of an assault

Mr. Giles's sadistic attack on Sylvia appears to have been provoked by an "older woman" who said ridiculous things. Mr. Giles never told me what they were. I had the impression that the older woman had her own opinions about things and that they probably contradicted Mr. Giles's views. Later, in the course of his psychotherapy, I learned that this older woman reminded him of his mother who did not take him into account and "pushed' her opinions into him. I also learned that he felt particularly defenseless and alone because his violent father was either away at work or sleeping off an alcoholic binge. The older woman's behavior revived these earlier experiences of helpless rage with his mother.

Mr. Giles set about reversing this experience of being unable to control the "older woman" by taking control of Sylvia. Mr. Giles identified with his father's use of violence to solve problems. First, by bullying, and then by inflicting physical pain with slaps and punches, Mr. Giles tried to get Sylvia to agree with him and see the older woman as he did. At the beginning, this was a premeditated sadistic attack because Mr. Giles assured himself that the neighbors were out as he "didn't want the police alerted".

At this point in Mr. Giles's narrative, we are aware that Sylvia is not a masochist in the conventional sense; that is, she does not immediately submit to her sadistic boyfriend. I think this is why Mr. Giles "chose" her. Ordinarily, a sadist is not interested in a masochist because he or she offers no resistance; there is nothing for the sadistic partner to overcome, to triumph over, to control. In this situation, we can see that, as Sylvia refuses to submit, Mr. Giles increases the level of pain he inflicts upon her.

Why did Mr. Giles move from slapping Sylvia to trying to gouge out her eyes? He said that he felt shame and guilt for making her feel "so worthless". I think this is the key to understanding the impact his mother's intrusiveness had on him and why he was desperate to force Sylvia to submit to his will. Mr. Giles had felt profoundly humiliated by his mother, just as the older woman had shamed him in front of his girlfriend. He was narcissistically destabilized and tried to reverse that experience of humiliation by projecting it, through violence, into Sylvia. Mr. Giles escalated his sadistic attacks because they were ineffective and, as a consequence, he was increasingly helpless and anxious. His sadistic attempts to control Sylvia were breaking down and Sylvia was not aware that she was increasingly at risk.

Later, Mr. Giles was able to acknowledge that he felt defeated by Sylvia. I wondered if the look in her eyes conveyed her indomitable defiance, which reinforced his helplessness and humiliation. He felt his only recourse was to get rid of the evidence of his failure.

While thinking about this assault with Mr. Giles in his therapy, it became clear that when his sadistic attacks failed, he panicked and regressed to a ruthless attack on Sylvia's eyes. He abandoned his attempt to take control of her mind and tried to get rid of her eyes. When he realized what he was doing, he stopped.

References

Cannon, W. B. (1939). *The Wisdom of the Body*. London: Kegan Paul, Trench, Trubner.
Freud, S. (1915c). Instincts and their vicissitudes. *S. E.*, *14*: 117–140. London: Hogarth.
Glasser, M. (1998). On violence: a preliminary communication. *International Journal of Psychoanalysis*, *79*: 887–902.
Sandler, J., & Sandler, A.-M. (1992). Psychoanalytic technique and the theory of psychic change. *Bulletin of the Anna Freud Centre*, *15*: 35–51.
Winnicott, D. W. (1958). Primitive emotional development In: *Collected Papers:Through Paediatrics to Psycho-Analysis* (pp. 145–156). London: Tavistock.

CHAPTER ELEVEN

Commentary on Donald Campbell's "Anatomy of a man's assault on a woman"

Justine Kalas Reeves

Introduction: the importance of studying the roots of violence from a psychoanalytic point of view

Dr. Donald Campbell presents a case of a man who voluntarily sought treatment after coming close to gouging out his girlfriend's eyes. We take as given that working with a person to understand what was in his or her mind *before* violating another person is precisely the detailed data that psychoanalytic treatment can provide. The forensic psychoanalyst is in a unique position to influence educational, legal, and mental health systems, and to make recommendations to parents, carers, and teachers who are in a position to intervene at nodal points of development when a perpetrator sounds an alarm in words or actions. Dr. Campbell's paper offers us helpful ideas towards these aims, using Mervin Glasser's indispensible papers on sadism (1996, 1998).

The developmental point of view in Glasser and Campbell

Donald Campbell is originally from the USA, and completed his child and adolescent psychoanalytic training at Hampstead (later called the

Anna Freud Centre) prior to completing adult analytic training at the British Society. He worked and did research with Mervin Glasser at the Portman Clinic in London for many years.

In his chapter, "Anatomy of a man's assault on a woman", he distinguishes between ruthless aggression and ruthless violence. Following Freud, Winnicott, and Glasser, ruthless aggression is a reaction to inner or outer dangers the sole aim of which is to preserve the ego. He uses as an example that if you were to see a lion and were unable to run, you would strike out with self-preservative aggression to get rid of the lion. The only reason for hurting the lion is to protect the self or "negate the threat," as Campbell writes. Ruthless violence, in contrast, comes about over the course of development when a parent and child mutually feel harmed in their exchanges such that the intersubjective feeling between them is dangerous and persecutory, leaving the child helpless and unprotected.

I would add that the parent who cannot modulate inner and outer threats for the child and is, therefore, perceived as a threat to the child, is also probably traumatized and abused, and is likely to have become sadistic over the course of his or her own development, again, to protect the self. To manage the conundrum—for the child—of being reliant upon the same parent who feels unsafe, self-preservative aggression becomes libidinized (the child feels pleasure in aggressing towards the parent to master the helplessness of feeling abandoned, starved, or treated as a cruel, persecutory child). Mother experiences the child as a threat to her survival, too, persecuted as she feels by her child's aggressing towards her. Campbell writes, "At this point, the child's development, and, in extreme cases, its survival, is at risk". Tragically, the child's mother (or carer) was likely to have been in the same predicament as a child, hence the extraordinary challenge in the clinical situation of influencing these intergenerational patterns of mutual harm.

The aim of this acceleration of sadomasochism is to take some control and feel some pleasure in that control. Yet, if the sadism in the child fails to control the dangerousness of the parent, the child might regress to ruthless aggression to get rid of painful reality—either through psychosis or destructiveness. Dr. Campbell's clinical example details how Mr. Giles's helplessness led to his use of violence for self-protection.

The effect of sadomasochism on the sexual development of the child, adolescent, and adult

In Campbell's experience, when a child repeatedly relies on sadomasochistic solutions to protect himself from abandonment or engulfment, "[when] sadomasochism permeates fantasies, masturbation fantasies, and the way his body is used in relationships, the foundations are laid for perverse sexual development, and/or the eroticism of aggression and, in some cases, the repetition of violence to generate sexual gratification" (p. 94). In other words, controlling and hurting an other is woven into the sexuality of the child. Rather than mutual pleasure, mutual hurting is sought in relationships to other people as well as in relationship to the self.

Campbell writes that violence is rarely just sadistic or ruthless, but some combination of the two. When the attempt to control her mind breaks down, as when Mr. Giles cannot persuade Sylvia to agree with him that the older woman said nonsense, his sadism morphs to ruthless violence. As Campbell writes: "He abandoned his attempt to take control of her mind and tried to get rid of her eyes". When Mr. Giles cannot change her mind, his helplessness intensifies and violence emerges. Sylvia is not under his omnipotent control, therefore Mr. Giles is impelled to gouge out her eyes to rid his psyche/self of her different point of view; hence, the use of "anatomy" in the chapter.

As a boy, Mr. Giles felt intruded by mother's "views" and he did not feel heard. His helplessness was reinforced as his father was at work or sleeping off an alcoholic binge. Father also modeled violence as a means to protect his own self. The role of the father in the evolution of Mr. Giles's violent modes of self-protection is discussed very little, as is intergenerational trauma.

Interventions that might have helped stem the evolution of violence in Mr. Giles optimally would have included help for the parents. Both parents are preoccupied with protecting and managing their own sense of self, which left Mr. Giles alone as a small boy to cope with overwhelming helplessness. Violence is born of the control a person wishes to obtain in the face of traumatic helplessness.

Discussion and summary

Dr. Campbell's work builds a portrait of what happens when a young boy's rightful need to feel validated, heard, understood, and loved from a mother and a father goes unanswered, leaving him with a limited range of solutions for self-preservation. The young Mr. Giles, it would appear, devised a means of feeling some sense of control in a home with unavailable, intruding, and violent parents by imagining himself mighty enough to change another person's mind. When he is unable to persuade his girlfriend that the older woman was ridiculous, he felt helpless again, as he did as a boy when mother pushed ideas into him and father was not there to offer an alternative. Feeling his selfhood diminish in Sylvia's defiance, he attacks the eyes, then feels conflict about the hurt he has inflicted. Mr. Giles had—I imagine—enough of a helpful and empathic voice in his mind to allow him to feel upset to see the harm he had done Sylvia, eventually getting himself to treatment. Although his impulse was to obliterate the defying eyes, he stopped himself. In the case Dr. Campbell presents, Mr. Giles himself intervened. Sadly, many who go on to perpetrate violence do not stop themselves. Early intervention services aimed at supporting parents with infants and toddlers that include supportive services for parents might well be the strongest deterrent to the evolution of violence. When a person jokes or makes glib remarks in reference to violent fantasies, particularly if in combination with social isolation and harm done to animals in childhood, such signals call for immediate, sustained, and thoughtful intervention and attention by mental health and law enforcement services. Psychoanalytic practitioners in the spirit of Campbell have much to contribute to solving the problems of intergenerational violence and we, too, need to ensure the significant data of psychoanalytic treatments are maintained within mental health and legal systems.

References

Glasser, M. (1996). Aggression and sadism in the perversions. In: I. Rosen (Ed.), *Sexual Deviation* (3rd edn) (pp. 279–299). Oxford: Oxford University Press.

Glasser, M. (1998). On violence: a preliminary communication. *International Journal of Psychoanalysis*, 79: 887–902.

CHAPTER TWELVE

End Rape On Campus (EROC) and the making of *The Hunting Ground*

Annie Clark

In 2013, Andrea Pino, Sofie Karasek, Danielle Dirks, Caroline Heldman, Kristin Brown, and I created an organization called End Rape On Campus out of necessity, as we wanted to share what we learned about our rights under Title IX and the Clery Act with a broader audience and respond to the survivors reaching out to us in a coordinated and organized way.

Today, EROC exists as a national US based non-profit organization. Our mission is threefold: to directly support survivors and their families/friends; to prevent sexual violence through education and to teach all students about their rights to an equitable education; to advocate for legislative reform to ensure our laws regarding gender-based violence are fair and equitable to all.

The Hunting Ground

In January 2013, a group of five women, myself included, filed federal complaints with the US Department of Education against the University of North Carolina at Chapel Hill (UNC), alleging the institution's mishandling of sexual assault cases. In a few months, our efforts were starting to gain attention beyond our own campus.

Filmmakers Kirby Dick and Amy Ziering happened to screen their documentary, *The Invisible War*, a film about sexual violence and institutional betrayal in the United States military, at UNC a few months after we filed these complaints. Many students went up to speak to the filmmakers at UNC after the screening, something that Kirby and Amy had experienced before at other colleges. These students explained that the issue of sexual assault and subsequent cover up, whether intentional or unintentional, was happening at their universities as well. One of the students who spoke to the filmmakers was a resident of Andrea Pino, a resident advisor at the time, and one of the five women who filed the federal complaints against UNC. She urged them to look into what was happening at the University of North Carolina at Chapel Hill.

The filmmakers also recognized the similarities between the collegiate system and the military system, and decided to start following the anti-campus sexual assault movement.

After a couple of years of filming myself and many other activists and survivors, their film team put together the documentary, *The Hunting Ground*, which chronicles this particular section of the sexual assault movement in real time. The film premiered at Sundance 2015, and later screened at theaters throughout the country, and at the White House. Although Andrea and I are featured, we are two of the many survivors and activists seeking to call attention to the issue of violence in educational settings.

One can currently find this film on Netflix, Amazon, and at various college and university screenings throughout the country.

We Believe You: Survivors of Campus Sexual Assault Speak Out

After the experience of filming *The Hunting Ground*, Andrea and I knew we wanted to do more to highlight survivor voices and focus on those who are most marginalized within this movement. While the film was a great 101 introduction to the issue of sexual violence in US higher education, we wanted to show more of whom survivors were before and after their assaults. We wanted to give people the power of sharing their own stories in an unfiltered, unedited way.

We also wanted to explore other aspects of identity; we wanted to give people the opportunity to share their identities in intersectional ways that are often left out of short media clips and headlines.

Therefore, in the book, *We Believe You* (Clark & Pino, 2016), we have the voices of thirty-six survivors, many of whom represent voices from the communities who are most impacted. In the book, survivors explore, in their own words, the intersections between their assaults and their identities, whether that be in regard to gender (including gender identity and gender expression), race, ethnicity, religion, immigration status, sexual orientation, and class, just to name a few.

Andrea and I entitled the book *We Believe You* because we currently live in a world where we, as a society, do completely the opposite.

In regard to the courage to fight violence against women, the book has a section entitled "Everyday activism", which shows how people can work to end rape culture, regardless of where they are personally or professionally in the world.

References

Clark, A. E., & Pino, A. (2016). *We Believe You: Survivors of Campus Sexual Assault Speak Out*. New York: Henry Holt.

Dick, K., & Ziering, A. (2015). *The Hunting Ground* (documentary film).

CHAPTER THIRTEEN

Sexual abuse of women in United States prisons: a modern corollary of slavery[1]

Brenda V. Smith

Introduction by Paula L. Ellman

Brenda Smith, Attorney and Professor at the American University School of Law, contributes an abbreviated version of her previously published paper from the *Fordham School of Law Journal*, which, by virtue of Smith's profession, presents this profound instance of "violence against women" from a legal perspective. Smith's crucial voice from the arena of law conveys her courage to fight violence against women by presenting us with her knowledge and research on the history of the legal tenets of our country. Complementing Smith's high standard of legal research in this chapter was her actual Conference presentation, where Smith stood out as the presenter who engaged her audience with her invitation to stand up and join her in a few yoga stretching positions before attending to her powerful PowerPoint and moving presentation.

Historical context of sexual abuse of women in custody

As long as there have been prisons and women in them, women have been sexually victimized (Garvey, 1998; Rafter, 1985; U.S. Department of Justice, Sourcebook on Criminal Statistics Online, 2002). Women in the earliest prisons were poor women, usually of the non-ruling or minority class, and women who had deviated from prevailing social norms for their gender (Rafter, 1985).

In the 1860s, women reformers in the USA raised public awareness about the increasing number of women in prison and the terrible conditions of confinement they faced, in particular the sexual abuse of women prisoners by male guards (Belknap, 2001). These reformers pointed out that men were luring women and girls into prostitution. Women prison reformers complained that prisons degraded rather than reformed women by subjecting them to sexual abuse (Freedman, 1981). Thus, the sexual abuse of women existed even in the earliest United States prisons. Around 1870, there was a movement to improve the conditions of incarcerated women. This "Reform Movement" was led, in large part, by Quaker men and women involved in, or sympathetic to, the abolition of slavery and gaining suffrage for women (Rafter, 1985, p. 103). They believed that women who had run afoul of the law were in need of reforming, and thus opened "reformatories" staffed by "matrons" to teach women the skills they needed to make their way in the world—sewing, gardening, laundry, and cooking (Pimlott & Sarri, 2002; Rafter & Stanley, 1999). The Reform Movement lasted until the 1930s, when it lost the support of some women's groups who felt that women's efforts needed to be focused on gaining the vote for women rather than prison reform (Rafter, 1985). This "abandonment" left the Reform Movement lethargic and left female prisoners languishing in institutions that retained the old characteristics of reformatories, without formal backing from established and respected women's groups (Belknap, 2001; Rafter, 1985). Even after suffrage was granted, there was a definite fracture of the women's movement, with some feminists voicing the idea that scarce resources were being wasted on the task of "reforming" women offenders (Rafter, 1985).

In the 1960s and 1970s, women correctional officers seeking job advancement used Title VII's[2] proscription against discrimination in employment to obtain positions in male prisons (42 U.S.C. § 2000e-2(a); *Dothard v. Rawlinson*, 1997). Concerned with the threat of Title VII litigation, prison officials supported women's entry into previously all-male settings, despite frequent challenges raised by male staff and male inmates (Smith, 2003). As a result, most restrictions on male officers' employment in women's prisons that predated the Title VII were removed and, by some estimates, male officers working in women's prisons now outnumber their female counterparts (Thomas, 1996).

Women's entry into male institutions and their abandonment of women's institutions created opportunities for male staff who had been prohibited by custom, if not by law, from working in women's institutions. Male and female correctional staff's entry into institutions housing female prisoners resulted in complaints, litigation, and reports of sexual abuse (Simon & Simon, 1993). These complaints were met with lawsuits requesting same-sex supervision. By and large, male prisoners have lost challenges to cross-gender supervision (Smith, 2003). However, female prisoners have had much greater success, with courts routinely recognizing a greater need and expectation of privacy for women.

Historical context of sexual abuse of women slaves

Sexual abuse was a prominent feature of the enslavement of African women in the United States. While slavery visited horrific and unimaginable abuse on all slaves, women slaves experienced abuse that was particularly related to their gender (Bridgewater, 2005). Women slaves were routinely used as concubines for male slave owners, their relatives, and their owner's guests. They were systematically impregnated by their owners, and, at their owner's request, by other slaves in order to produce children that were sold, worked, or in turn bred to raise other slaves. Much of the early abolitionist work by women reformers, the same reformers who led the movement to create women's prisons, focused on sexual abuse of female slaves (Hewitt, 2006).

In fact, Harriet Jacobs, one of the early female abolitionists and a former slave, wrote extensively of the sexual exploitation of female slaves (Jacobs, 1987). At the same time, the sexual degradation of female slaves was also used rhetorically by early women's rights groups who compared their lack of rights to that of female slaves—making the plea that their treatment should be better than that of female slaves (Declaration of Sentiments, 1848). Their failure to get that "better" treatment moved them to abandon both the abolition movement and the reform of women's prisons, in favor of gaining suffrage (Stanton, 1854).

Sexual abuse of women in prison and slavery: congruent oppression(s)?

Slavery and sexual abuse of women in prison share many congruencies and certainly obvious differences (Slavery Convention of 1926, 46 Stat. 2183, 1926). The sexual abuse of slaves differed from sexual abuse of women in prison in at least one fundamental and important way—its legality. Slavery and the sexual abuse of slaves that occurred as a result of it were legally sanctioned in the USA, while arguably sexual abuse of women in custody is not (42 U.S.C. §1560, 2003). It would be tempting to say that sexual abuse in institutional settings primarily affects women, and therefore—like slavery—an identifiable group is targeted for discriminatory treatment. That, however, is not true. Both male and female prisoners frequently face sexual abuse by both staff and other inmates as a means of domination (Mariner, 2001).

Similar to sexual abuse in prisons, sexual abuse of slaves also was not limited to abuse of females. Although sexual abuse of male slaves did not take the same form as sexual abuse of women slaves, male slaves were targeted for abuse related to their sexuality—often facing castration as a form of oppression (Bourne, 2008). Thus, a congruency of both sexual abuse of women in prison and women in slavery is that sexual abuse was and is used as a tool of oppression.

Sexual violence as a tool of oppression

Sexual violence has been used as a means of oppression, control, and retribution against women in custody both domestically and internationally (Giddings, 1984; U.N. Economic & Social Council, Commission on Human Rights, 1999). On the international stage, in times of war, sexual abuse, usually against women, is frequently used during investigation as a means of intimidation or torture (Goodwin, 2004). The literature on the experience of women in slavery and that of women prisoners is replete with accounts of the sexual abuse of women (Jacobs, 1987).

An offshoot of sexual violence is the complicated relationships that sometimes emerge between captive and captor (Soh, 2000). Both in slavery and in prison, the roles of the oppressed and the oppressor can become confused, sometimes resulting in relationships that stretch traditional boundaries of captor and captive (*Judgment Day*, part 4:

1832–1865, 1999). There are many accounts of women slaves bearing children and having long-term relationships with their owners (Bartlett & Harris, 1998). The same is true for women in custody (Worley, 2003). The reasons for these relationships are quite complex. They can certainly be motivated by love, sexual desire, or desire to bear children—even under oppressive conditions (Franke, 2001; Phillips, 1997). These relationships, in the context of slavery, were often motivated by need (the oppressor had access to items that would make slavery or imprisonment more bearable), better food or clothing, better work assignments, protection from other oppressors, and increased status within the framework (White, 1990). The same is true for women prisoners (Dinos, 2000).

Because of the imbalance of power inherent to the position of authority that captors hold over the captured, the concept of consent might have only limited value in evaluating these relationships (*Carrigan v. Davis*, 1999). In slavery, however, consent was not an issue. Slave masters owned slaves and their wives. Neither wife nor slave could protest against sexual relations and had little power over what happened to the products of those unions (Offen, 2005). Wives and slaves also had little say over the custody, disposition, and education of children (Mellon, 1998). Unless state law provided otherwise, or separate arrangements were made prior to marriage, all of a woman's property belonged to her husband (Basch, 1982). As for slaves, anything they produced—human or material—belonged to the slave owner.

In prison, staff—primarily male—have exploited the prison setting as an opportunity to abuse women prisoners (*Daskalea v. District of Columbia*, 2000). When courts and state law fail to respond to sexual abuse against women prisoners, they effectively "privatize" it (Buchanan, 2005). Like slaves, women prisoners have few means to protest against these sexual relations (Dirks, 2004). Thus, the authority of the corrections personnel who have the power to protect women from sexual abuse or ignore and perpetrate that abuse becomes similar to the patriarchal authority of the husband and slave-owner seen in the nineteenth century.

The impact of economic and political forces on the institution

Undoubtedly, there were powerful political and economic interests supporting slavery (Bridgewater, 2005). The political and economic forces that shape criminal justice policy, and which, in turn, support imprisonment, are powerful as well. Slavery helped stabilize the economy of the early colonies by providing a cheap source of labor for the benefit of a few wealthy landowners (Sheldon, 2005). Cheap slave labor was a standard means of economic growth until emancipation, when slave plantations were dismantled—and then quickly replaced by prisons (Hindus, 1980). Soon after emancipation, the composition of prisons shifted from predominantly white to predominantly black (Sheldon, 2005). Thus, in spite of—or perhaps because of—emancipation, the enslavement of blacks was quickly converted to the subjugation of blacks through imprisonment, furthering the goal of feeding the economy (Hindus, 1980).

Prisons have become the primary economic development project in many communities, providing economic growth and stability to economically marginal communities (Brooke, 1997). Private prison concerns such as Wackenhut and Corrections Corporation of America are publicly traded on the New York Stock Exchange and build prisons not just in this country, but also around the world (Brooks, 1999; Corrections Corporation, n.d.). Prisoners are seen as a commodity that these corporate entities house as a service to states. In many states, the most powerful labor unions are police and correctional employee unions (American Federation of State, County and Municipal Employees, 2002).

Political forces are also strong in promoting imprisonment. Getting "tough on crime" is a certain way to enhance the political standing of elected officials (Anderson, 2002). With such strong political forces and economic benefit, like the slave plantations of the past, it is not surprising that sexual abuse of women in the prison system, much like the rape and breeding of slave women, is often overlooked as one of the by-products of a necessary institution (Garvey, 1998).

Legal protection from unwanted sexual relations

It goes without saying that there was no legal protection from sexual abuse for female slaves (Bridgewater, 2005). Women prisoners, at least, have some legal protection from forced sex by correctional staff (42 U.S.C. §1560, 2003). Twenty-three states specifically provide by law that a prisoner's consent is not a defense to criminal prosecution of staff sexual misconduct (Smith, 2003). These states recognize that the difference in power between prisoners and correctional staff negates claims of consent. Notwithstanding this majority view, there continues to be debate among courts about the ability of prisoners to consent and the impact this consent should have on the availability of relief for violations of constitutional rights (*Carrigan v. Davis*, 1999). Several states have made it a separate criminal offense for an offender to have "consensual" sex with a staff person (Smith, 2003). These states, Arizona, Nevada, and Delaware, can separately sanction prisoners and staff for "consensual" sex (Arizona Revised Statutes Ann. § 13–1414(B), 1989; Delaware Code Ann. tit. 11, § 1259, 1995; Nevada Revised Statutes § 212.187(1), 1997). Not surprisingly, there are few criminal prosecutions for custodial sexual misconduct in states against correctional staff.

While there is legal protection in the modern context for sexual abuse of women in custody, women prisoners still have little choice about whether to become sexually involved with correctional staff. Like slaves, women prisoners are often wholly dependent upon correctional staff for their lives and their livelihoods. Correctional staff, like slave owners, determine the ways in which women will serve their time: where they will be housed; where they will work; how much contact they will have with the outside; what they will eat; how they will be clothed. This exercise of dominion and control severely limits—if not obviates—consent. Like slaves who lacked freedom of choice, women prisoners must often use their sexuality to negotiate within the prison system. Thus, the sexual abuse of female slaves and female inmates are congruent and merit legal protection.

The Thirteenth Amendment of the Constitution outlawed slavery and slavery-like conditions by both private and state conduct (Amar, 1992; U.S. Const. Amend. XIII). Courts have construed the Thirteenth Amendment to abolish not only chattel slavery but to "abolish all prospective forms of slavery" as well (McConnell, 1992). The Thirteenth Amendment, however, has a specific exclusion allowing such conditions as a punishment for crimes that result from a legitimate conviction. Nevertheless, sexual abuse is "not part of the penalty" that women prisoners are expected to pay for their crime (*Rhodes v. Chapman*, 1981) and, thus, women prisoners should receive protection from sexual abuse notwithstanding the Thirteenth Amendment exclusion. The Thirteenth Amendment applies both in letter and spirit to the protection of slaves and prohibits slavery-like conditions or treatment, even if the "slave" is a woman prisoner subjected to sexual abuse by the state and its agents: Well beyond the boundaries of punishment for her crimes.

In the early twentieth century case *Butler v. Perry*, the United States Supreme Court held that involuntary servitude included "those forms of compulsory labor akin to African Slavery which in practical operation would tend to produce undesirable results" (1916; see also *Robertson v. Baldwin*, 1897). "Involuntary servitude" is broader than the term slavery (*Clyatt v. United States*, 1905). Involuntary servitude is "control by which the personal service of one [person] is disposed of or coerced for another's benefit," whereas slavery, at least in the U.S. context, is tied to race (Amar, 1992; Koppelman, 1990).

Contemporary criminal involuntary servitude cases reflect an economic view of the Thirteenth Amendment and have focused primarily on forced labor and peonage (Amar, 1992). This narrow view, however, fails to recognize that slavery and involuntary servitude were more than forced labor. In the case of female slaves, it was forced sex and reproduction. The international human rights view of slavery is much more nuanced and has recognized that slavery and slavery-like conditions included sexual violence, which violates the International Covenant on Civil and Political Rights, the Convention Against Torture, and the Slavery Convention.

A competing and more accurate view is that slavery and involuntary servitude were more than economic systems of free labor, they were complex social systems (*Gratz v. Bollinger*, 1998). For example, women's services included not only those that could have been provided by substitute wage labor, but also sexual and reproductive services that clearly fall outside the wage–labor system (Scales-Trent, 1989). Given that, courts have found that Congress intended for the Thirteenth Amendment to prohibit anything with characteristics of chattel slavery and that there is ample evidence that sexual exploitation of women slaves was a recognized evil of the chattel slavery system. In much the same way, coerced sexual services of women prisoners should be considered as falling within the scope of the involuntary servitude prohibition.

Women who are sexually abused while incarcerated are protected by §1983, a provision enacted pursuant to the Thirteenth Amendment. (*Riley v. Olk-long*, 2002; *Women Prisoners of the D.C. Department of Corrs. v. District of Columbia*, 1994; *Daskalea v. District of Columbia*, 2000).

Section 1983 prohibits deprivation of any rights guaranteed by the constitution, law or ordinance by a person acting under color of state laws. Agencies, city officials and individual correctional staff are persons acting under color of state law for purposes of § 1983 (*Gilmore v. Salt Lake City*). Women in custody have successfully used this statute in litigating cases of sexual abuse in custody, and courts have consistently found sexual abuse creates a cause of action under § 1983 and violates the Eighth Amendment prohibition on cruel and unusual punishment. Likewise, courts have that other degrading treatment that does not rise to the level of rape—including violations of women's privacy—are actionable under §1983 and violate the Eighth Amendment of the Constitution. This protection is aimed at protecting vulnerable citizens from the power of the state.

Feminist advocacy on behalf of women in prison

Given that the focus of feminist efforts has always been to right the power imbalance between men and women, perhaps the most surprising congruency between slavery and abuse of women in custody is the lack of consistent and forceful feminist advocacy. As with slavery, the feminist response to the abuse of female prisoners has been varied and sporadic, with mixed results as to its impact on the problem.

The history of feminist activism on slavery is mixed. While white feminists often tied their struggle to that of slaves—comparing their lack of rights to that of slaves—they just as often distinguished themselves based on race and privilege. For example, in the struggle for the vote, some white feminists parted ways with abolitionists on giving the franchise to newly emancipated male slaves (Stanton, 1854). They felt strongly that white women should have the right to vote before black men (hooks, 1981). Lost completely in that discourse was the situation of black women—who were dually burdened by gender and race.

Similarly, modern feminist advocacy on behalf of women in custody has been mixed. In the struggle to address sexual abuse of women in custody, national feminist organizations such as National Partnership on Women and Families, Legal Momentum, and National Women's Law Center have been slow to react. The primary advocates have been individual women with a background of work on criminal justice issues, poverty issues or international law. For example, national women's organizations that were very vocal in lobbying for the passage of the Violence Against Women Act of 1994 (VAWA I) have, by and large, not taken up the issue of abuse of women in custody (42 U.S.C., 22 U.S.C. §7101–7710; *Women Prisoners of the D.C. Department of Corrections v. District of Columbia,* 1994). There was a significant debate among women's groups and church-based organizations about whether to support VAWA I's initial approach of enhanced penalties and criminalization as the primary method to battle violence against women. As initially enacted, VAWA I, and as reauthorized in 2000, as VAWA II, the statute has prohibited the use of its funds for any persons in custody (42 U.S.C., 22 U.S.C. §7101–7710). While initially enacted to prevent male perpetrators from gaining access to funds meant to assist female victims, the prohibition found in both VAWA I and VAWA II on the use of funds for any individual in custody means that the significant number of women in prison with histories of physical and sexual abuse, both prior to and during imprisonment, are ineligible for services funded by VAWA II, the largest source of funding nationally for these programs (Browne, 1999).

In actuality, modern feminist organizations have been slow to stake out any position on criminal justice except one related to women as victims of crime (Bruch, 2004; Kapur, 2002; Volpp, 1996). According to Ratna Kapur, this reticence directly rejects the mainstream feminists' tendency to adopt the "victim subject" as an ideal model (2002). Kapur attributes such a tendency to the movement's constant reliance on essentialism as a basis for making claims and seeking relief. Kapur goes on to note that gender essentialism is seriously flawed because it lumps a large group of women together based on a single shared experience. In the case of women slaves and women prisoners, the shared experience is sexual violence. Such a stance, argues Kapur, is oversimplification in its worst form, as this "victim" theory "cannot accommodate a multi-layered experience," which is obtained through the lens of varying cultures, races, religions, and sexual orientations. This essentialism fails to consider the complexities of individual women's experience of sexual oppression and the accommodations they make in order to survive and achieve some "normalcy" within the confines of the oppression (Worley, 2003, p. 178).

Very little feminist advocacy is devoted to the many primarily poor and non-white women who are prisoners. This contrasts with the historical movement, where women and women's organizations were the primary movers for improvement and reform of women in the justice system. There exists legitimate critique that this advocacy was religiously based and focused on making white women who had strayed conform to the middle class standard of womanhood and motherhood, as women of African descent were not incarcerated in the earliest prisons (Rafter, 1985).

In recent efforts to combat the sexual abuse of women in custody, advocates—not associated with national women's organizations—have used a multi-pronged approach that has included litigation aimed at systematic reform, public education, and legislative reform.

Litigation on behalf of women

One approach to litigating on behalf of women prisoners is embodied in *Canterino v. Wilson* where director of the National Women's Law Center's International Human Rights Clinic, Susan Deller Ross, who was employed as an attorney at the U.S. Justice Department, Civil Rights Division, Special Litigation Division, argued for better programming for a class of women prisoners on equal protection grounds (1982). The prisoners were contesting the prison's refusal to allow them to take vocational classes viewed as "traditionally male" disciplines, and instead limited the women's choices to "business office education" and upholstery. The women were ultimately successful due to Ross's attack on the disparate treatment of men and women prisoners on equal protection grounds; however, nowhere in the case did any issues regarding sexual abuse of the women prisoners arise.

In 1993, while at the National Women's Law Center, I co-counseled a case, *Women Prisoners of the D.C. Department of Corrections v. District of Columbia*, which challenged a pattern and practice of discrimination against a class of female prisoners in the District of Columbia (1994). The claims in *Women Prisoners* included the sexual abuse of women in three District of Columbia prisons and female prisoners' unequal access to educational, vocational, and religious opportunities. The court found that the District of Columbia and its officials had violated the Fifth and Eighth Amendments of the Constitution and D.C. Code Section 24–442, which provided for the care and safekeeping of prisoners and ordered the District to implement practices that remediated the identified problems (pp. 664–665).

This case represented an "equality plus" approach, in which women's rights were asserted within the framework of Eighth Amendment's cruel and unusual punishment violations. Evidence of these constitutional violations was in the form of compelling prisoner testimony that detailed numerous incidents of sexual abuse (pp. 639–641). Yet another approach to the problem of sexual abuse has been to combine human rights and equality advocacy to change female prisoners' conditions of confinement.

Deborah LaBelle, a Michigan sole practitioner, has litigated several cases in which she has combined international human rights principles and United States constitutional law to obtain victories on behalf of women prisoners suffering sexual abuse at the hands of corrections officers. Using human rights in the context of sexual abuse of women in custody was precipitated by a "confluence of factors", including both domestic and international attention and directives (Fox & Thomas, 2004). Ellen Barry, the founder of Legal Services for Prisoners with Children in California, however, took another approach, and focused on maternal and child health issues as a litigation targets. For example, in *Shumate v. Wilson*, the complaint alleged that the California Institute for Women and the Central California Women's Facility had

> furnished inadequate sick call, triage, emergency care, nurses, urgent care, chronic care, specialty referrals, medical screenings, follow-up care, examinations and tests, medical equipment, medications, specialty diets, terminal care, health education, dental care, and grievance procedures, and that the provision of medical care featured unreasonable delays and disruptions in medication. (2000; see also *Plata v. Davis*, 2003)

While these approaches have been quite different, they have all resulted in positive change for women prisoners (Fox & Thomas, 2004). In fact, they represent an evolution of litigation; rather than being formulaic in its approach, essentializing women in custody, advocacy on behalf of women prisoners has taken many forms and addressed a broad range of women's experience in custody—worker, victim, and mother. While litigation is an important tool in combating past abuses, public education holds the greatest promise of preventing sexual abuse of women prisoners.

Public education

To some extent, the visibility of staff sexual misconduct with inmates and other examples of abuse in institutional settings in the media have informed the public's perception about the problem of sexual abuse in institutional settings. These accounts have convinced a once skeptical public[3] that sexual abuse can and does occur in institutional settings (2001 Country Reports on Human Rights Practices, 2001).

A more difficult group to convince has been those in the corrections hierarchy. Schooled to believe that prisoners always lie—women prisoners' corrections agencies especially, have been slow to recognize that sexual misconduct is a pervasive problem in institutional settings (Cornelius, 2001). At about the time that the directors of Departments of Corrections began losing their jobs over sex scandals in prisons, heads of corrections agencies identified sexual abuse of individuals in custody as a major problem and took positions decrying these practices (National Sheriffs Association, Resolution, 2002; Sigal, 2002).

Recognizing the need for training and technical assistance on this issue, the National Institute of Corrections (NIC), under the leadership of Anadora Moss, who had been involved in directing Georgia's response to a sexual abuse scandal, began to develop a systemic approach to addressing staff sexual misconduct with offenders (*Cason v. Seckinger,* 2000). NIC began an aggressive campaign in 1995 to assist state departments of corrections to address staff sexual misconduct with inmates, focusing on leadership, policy, law, management, investigation, and agency culture. NIC offered training programs for key state corrections' decision makers, on-site technical assistance on policy development and the drafting of legislation, and developed training programs for corrections staff.

While the correctional hierarchy has begun to address its lack of awareness through training and technical assistance, they have been slow to permit similar training for inmates (National Sheriffs Association, Resolution, 2002). Correctional officials believed that inmates would use the information to control staff by making false complaints of sexual abuse (*Riley v. Olk-Long,* 2002). Many states only mention sexual violence as part of the brief orientation that inmates received when they entered the correctional system (U.S. Department of Justice, 2010). The majority of those that provided more detailed training to inmates did so as part of an agreement reached in litigation

(*United States v. Arizona*, 1999). In recent years, however, several states have begun voluntarily to offer training about sexual violence to inmates (Arlington County Detention Facility, 2000; California Department of Corrections, 2000; Michigan Department of Corrections, 2001). Advocates critical of the correctional hierarchy have tried remedying this situation by providing materials to inmates and the public on preventing and addressing staff sexual misconduct with inmates (Smith, 2003). Moving beyond public education and training, legislators have begun to draft and enact legislation penalizing women prisoners' abusers.

Legislation addressing staff sexual misconduct with inmates

The moving force behind the first piece of modern legislation addressing sexual abuse of women in custody was the Women's Rights Division of Human Rights Watch, under the leadership of Dorothy Q. Thomas. The Women's Rights Division had published numerous reports dealing with sexual abuse of women in custody, seeking to document human rights abuse in the USA, and had received positive response to these reports. For example, Radhika Coomaraswamy, the United Nations Special Rapporteur on Violence Against Women, Its Causes and Consequences, issued a highly critical report of the United States' practices with regard to women in custody (Thomas, 1996; the report was delivered at the Fifty-Fifth Session of the United Nations Human Rights Commission in April 1999. Prior to that meeting, however, the United States Department of Justice embarked on a visual campaign to highlight its interest in improving the conditions of women in custody (speech, December, 1999). Following up on those reports, the Women's Division gained the support of Michigan Congressman John Conyers, who introduced the Prevention of Custodial Sexual Assault by Correctional Staff Act (Custodial Sexual Assault Act) as part of omnibus legislation reauthorizing the Violence Against Women Act (VAWA) (§341–346, 1999).

The legislation called for the establishment of a registry for correctional employees found involved in custodial sexual misconduct American Federation of State, County and Municipal Employees, 1999). It also called for withholding federal law enforcement funds from those states that failed to enact legislation criminalizing staff sexual misconduct with inmates (VAWA, 1999). While VAWA passed, the Prevention of Custodial Sexual Assault by Correctional Staff Act did not (VAWA II, 1999).

Two years later, Human Rights Watch, under the leadership of Wendy Patten, authored another report, *No Escape: Male Rape in U.S. Prisons*, this time documenting the sexual abuse of male prisoners (Mariner, 2001). Teaming with Stop Prisoner Rape, an organization originally founded by male prison rape survivors, but led by a woman, Lara Stemple, Human Rights Watch pushed for the enactment of another piece of legislation, the Prison Rape Reduction Act of 2002 (H.R. 4943, 2002; McFarlane & Lerner-Kinglake, 2016). The initial legislation, which was introduced with bipartisan support, focused primarily on prisoner-on-prisoner sexual assault and provided for penalties only in cases of prison rape (Hearing on the Rison, 2002; Mariner, 2001). While there was bipartisan support for the bill, the failure to include the perspectives of accrediting organizations such as the American Correctional Association, the Association of State Correctional Administrators, and groups who had worked primarily on issues related to sexual abuse of prisoners by staff slowed enactment of the bill.

The Prison Rape Reduction Act was reintroduced in 2003, with significant amendments—changing the name to the Prison Rape Elimination Act (PREA), and including coverage of staff sexual abuse of persons in custody and grants to assist states in their efforts to prevent, reduce, and prosecute prison rape (H.R. 1707, 2003). The legislation passed unanimously on September 23, 2003 (42 U.S.C.S.).

As enacted, PREA establishes a "zero tolerance" policy for rape in custodial settings, requires data collection on the incidence of rape in each state, and establishes a National Prison Rape Elimination Commission (42 U.S.C.S. §15609, 2003). The Commission is required to issue a report on the causes and consequences of prison rape, and to develop recommendations for national standards on the prevention, detection, and punishment of prison rape (42 U.S.C.S., §15606, §15602, 2003). While PREA does not create a private cause of action for prisoners, it does create a system of incentives and disincentives for states, correctional agencies and correctional accrediting organizations that fail to comply with its provisions (§15602(7); *Alexander v. Sandoval*, 2003). Each correctional agency must, upon request by the Bureau of Justice Statistics (BJS), report the number of instances of sexual violence in its facilities (PREA, 2003). On an annual basis, the three states with the highest incidence and two states with the lowest incidence of prison rape will appear before the Review Panel on Prison Rape to explain what they are doing in their facilities (§16503(b)(3)(A)). States and accrediting organizations stand to lose five percent of federal funds for criminal justice activities for failure to implement or develop national standards (§15607(c)(2)). As an incentive to comply, PREA provides grant assistance to states to implement practices that reduce, prevent, or eliminate prison rape (§16505).

Like litigation, the enactment of legislation is a critical element in responding to staff sexual abuse of women in custody. Legislation sends a message to the public, prisoners, and correction staff that sexual misconduct is a serious public policy concern that merits prosecution and appropriate penalties. Yet, state legislation has not had the broad prophylactic effect that policymakers, advocates, and many corrections officials anticipated. Unfortunately, sexual abuse in institutional settings is even less likely to be reported and prosecuted than sexual assault in the community (U.S. Department of Justice, 2005). Interestingly, major legislative efforts to address sexual abuse of persons in custody, particularly women in custody, were, for the most part, engineered by women who had strong feminist credentials but worked in organizations that were more aligned with prisoners rights and human rights. While the influence of feminism is clear, the lack of involvement of women's organizations in leading this effort was a missed opportunity for feminists and women in custody.

Conclusion

The sexual abuse of women in custody is akin to the sexual abuse of female slaves. At base, both slave-owners and correction officers used sexual domination and coercion of women to reinforce notions of domination and authority over the powerless. Like women slaves, women prisoners are seen as untrustworthy, promiscuous, and seductive. They are the archetypal "Dark Lady" who is responsible not only for her own victim-hood, but also for the corruption of men. Like women slaves, women in custody have sometimes "chosen" to align with their captors—for reasons of convenience, sexual expression, desire, material need, or survival (Abrams, 1999; Dinos, 2000; Franke,

2001; *Ice v. Dixon,* 2005; Jacobs, 1987). Because she is the "other" woman, poor, and often black, she is relegated to the margins, outside of the coalition by traditional feminists, black men, and those advocating for poor people (hooks, 1981; Rubenstein & Mukamal, 2002).

While litigation, public education, and legislation, have yielded concrete gains in addressing abuse of women in custody, much remains to be done. Demands for supervision of women inmates by women correctional staff have met with some success (*Jordan v. Gardner,* 1992). Poor record keeping by federal, state, and county correctional authorities, however, makes it difficult to gauge the prevalence of the problem, thereby rendering it anecdotal at best and invisible at worst. This lack of record keeping or naming the problem means that bad actors can resign prior to, or in lieu of, firing or prosecution, free to obtain employment in other corrections institutions. It also means that little accountability exists for states that fail to remedy the abuse of women in custody (42 U.S.C. §15602 6, 2003).

The lack of support or services for women who are abused in custody or who come into custodial settings at greater risk for abuse because of past histories of physical and sexual abuse remains despite the enactment of VAWA, the largest appropriation of funds to combat violence against women in this nation's history (Smith, 2003). Moreover, the lack of visible prosecutions of sexual abuse in custody and appropriate sanctions for those found guilty sends the message that corrections officials, employees, and agencies can act with impunity (Smith, 2003; Report of the Special Rapporteur, n.d.). It is to be hoped that the passage of the Prison Rape Elimination Act, with its focus on documentation, data collection, and the development of standards, will begin to remedy the sexual abuse of women in custody and increase the accountability of states and correctional officials.

Finally, the record of advocacy by national women's organizations of addressing the concerns of women in custody is mixed at best. Fortunately, there are a host of creative and determined women advocates who were trained or worked in women's organizations and took up the concerns of women in custody. These women advocates have addressed not only sexual violence of women in custody, but health, education, and vocation needs of female inmates. In this way, they have claimed the history of early feminist abolitionists, such as Rhoda Coffin, who were able to reconcile advocacy for women in custody with advocacy that advanced women as a whole.

Notes

1. A version of this paper was previously published as: Brenda V. Smith, *Sexual Abuse of Women in United States Prisons: A Modern Corollary of Slavery*, 33 Fordham Urb. L.J. 571 (2006). SSRN Link.
2. 42 U.S.C. § 2000e-2(a) (1994).
3. *See generally* U.S. Department of State, Bureau of Democracy, Human Rights, and Labor, Country Reports on Human Rights Practices for 2001 (2002), available at: www.state.gov/g/drl/rls/hrrpt/2001/ (providing comprehensive information on the human rights practices of all countries who are members of the United Nations).

References

Abrams, K. (1999). From autonomy to agency: feminist perspectives on self-direction. *William and Mary Law Review*, 95: 353–386.

Alexander v. Sandoval, 532 U.S. 275, 291 (2003).

Amar, A. (1992). Child abuse as slavery: a Thirteenth Amendment response to DeShaney. *Harvard Law Review*, 105(6): 1359–1385.

American Federation of State, County and Municipal Employees Newsletter (1999). AFSCME opposes measure on sexual assault. Spring. Accessed at: AFSCME Corrections United News website: www.afscme.org/news/publications/newsletters/afscme-corrections-united/spring-1999-acu-newsletter/afscme-opposes-measure-on-sexual-assault.

American Federation of State, County and Municipal Employees Newsletter (2002). COs a major part of union's success. Spring. Accessed at: AFSCME website: www.afscme.org/news/publications/newsletters/afscme-corrections-united/spring-2002-acu-newsletter/cos-a-major-part-of-unions-success.

Anderson, G. (2002). Parole revisited. *American Magazine*, March 14. Accessed at: http://americamagazine.org/issue/363/article/parole-revisited.

Arlington County Detention Facility (2000). *Sexual Misconduct Brochure*.

Bartlett, K., & Harris, A. (1998). *Gender and Law: Theory, Doctrine, Commentary*. New York: Aspen.

Basch, N. (1982). In the eyes of the law. In: K. Bartlett & A. Harris (Eds.), *Gender and Law: Theory, Doctrine, Commentary* (pp. 11–12). New York: Aspen Law & Business, 1998.

Belknap, J. (2001). *The Invisible Woman: Gender, Crime and Justice* (2nd edn). New York: Wadsworth.

Bourne, J. (2008). Slavery in the United States, March 26. Accessed at: EH.Net Encyclopedia website: https://eh.net/encyclopedia/slavery-in-the-united-states/.

Bridgewater, P. (2005). Ain't I a slave: slavery reproductive abuse, and reparations. *UCLA Women's Law Journal*, 14: 115–118.

Brooke, J. (1997). Prisons: a growth industry for some; Colorado County is a grateful host to 7,000 involuntary guests. *New York Times*, November 2.

Brooks, R. (1999). Prison concern agrees to settle inmate lawsuit. *Wall Street Journal*, March 2.

Browne, A. (1999). Prevalence and severity of lifetime physical and sexual victimization among incarcerated women. *International Journal of Law and Psychiatry*, 22: 319.

Bruch, E. (2004). Models wanted: the search for an effective response to human trafficking. *Stanford Journal of International Law*, 40(1): 23.

Buchanan, K. (2005). Beyond modesty: privacy in prison and the risk of sexual abuse. *Marquette Law Review*, 88: 754.

Butler v. Perry, 240 U.S. 328 (1916).

California Department of Corrections (2000). *Sexual Abuse/Assault Prevention and Intervention: An Overview for Offenders, Know your Rights & Responsibilities*.

Canterino v. Wilson, 546 F. Supp. 174 (W.D. Ky. 1982).

Carrigan v. Davis, 70 F. Supp. 2d 448, 459–461 (D. Del. 1999).

Cason v. Seckinger, 231 F.3d 777 (11th Cir. 2000).

Clyatt v. United States, 197 U.S. 207, 215–218 (1905).

Cornelius, G. (2001). *The Art of the Con: Avoiding Offender Manipulation*. Alexandria, VA: American Correctional Association.

Corrections Corporation (n.d.). Accessed at: CCA website: www.cca.com/.

Country Reports on Human Rights Practices. (2001). Accessed at: U.S. Department of State website: www.state.gov/g/drl/rls/hrrpt/2001/.

Daskalea v. District of Columbia, 227 F.3d 438, 443 (D.C. Cir. 2000).

Dinos, A. (2000). Custodial sexual abuse: enforcing long-awaited policies designed to protect female prisoners. *New York Law School Review*, 45: 283–284.

Dirks, D. (2004). Sexual revictimization and retraumatization of women in prison. *Women's Studies Quarterly*, 32: 107, 110.

Fox, L., & Thomas, D. Q. (Eds.) (2004). Sexual abuse of women in prison: a thematic case study 99–101. Available at https://ffcontentgrantsviz.blob.core.windows.net/media/1737/2004-close_to_home.pdf.

Franke, K. (2001). Theorizing yes: an essay on feminism, law, and desire. *Columbia Law Review*, 181: 205.

Freedman, E. (1981). *Their Sister's Keepers: Women's Prison Reform in America, 1830–1930*. Ann Arbor, MI: University of Michigan Press.

Garvey, S. (1998). Freeing prisoners' labor. *Stanford Law Review, 50*(2), 339–398.

Giddings, P. (1984). *When and Where I Enter*. New York: William Morrow.

Gilmore v. Salt Lake City. Action Program, 710 F.2d 632, 637 (1983).

Goodwin, J. (2004). Silence=rape: while the world looks the other way, sexual violence spreads in the Congo. *The Nation*, available at: https://www.thenation.com/article/silencerape/.

Gratz v. Bollinger, No. 97-75321 (E.D. Mich. 1998).

Hewitt, N. (2006). Abolition & suffrage. Accessed at: www.pbs.org/stantonanthony/resources/index.html?body=abolitionists.html.

Hindus, M. (1980). *Prison and Plantation: Crime, Justice, and Authority in Massachusetts and South Carolina, 1767–1878*. Chapel Hill, NC: University of North Carolina Press.

hooks, b. (1981). *Ain't I A Woman?* London: Pluto Press.

H.R. 1707, 108th Cong. (2003). Available at: https://www.congress.gov/bill/108th-congress/house-bill/1707/text?q=%7B%22search%22%3A%5B%22H.R.+1707%22%5D%7D&r=1.

H.R. 4943 (2002). Available at: https://www.congress.gov/bill/107th-congress/house-bill/4943/text?q=%7B%22search%22%3A%5B%22H.R.+4943%2C%22%5D%7D&r=1.

Ice v. Dixon, No. 4:03CV2281, 2005 U.S. Dist. LEXIS 13429 (N.D. Ohio July 6, 2005).

Jacobs, H. (1987). *Incidents in the Life of a Slave Girl*. Cambridge, MA: Harvard University Press.

Jordan v. Gardner, 986 F. 2d 1521, 1530-31 (9th Cir. 1992).

Judgment Day, part 4: 1832–1865 (1999). In: *Africans in America*. (Television series.)

Kapur, R. (2002). The tragedy of victimization rhetoric: resurrecting the "native" subject in international/post-colonial feminist legal politics. *Harvard Human Rights Journal, 15*: 5–6.

Koppelman, A. (1990). Forced labor: a Thirteenth Amendment defense of abortion. *Northwestern University Law Review*, col. 84, p. 491.

Mariner, J. (2001). *No Escape: Male Rape in U.S. Prisons*. New York: Human Rights Watch.

McConnell, J. C. (1992). Beyond metaphor: battered women, involuntary servitude and the thirteenth amendment. *Yale Journal of Law & Feminism, 4*: 212.

McFarlane, L., & Lerner-Kinglake, J. (2016). The Prison Rape Elimination Act and beyond: sexual violence in detention. Available at: http://justdetention.org/.

Mellon, J. (1998). *Bullwhip Days: The Slaves Remember, An Oral History*. New York: Grove Press.
Michigan Department of Corrections (2001). *Women Prisoners' Guide to Identifying and Addressing Gender-based Misconduct*. Available at: https://www.law.umich.edu/special/policyclearinghouse/Documents/Michigan%20Trifold%20July%202011%20-%20WHV.pdf.
National Sheriffs Association, Resolution (2002). Development of policies on standards of conduct for jail and local corrections facility staff. Accessed at: www.wcl.american.edu/faculty/smith/0507conf/nsaresolution.cfm.
Offen, K. (2005). How (and why) the analogy of marriage with slavery provided the springboard for women's rights demands in France, 1640–1848. http://dx.doi.org/10.12987/yale/9780300115932.003.0004.
Phillips, S. (1997). Claiming our foremothers: the legend of Sally Hemmings and the tasks of black feminist theory. *Hastings Women's Law Journal*, *8*(2): 405.
Pimlott, S., & Sarri, R. C. (2002). The forgotten group: women in prisons and jails. In. J. Figueira-McDonough & R. C. Sarri (Eds.), *Women at the Margins: Neglect, Punishment and Resistance* (pp. 55–86). Bighamton, NY: Hawthorne Press.
Plata v. Davis, 329 F.3d 1101, 1103 (9th Cir. 2003).
Prison Rape Elimination Act, 42 U.S.C. (2003). Available at: https://www.congress.gov/108/plaws/publ79/PLAW-108publ79.pdf.
Rafter, N. H. (1985). *Partial Justice: Women in State Prisons, 1800–1935*. Lebanon, NH: Northeastern University Press.
Rafter, N. H., & Stanley, D. (1999). *Prisons in America: A Reference Handbook*. Santa Barbara, CA: ABC-CLIO.
Rhodes v. Chapman, 452 U.S. 337, 347 (1981).
Riley v. Olk-long, 282 F.3d 592, 597 (8th Cir. 2002).
Robertson v. Baldwin, 165 U.S. 275, 282 (1897).
Rubenstein, G., & Mukamal, D. (2002). Welfare and housing—denial of benefits to drug offenders. In: M. Chesney-Lind & M. Mauer (Eds.), *Invisible Punishment: The Collateral Consequences of Mass Imprisonment* (pp. 37–50). New York: New Press.
Scales-Trent, J. (1989). Black women and the constitution: finding our place, asserting our rights. *Harvard Civil Rights–Civil Liberties Law Review*, *24*: 10–44.
Sheldon, R. (2005). Slavery in the third millennium. Accessed at: Center on Juvenile and Criminal Justice website: www.cjcj.org/news/5873.
Shumate v. Wilson, No. CIV S–95–0619 (E.D. Cal. Aug. 21, 2000).
Sigal, P. (2002). Bucks warden resigns after turbulent year county commissioners had asked him to step down. *Philadelphia Inquirer*, February 7.

Simon, R., & Simon, J. (1993). Female guards in men's prisons. In: R. Muraskin & T. Alleman (Eds.), *It's a Crime: Women and Justice* (pp. 226–241). Englewood Cliffs, NJ: Prentice Hall.

Smith, B. (2003). Watching you, watching me: cross-gender supervision of prisoners. *Yale Journal of Law and Feminism, 15*: 225.

Soh, C. (2000). Human dignity and sexual culture: a reflection on "comfort women" issues. Speech presented to the Institute for Korean–American Studies Spring Symposium, University of Pennsylvania, May 1.

Stanton, E. (1854). Address to the legislature in the state of New York. In: K. Bartlett & A. Harris (Eds.), *Gender and Law: Theory, Doctrine, Commentary* (pp. 57–63). New York: Aspen Law & Business. 1998.

Thomas, D. (1996). Human rights watch, all too familiar: sexual abuse of women in U.S. state prisons. *Human Rights Watch*. Available at: https://www.hrw.org/reports/1996/Us1.htm#_1_1.

U.N. Economic & Social Council, Commission on Human Rights (1999). Report of the Special Rapporteur on Violence Against Women, Its Causes and Consequences. Available at: https://documents-dds-ny.un.org/doc/UNDOC/GEN/G99/100/12/PDF/G9910012.pdf?OpenElement.

United States Government (2002). The Prison Rape Reduction Act of 2002 Hearing before the Senate Committee on the Judiciary. Accessed at: https://www.gpo.gov/fdsys/pkg/CHRG-107shrg87677/pdf/CHRG-107shrg87677.pdf.

United States v. Arizona, No. 97--476--PHX--ROS (D. Ariz. Mar. 11, 1999).

U.S. Constitution Amendment XIII, §1.

U.S. Department of Justice (2005). Deterring staff sexual abuse of federal inmates. Office of the Inspector General. Available at: https://oig.justice.gov/special/0504/final.pdf.

U.S. Department of Justice (2010). *Sourcebook on Criminal Justice Statistics Online*. Accessed at: http://www.albany.edu/sourcebook/pdf/t6412010.pdf.

Violence Against Women Act, H.R. 357, 106th Congress (1999). Available at: https://www.congress.gov/bill/106th-congress/house-bill/357/text?q=%7B%22search%22%3A%5B%22hr+357%22%5D%7D&r=2.

Volpp, L. (1996). Talking "culture": gender, race, nation, and the politics of multiculturalism. *Columbia Law Review, 96*: 1585.

White, D. (1990). *Ar'n't I A Woman: Female Slaves in the Plantation South.* New York: W. W. Norton.

Women Prisoners of the D.C. Department of Corrs. v. District of Columbia, 877 F. Supp. 634 (D.D.C. 1994).

Worley, R. (2003). Prison guard predators: an analysis of inmates who established inappropriate relationships with prison staff, 1995–1998. *Deviant Behavior, 24*: 181–193.

CHAPTER FOURTEEN

Commentary on "End Rape on Campus (EROC)" and "Sexual abuse of women in United States prisons"

Joy Kassett

Violence prevention is where child psychoanalysts, scholars, and activists can come together to make lasting changes in our society. In the two preceding chapters, both authors discuss violence and aggression towards women, in particular sexual assault and rape. The first, Chapter Twelve, discusses sexual assault on college campuses with a focus on activism, and the second, Chapter Thirteen, discusses with a scholarly focus sexual assault in prison facilities.

Research has shown that there are many early pathways to aggression with no single pathway identified as the leading cause of aggression. These pathways include, but are not limited to, individual factors (intrauterine environment, gender differences, temperament, and emotional traits), disturbed family dynamics, parental characteristics and parenting practices, exposure to violence and behavioral aggressiveness, living in violent neighborhoods, disrupted attachment relationships, and maternal reflective capacity. Understanding the pathways to aggression informs our thinking about prevention. Research has shown that early aggressive behavior is predictive of later aggressive behavior, confirming findings that have shown that the critical window of intervention is in the early years of life (Reebye, 2005).

Child psychoanalysts understand the importance of early intervention. The theory and practice of child psychoanalysis is designed to help aggressive children, in the early years of life, begin to identify their angry feelings, elaborate upon them, and understand their origins. From my experience as a child analyst, and in my work with aggressive children, I have come to understand that, internally, these children live in fear where imagined or real danger surrounds them. Yet, unlike other children who use imaginative play to work through their fears, the fears of these children invade their real world. In danger of being attacked, they attack others-scaring them, terrorizing them, shocking them, making others feel as they do. These children can become so violent that they cannot function in school, at home, with peers; yet, behind every violent act towards another is a fear that runs so deep and it is those fears that must be known for the aggression to be understood and contained. Working with aggressive children is not easy, for we, as analysts, are often seen as a dangerous threat too, worthy of attack. In no uncertain terms, we let these children know we can tolerate the attacks and other forms of aggression. We work closely with caregivers so that the treatment is maintained long enough to help us understand the fears, knowing that if these children do not get the mental health attention they need, the risk to themselves and society, down the road, is great. Without help, these could be the very same children, who, as adults, become prison guards who rape inmates or college students who sexually assault fellow students.

Like victims and survivors, children need to be heard and understood and if children are heard and understood, there will be fewer victims and survivors. To quote a famous child psychoanalyst, Selma Fraiberg,

> The permission of psychoanalytic therapy is the permission to speak of the dangerous and forbidden thoughts; it is not the permission to act on them. The process enables the patient to bring the forbidden impulses under control of the higher mental processes of reason and judgment, a process which automatically strengthens the moral side of man by partially freeing it from its primitive and irrational sources. (Fraiberg, 1959, p. 29)

Hence, child psychoanalysis can be viewed as a model of early intervention and prevention; a model that is quite relevant to the two chapters that have preceded this commentary, both of which address the importance of the prevention of a problem that has been ongoing and needs to be stopped; more specifically, in relation to college campus and prison sexual assault and violence.

While there are underlying differences between the culture of sexual assault on college campuses and in correctional facilities, both chapters outline similar necessary strategies in an effort to confront, address, and prevent these crimes. As featured in Brenda Smith's chapter (Chapter Thirteen), recent efforts to combat the sexual abuse of women in custody have included a multi-pronged approach of litigation aimed at systematic and legislative reform. Both types of reform "send a message to the public, prisoners and corrections staff that sexual misconduct is a serious public policy concern that merits prosecution and appropriate penalties." Public education is another approach to reform that, according to Smith, "holds the greatest promise of preventing sexual abuse for women in prisons." Media exposure, staff trainings related to sexual misconduct with offenders, and technical assistance are just a few of the ways that education is having an impact.

Annie Clark writes a personal account of her activism from starting an organization called End Rape on Campus (EROC) to being featured in the documentary, *The Hunting Ground*, and, finally, a publication of her most recent work with Andrea Pino entitled, *We Believe You: Survivors of Campus Sexual Assault Speak Out*. Like Smith, Clark believes that media exposure and other forms of public education about campus sexual assault go a long way towards prevention. This is clearly spelled out in the mission statement of EROC.

> EROC works to end campus sexual violence through direct support for survivors and their communities; prevention through education; policy reform at the campus, local, state, and federal levels, including federal accountability for Title IX, Title II, and Clery Act enforcement.

Prevention of any kind of violent act from sexual assault to gun violence must be the focus of all levels of intervention including early individual and family mental health treatment, educational programs in schools, community services, financial support on the local, state, and federal level, legislation, and litigation. We must all work together to "strengthen the moral side of man" and do what is right for our future, a future where EROC "envisions a world in which each individual has an educational experience free from violence, and until then, that all survivors are believed, trusted, and supported."

References

Fraiberg, S. (1959). *The Magic Years*. New York: Scribner (Simon and Schuster).

Reebye, P. (2005). Aggression during early years-infancy and preschool. *Canadian Child & Adolescent Psychiatric Review*, 14(1): 16–20.

CHAPTER FIFTEEN

Combatting femicide in Mexico: achievements and ongoing challenges

Maureen Meyer

Mexican and international media is often filled with gruesome news about Mexico. In the first three months of 2016, a mayor was killed the day after she took office, a journalist was kidnapped from her home and later found killed, and the number of people who have disappeared in the country has kept rising, reaching over 27,000 cases since 2007. In the context of this widespread violence, the gender-based violence that affects Mexican women in specific ways is often overlooked, although it is an equally pressing problem.

Femicides, defined in general terms in Mexico as the violent and deliberate killing of women, came under the spotlight in Mexico in the mid-1990s and early 2000s due to the wave of killings of girls and women in Ciudad Juarez and Chihuahua city, both in the northern state of Chihuahua. That these killings became so noteworthy was, in large part, due to the tireless efforts of mothers, daughters, sisters, women's rights activists, and others who spoke out against these deaths and denounced the government's grossly inadequate response.

Although there is now less national and international attention on femicides in Mexico, it is not because the problem has gone away; indeed, gender-based killings are on the rise in many states. What have changed in the past decade are the legal protections and mechanisms available to address this widespread problem. This chapter examines the current state of femicide in Mexico. It then describes how the struggle to address femicides in the state of Chihuahua raised awareness of the issue and shifted the national debate, leading to important victories, particularly on the legal front. Last, the chapter examines the mechanisms currently available to address femicide in Mexico and what is needed to ensure that they become effective tools capable of combatting this widespread and grave crime.

Current state of femicide in Mexico

In the past two years, six pregnant women in the Mexican state of Puebla were killed by their partners, who did not want to be fathers; the most recent of these murders was of twenty-five-year-old Samaí Alejandra Márquez Salgado in February 2016 (*El Diario*, 2016). These cases in Puebla are just the tip of the iceberg. The State of Mexico, Mexican President Enrique Peña Nieto's home state, has the most homicides of women in the country in absolute numbers. Between 2007 and 2013, the state's homicide rate for women increased by 155% (Molina, 2015). Ecatepec, a municipality in the State of Mexico and where Pope Francis recently visited, is considered the most violent place in Mexico to be a woman.

Unfortunately, there is a lack of concrete statistics regarding femicides in the country. In an April 2016 report titled *La violencia feminicida en México: aproximaciones y tendencias, 1985–2014* (Femicide violence in Mexico: approximations and tendencies 1985–2014), the Mexican Ministry of the Interior (*Secretaría de Gobernación*, SEGOB), Mexico's National Women's Institute (*Instituto Nacional de las Mujeres*), and UN Women stated that because Mexico does not have a fixed system to register gender-based killings and local prosecutors often fail to report crimes as such, it is impossible to know how many of these killings were femicides (SEGOB, INMUJERES, ONU Mujeres, 2016).

The most comprehensive information available in Mexico is from Mexico's National Statistics and Geography Institute (*Instituto Nacional de Estadística y Geografía*, INEGI), which records its data based on death certificates. INEGI released a study on November 25, 2015, the International Day for the Elimination of Violence Against Women, in which it concluded that, on average, seven women were killed in Mexico every day in 2013 and 2014. INEGI found that, in 2011, 63% of all Mexican women over the age of fifteen had been victims of violence by their partners or another individual. While there was a significant increase in homicides of men, particularly between 2008 and 2011, INEGI's statistics show that for women, homicides are more constant and less subject to current events, indicating that the killing of women is more of a structural phenomenon derived from a cultural pattern and less due to the organized crime-related violence that has impacted the country in the past decade (*Instituto Nacional de Estadistica y Geografia* (INEGI), 2016).

INEGI's analysis of data from 2013 also showed concerning trends in the killings of women. In this year, seven out of every 100 women that were killed were 0–14-year-old girls. INEGI also highlighted that women and girls are more likely to be attacked where they live: 29.4% of women compared to only 10% of men are killed in their homes. Women and girls are also killed with more violence and cruelty, using methods that produce more pain and which prolong death. In 2013, thirty-two out of every 100 women that were killed were hung, strangled, burned, stabbed, or hit with blunt instruments, while over 65% of men were killed with a gun (INEGI, 2016).

Combatting femicide in Mexico, the Juarez experience

Although the overall number of murders of women and girls may be more prevalent in other Mexican states, it was the struggle of the families from Ciudad Juarez and Chihuahua city, Chihuahua, which put this issue on the national and international agenda for Mexico. Beginning in the early 1990s and throughout the next decade, there was an increase in the killings of women and girls in the state; others disappeared and were never heard from again. Between 1993 and 2014, at least 1,530 women were murdered in Ciudad Juarez alone (Becerra, 2015).

The Ciudad Juarez cases were noteworthy for many reasons. From 1993–2003, of the 370 murders analyzed by Amnesty International, at least 137 had been sexually assaulted before death. Amnesty International noted that, "many of the women were abducted, held captive for several days and subjected to humiliation, torture and the most horrific sexual violence before dying, mostly as a result of asphyxiation caused by strangulation or from being beaten" (Amnesty International, 2003). Although many other cases did not involve sexual assault, they were often vicious, including many cases of domestic violence. The majority of the victims were young and poor, working in the many *maquiladoras* (factories) in this border city; others were waitresses, students, and women employed in the informal economy.

Beyond the brutality of many of the cases, the response from the government was grossly inadequate. The police were slow to act when girls were reported missing and on many occasions, they blamed the victims themselves. Authorities called some victims prostitutes, or blamed them for wearing short skirts, going out dancing, or being "easy" (Robertua, 2012). A statement made by the Chihuahua state attorney general who was in office between 1998 and 2002 clearly illustrates this "blame the victim" mentality:

> "Regretfully, there are women who because of the [circumstances of their lives], the places where they carry out their activities, are at risk; because it would be very difficult for anyone going out into the street when it is raining, well, it would be very difficult not to get wet." (Monárrez Fragoso, 2002)

Given the government's indifference, obstruction, and, at times, hostility towards the families, the mothers of murdered girls began to organize. These brave women were then joined by human rights and feminist activists and others to raise awareness about violence against women in Ciudad Juarez and Chihuahua city and, indeed, the pressing problem of violence against women in Mexico in general.

Several mothers founded their own organizations, such as Justice for our Daughters (*Justicia para Nuestras Hijas*) and May Our Daughters Return Home (*Nuestras Hijas de Regreso a Casa*). The organization Friendship House (*Casa Amiga*) began to document the deaths of women and publicize them. The phrase "Not one more" ("*Ni Una Más*") was coined to protest about these killings, often appearing alongside a pink cross, many of which scattered the landscape in Ciudad Juarez and continue to be visible today.

Because of the irregularities in the investigations, the significant number of unidentified remains, and doubts of victims' families about the identity and/or cause of death of the remains they received, families and national and international human rights organizations secured the participation of the Argentine Forensic Anthropology Team (*Equipo Argentino de Antropólogos Forensese*, EAAF), a non-governmental, independent team established in the 1980s that provides forensic services in cases of human rights violations worldwide.

The EAAF began forensic work for several cases in Ciudad Juarez in 2004. Its work revealed insufficient information in the forensic files of women and girls, files that were missing or misplaced, remains that were misplaced or went missing, and multiple irregularities in the final destination of remains: they could be stored in the medical examiner's office, buried in municipal cemeteries, donated to the Medical School of the Autonomous University of Ciudad Juarez, or cremated. Several remains were initially misidentified and, although the EAAF was able to positively identify thirty-three remains of the eighty-three that it examined, fifty remained unidentified at the end of its work in 2010 (Torres Ruiz, 2015).

One of several cases presented by Mercedes Doretti from the EAAF in a hearing before the Inter-American Court of Human Rights, discussed below, is telling of Mexican authorities' disregard in these investigations. In this case, a twenty-four-year-old mother of five went missing in 1999; her family looked for her for seven years. The EAAF was able to ascertain that, a few days after she went missing, the woman died in a hospital in Ciudad Juarez, but her family was never notified. Her remains, along with her full name, were then sent to the city's medical examiner's office. One month later, her body was transferred to the city's Medical School, where it remained until 2002 when it was placed in a common grave in a local cemetery. Her remains were only identified after EAAF exhumed the common grave and conducted an extensive examination of photos and official documents that were dispersed among many agencies (Doretti, 2009).

Local and national advocacy around the femicides in Ciudad Juarez also led to strong international condemnation and widespread attention on the situation. Amnesty International, Human Rights Watch, the Washington Office on Latin America (WOLA), and other organizations all became involved in denouncing the situation in Ciudad Juarez and the government's failure to address these killings, sanction those responsible, and provide answers to the families. The Inter-American Commission on Human Rights (IACHR) and various

UN agencies (such as the Committee on the Elimination of All forms of Discrimination against Women, the Committee on Torture, and the special rapporteurs for: extrajudicial, summary, or arbitrary executions; the independence of judges and lawyers; violence against women) all criticized the murders of women and girls in Ciudad Juarez and the government's failure to investigate and prosecute those responsible (Anaya, 2009).

Progress made in Mexico

The momentum provided by the attention on femicide in Ciudad Juarez led to broader movements in Mexico, such as the creation of the National Citizen Observatory on Femicide (*El Observatorio Ciudadano Nacional del Feminicidio*, OCNF), an alliance of thirty-six organizations which works to document the murders of women in order to identify patterns that can contribute to these crimes being classified as femicide.

Additionally, in response to mounting pressure by victims' families and national and international organizations and human rights bodies, the Mexican government created the Federal Commission to Prevent and Eradicate Violence Against Women in Ciudad Juarez (*Comisión para Prevenir y Erradicar la Violencia contra las Mujeres en Ciudad Júarez*) in February 2004, with the stated purpose of providing a government response to the murders and disappearances of women in the city. Following this commission, the federal government established in 2006 the Special Prosecutor's Office for Crimes of Violence Against Women and Human Trafficking (*Fiscalía Especial para los Delitos de Violencia contra las Mujeres y Trata de Personas*, FEVIMTRA) within the federal Attorney General's Office (*Procuraduría General de la República*, PGR). FEVIMTRA is tasked with carrying out criminal investigations and prosecutions for these crimes throughout Mexico, as well as providing comprehensive attention to victims of violence against women and trafficking, contributing to the development of public policies to prevent these crimes, and collaborating in the search for disappeared women and girls.

Notable Mexican feminists, such as Marcela Largarde, also pushed to create a stronger legal framework to address gender-based violence. As a federal deputy, Lagarde promoted the creation of the

General Law on Women's Access to a Life Free from Violence, which was signed into law in February 2007. The purpose of the law is to establish coordination between the federal government, the states, and the municipalities to prevent, sanction, and eradicate violence against women. It also establishes methods to guarantee women's access to a life free from violence that favors women's development and wellbeing in accordance with the principles of equality and non-discrimination. Importantly, the law includes the term "femicide violence," which is defined as

> an extreme form of gender-based violence against women, resulting from the violation of their human rights, in the public and private spheres, consisting of misogynistic conduct that can lead to social and state impunity and may culminate in homicide and other forms of violent death of women. (IACHR, 2015)

In 2011, a process was also started to classify femicide as a crime at the state level. It is now part of the criminal code in all states except Chihuahua, whose code already included strict penalties for the murders of women as a result of the mobilization around femicides and the progress made in state judicial reform (OCNF, 2015).

Another important element of the general law is that it established the Alert of Gender Violence Against Women (*Alerta de Violencia de Género contra las Mujeres* (AVGM)). The AVGM is a set of emergency governmental measures designed to address and eradicate violence against women in the Mexican states. It can be declared based on an increase in crimes against women; state human rights commissions, the National Human Rights Commission (*Comisión Nacional de los Derechos Humanos*, CNDH), civil society organizations, or international bodies can also request that an AVGM be declared (*Cámara de Diputados*, 2015).

While progress was being made to strengthen Mexico's legal framework to combat femicide and violence against women, several human rights organizations, together with the victims' families, began bringing cases before the IACHR to denounce the failure of the Mexican government to adequately investigate the crimes and prosecute those responsible. For example, in March 2009, the IACHR admitted the cases of the murders of Paloma Angélica Escobar Ledezma and Silvia Arce as representative of the pattern of discrimination and violence against women in the state (Center for Justice and International Law (CEJIL), 2009).

Another case, known as the Cotton Field Murders, went to the Inter-American Court of Human Rights. The case involved the 2001 murder of three women in Ciudad Juarez: Esmeralda Herrera Monreal, Laura Berenice Ramos Monarrez, and Claudia Ivette Gonzales, whose remains were found in a cotton field in the outskirts of Ciudad Juarez along with the remains of five other women. The investigations into these murders were wrought with irregularities, beginning with the fact that the authorities refused to look into the whereabouts of these women until seventy-two hours after their disappearances had been reported. Three months after the bodies were found, volunteers searching the site discovered clothing that was recognized by the mother of one of the victims, as well as hair, shoes, and clothing remnants, none of which had been gathered by police investigators during their search.

The cases of the murders of Esmeralda Herrera Monreal, Laura Berenice Ramos Monarrez, and Claudia Ivette Gonzales were originally presented separately before the Inter-American Commission on Human Rights.[1] In 2007, after holding hearings and several deliberations, the Commission decided to unify the three cases and petitioned the Inter-American Court to assume the case against the Mexican government

> regarding the responsibility it has incurred in failing to provide measures of protection to [the victims]; the lack of prevention of gender crimes, despite full knowledge of the existence of a pattern of violence that had left hundreds of women and girls murdered by the time of these events occurred; the authorities' lack of response to the disappearance of the victims; the lack of due diligence in the investigation of the victims' murders, as well as the denial of justice and the failure to provide adequate compensation to their next of kin. (IACHR, 2007)

After a lengthy process, on November 16, 2009, the Court issued a sentence against Mexico for failing to investigate the disappearance, mistreatment, and murder of these girls and to prosecute and sanction those responsible (IACHR, 2009). This was the first case heard before the Inter-American Court whose central issue was gender violence and it was only the third case to be brought against the Mexican government in the Court.

The sentence, which is legally binding for Mexico, requires the government to: investigate and sanction those responsible for the murders, including the intellectual authors, investigate the authorities responsible for the irregularities in the investigations into the murders, provide reparations for the family members, and carry out a public act within a year in which the government recognizes its international responsibility for these crimes and constructs a monument for the victims, among other resolutions (IACHR, 2009).

On the national front in Mexico, and more recently, in January 2015, a panel of three women judges handed down unprecedented prison sentences of 697 years and six months each to five men convicted of trafficking and killing eleven girls and women from Ciudad Juarez. Arrested in 2013, the defendants were accused of systematically abducting and sexually exploiting young, working-class girls before killing them and disposing of their remains in the rural Juarez Valley. According to media coverage,

> a three-month trial exposed how the ring systematically abducted, enslaved, and murdered women between at least 2009 and 2011, even as thousands of federal police and soldiers were deployed to the Mexican city to confront warring drug cartels. The court heard that the gang regularly paid off corrupt police officers and soldiers, who sometimes participated in the sexual exploitation of the women. (Tuckman, 2015)

The panel's sentence is important as the first conviction for the crime of human trafficking in the new adversarial judicial system in the state of Chihuahua. It is also significant because, although the gang's leaders and corrupt officials who enabled this violence still need to be investigated, the public prosecutor—working with the Women's Network in Ciudad Juarez (*Red Mesa de Mujeres*) and Justice for Our Daughters—was able to demonstrate, based on documented evidence and testimonies, the reality of femicide in Ciudad Juarez (Gurrea, 2015).

Next steps

As was described in the previous section, the efforts by families, experts, legislators, civil society organizations, and the international community to denounce femicide in Mexico have resulted in important victories to prevent gender-based violence and provide legal protections for women who are victims of violence, and they have led to key resolutions on paradigmatic cases.

In spite of this progress, the high numbers of femicides that continue to occur in Mexico point to the many challenges that remain. One overarching challenge is overcoming discrimination that leads to gender-based violence in Mexico. In addition to the discriminatory violence, discrimination is also reflected in the impunity that prevails in the majority of the cases of femicide and other cases of violence against women in Mexico. As Mexican lawyer Andrea Medina Rosas highlighted in an article about the significance of the Cotton Field Murders case,

> in Mexico, in cases of violence against women, impunity is a constant feature that practically results in preventable acts of violence escalating to attempted murder and murder. In this way, highlighting impunity in cases of violence against women is central to show who is responsible for these acts and to leave behind the discriminatory prejudice of blaming women for the violence that they suffer. (Medina Rosas, 2011, translated for this edition)[2]

In an analysis of the classification of femicide as a crime, the OCNF found that of the 613 femicide cases investigated by state prosecutors between 2012 and 2013, charges had only been presented in 25% of the cases and only 1.6% had resulted in a conviction; 24% of the cases were still under investigation, while information was not available for the other cases (*Observatorio Ciudadano Nacional del Feminicidio* (ONCF), 2015).[3] In some states' criminal codes, the classification of femicide as a crime is difficult to prove. Even in states with clear definitions, judicial officials often lack an understanding of the crime and discrimination still impedes comprehensive investigations and sanctions of murders of women (Mejía Piñeros, 2014).

In compliance with the 2009 Inter-American Court sentence on the Cotton Field Murders, FEVIMTRA published in November 2014 the Protocols for Criminal, Police and Expert Investigation with a Gender Perspective for the Crime of Femicide and Sexual Violence. The protocols provide guidelines with a gender perspective for how officials should investigate these crimes. While long in coming, it is hoped that through training on the protocols and their full use, there will be improved attention to and prosecution of cases of femicide and sexual violence in the country.

At the same time, the AVGM is finally gaining some traction. Although the Alert is an important mechanism included in the 2007 General Law on Women's Access to a Life Free from Violence, it was not until 2015, eight years after the law was enacted, that the only two existing AVGM's to date were issued in Mexico. On July 31, 2015, the alert was declared in eleven municipalities of the State of Mexico. This important step was taken after five years of litigation by the Mexican Commission for the Defense and Promotion of Human Rights (Comisión Mexicana de Defensa y Promoción de los Derechos Humanos) and the ONCF. As the petitioning organizations have highlighted, "if the alert had been declared in time, many deaths and disappearances could have been avoided" (Comisión Mexicana, 2015, translated for this edition).

In August 2015, an AVGM was declared in eight municipalities in the state of Morelos at the request of the governor and the organization the Independent Human Rights Commission of Morelos (*Comisión Independiente de Derechos Humanos de Morels*). The request was originally made by the Commission in 2013 after registering 500 femicides in the state between 2000 and 2013. By the time the alert had been declared, 633 cases had been registered (Xinhua, 2015).

Currently, Mexican authorities have requests to activate the alert in thirteen additional states (*Secretaría de Gobernación* (SEGOB), 2016). In spite of requests made by civil society organizations, many governors have resisted making use of the alert, denying the magnitude of the problem in their states and arguing that there are already state policies in place to protect women. Although criminal prosecutions are important to prevent further cases, an analysis of the effectiveness of the alerts in the State of Mexico and Morelos and granting alerts in additional states might also contribute to combatting the widespread number of attacks and murders of women in the country.

Courageous women

The International Psychoanalytical Association Committee for Women and Psychoanalysis conference held on March 4 and 5, 2016 was aptly titled, "The Courage to Fight Violence Against Women." In the past two decades in Mexico, violence against women—and femicide as a brutal expression of this violence—became a public issue thanks to the tireless work of experts, legislators, women's rights and human rights organizations, but also many, many mothers and their families, who had the courage to speak out and denounce their daughters' disappearances, demanding the truth about what happened to them and justice for those responsible. Many challenges remain to combat violence against women in Mexico, but it is clear that progress will continue to be made thanks to civil society activism to raise awareness, denounce crimes, and push the government for accountability in cases of gender-based violence.

In closing, I wanted to speak of one of the courageous women that my organization and I have had the good fortune of working with, Norma Ledezma. Norma's sixteen-year-old daughter, Paloma, left her house on March 2, 2002 to go to school and never returned. Her body was found with signs of sexual violence three weeks later on the highway between Chihuahua City and Aldama City. Mexican authorities were slow to act and, at times, obstructed the investigation. Norma, together with human rights organizations, took Paloma's case to the Inter-American Commission on Human Rights.

Since her daughter's murder, Norma has worked tirelessly on many other cases of women and girls who were killed or disappeared in Chihuahua. She founded, with other activists, the organization Justice for Our Daughters, she has advocated for Mexican authorities to investigate cases of femicide and disappearances, and she has provided counsel on many legal cases, including the historic ruling in Ciudad Juarez last year. As a result of this work, she has been subject to multiple threats, attacks, and defamation over the years.

In 2011, after years of hearings and meetings at the Inter-American Commission, Norma and her lawyers reached an agreement with the Mexican government on the case, nine years after Paloma's murder. As part of the agreement, the Mexican government issued a public recognition of its failure to investigate the case and prosecute those responsible, it committed to continue the investigation into her murder, and to enact measures so that cases such as Paloma's do not happen again (Comisión Mexicana, 2012). Additionally, one of Chihuahua's Centers for Justice for Women, which operate under the state public prosecutor's office, now bears the name Paloma Angélica Escobar Ledezma. In February 2016, Norma celebrated another important step in the search for justice for women and to remember her daughter Paloma: she obtained her law degree so that she can fully work as legal counsel on many cases of violence against women in the future (Mayorga, 2016).

Notes

1. The cases were supported by the families of the girls, the *Red Ciudadana de No Violencia y por la Dignidad Humana, Centro para el Desarrollo Integral de la Mujer A.C.* (CEDIMAC), *Asociacion Nacional de Abogados Democratics* (ANAD) and Comité de América Latina y el Caribe para la Defensa de los Derechos de la Mujer (CLADEM).
2. Original quote: *En México, en los casos de violencia contra las mujeres, la impunidad es una característica constante que prácticamente lleva de la mano los actos de violencia prevenibles al extremo de atentar contra la vida y causar muertes. Así, señalar la impunidad en los casos de violencia contra las mujeres es central para evidenciar quién es responsable de esos actos, y dejar el prejuicio discriminatorio de responsabilizar a las mujeres de la violencia que sufren.*
3. The low conviction rate for these crimes is similar to overall impunity rates in Mexico, with some estimates affirming that those responsible are sanctioned in less than one percent of all crimes committed in Mexico (*Centro de Estudios Sobre Impunidad y Justicia* (CESIJ), 2016).

References

Amnesty International (2003). Mexico: intolerable killings: 10 years of abductions and murders of women in Ciudad Juarez and Chihuahua: summary report and appeals cases, August. Accessed at: www.amnesty.org/en/documents/AMR41/027/2003/en/.

Anaya, A. (2009). Altos niveles de presión transnacional sobre México por violaciones de derechos humanos: el caso de las desapariciones y asesinatos de mujeres en Ciudad Juárez, *Documentos de Trabajo de CIDE, 190*(November): 1–32.

Becerra, L. (2015). Estado de Mexico en focos rojos, centro de investigación para el Desarrollo (*CIDAC*), August. Accessed at: http://cidac.org/estado-de-mexico-en-focos-rojos/.

Cámara de Diputados del Congreso de la Unión (2015). Ley general de acceso de las mujeres a una vida libre de violencia, December. Retrieved from: www.diputados.gob.mx/LeyesBiblio/pdf/LGAMVLV_171215.pdf.

Center for Justice and International Law (2009). Comisión Interamericana de Derechos Humanos admite dos casos mexicanos de feminicidio, September. Accessed at: www.cejil.org/es/comision-interamericana-derechos-humanos-admite-dos-casos-mexicanos-feminicidio.

Centro de Estudios Sobre Impunidad y Justicia (2016). Índice global de impunidad México IGI-MEX 2016, *Universidad de las Americas—Puebla*, February. Accessed at: www.udlap.mx/igimex/assets/files/IGI-MEX_CESIJ_2016.pdf.

Comisión Mexicana de Defensa y Promoción de los Derechos Humanos (2012). Caso Paloma Angélica Escobar Ledezma. Accessed at: http:/cmdpdh.org/casos-paradigmaticos-2–2/casos-defendidos/caso-paloma-escobar-ledezma/.

Comisión Mexicana de Defensa y Promoción de los Derechos Humanos (2015). Alerta de género en el estado de Mexico. Accessed at: http://cmdpdh.org/temas/violencia-contra-las-mujeres/alerta-de-genero-edomex/.

Comité de América Latina y el Caribe para la Defensa de los Derechos de la Mujer (CLADEM), Caso Campo Algodonero. Accessed at: www.cladem.org/programas/litigio/litigios-internacionales/12-litigios-internacionales-oea/22-caso-campo-algodonero-mexico-femicidio-feminicidio.

Doretti, M. (2009). Testimony of Mercedes Doretti before the Inter-American Court of Human Rights, *Equipo Argentino de Antropología Forense* (EAAF), April. Accessed at: www.corteidh.or.cr/docs/casosexpedientes/Doretti.pdf.

El Diario (2016). ¿Qué pasa en puebla? Asesinan a embarazada; empresario y escoltas descuartizan a jóvenes, February 22. Accessed at: www.eldiariony.com/2016/02/22/que-pasa-en-puebla-asesinan-a-embarazada-y-empresario-y-escoltas-descuartizan-a-jovenes/.

Gurrea, C. J. A. (2015). Los saldos de un juicio histórico, *El Universal*, July 29. Accessed at: www.eluniversal.com.mx/articulo/estados/2015/07/29/los-saldos-de-un-juicio-historico.

Instituto Nacional de Estadistica y Geografia (INEGI) (2016). Estadisticas a proposito del Dia Internacional de la Eliminacion de la Violencia Contra la Mujer, November 23. Accessed at: www.inegi.org.mx/saladeprensa/aproposito/2015/violencia0.pdf.

Inter-American Commission on Human Rights (2007). Demanda ante la Corte Interamericana de Derechos Humanos en el caso de Campo Algodonero: Claudia Ivette González, Esmeralda Herrera Monreal y Laura Berenice Ramos Monárrez (Casos 12.496, 12.497 y 12.498) contra los Estados Unidos Mexicanos, November. Accessed at: www.cidh.

org/demandas/12.496–78%20Campo%20Algodonero%20Mexico%204%20noviembre%202007%20ESP.pdf.

Inter-American Commission on Human Rights (2009). *Technical Data: González y otras ("Campo Algodonero") Vs. México*, March. Accessed at: www.corteidh.or.cr/cf/jurisprudencia/ficha.cfm?nId_Ficha=347&lang=en.

Inter-American Commission on Human Rights (2015). Situation of human rights in Mexico, December. Accessed at: www.oas.org/en/iachr/reports/pdfs/Mexico2016-en.pdf.

Inter-American Court of Human Rights (2009). Caso González y Otras ("Campo Algodonero" vs. México, November. Accessed at: www.corteidh.or.cr/docs/casos/articulos/seriec_205_esp.pdf.

Mayorga, P. (2016). Norma Ledezma: la madre que estudió Derecho para hacerle justicia a su hija asesinada, *Proceso*, February 22. Accessed at: www.proceso.com.mx/430919/norma-ledezma-la-madre-que-estudio-derecho-para-hacerle-justicia-a-su-hija-asesinada.

Medina Rosas, A. (2011). Campo Algodonero definiciones y retos ante el feminicidio en México, March. Accessed at: www.corteidh.or.cr/tablas/r26767.pdf.

Mejía Piñeros, M. C. (2014). Estudio de la implementación del tipo penal de feminicidio en México: causas y consecuencias 2012–2013. *Católicas por el Derecho Decidir A.C*, November. Accessed at: http://observatoriofeminicidiomexico.org.mx/wp-content/uploads/2015/01/17-NOV-Estudio-Feminicidio-en-Mexico-Version-web-1.pdf.

Molina, J. (2015). En México ocurre un feminicidio cada 3 horas: ONG; "El Problema Se Ha Naturalizado", Alerta, *El Diario*, October 13. Accessed at: www.sinembargo.mx/13–10–2015/1517190.

Monárrez Fragoso, J. (2002). Serial sexual femicide in Ciudad Juárez. *Debate Feminista*, 25(13). Accessed at: www.womenontheborder.org/sex_serial_english.pdf.

Observatorio Ciudadano Nacional del Feminicidio (2015). Estudio de la implementación del tipo penal de feminicidio en Mexico: causas y consecuencias 2012, 2013, & 2014, November. Accessed at: http://observatoriofeminicidiomexico.org.mx/wp-content/uploads/2015/01/17-NOV-Estudio-Feminicidio-en-Mexico-Version-web-1.pdf.

Robertua, V. (2012). Femicide: is this an important issue? Verdinand Robertua's Blog, April 9. Accessed at: https://verdinand633.wordpress.com/2012/04/09/femicide-in-global-regional-and-ciudad-juarez/.

Secretaría de Gobernación (2016). Alerta de Violencia de Genero contra las Mujeres, Ficha Informativa. Accessed at: www.conavim.gob.mx/en/CONAVIM/Informes_y_convocatorias_de_AVGM.

Secretaria de Gobernación, Instituto Nacional de las Mujeres, and Entidad de las ONU para la Igualdad de Género y el Empoderamiento de las Mujeres (2016). La violencia feminicida en México, aproximaciones y tendencias 1985–2014, April. Accessed at: www2.unwomen.org/~/media/field%20office%20mexico/documentos/publicaciones/2016/02/violencia%20feminicida%20en%20m%C3%A9xico%20aproximaciones%20y%20tendencias%201985_2014.pdf?v=1&d=20160418T214527.

Torres Ruiz, G. (2015). Gobierno de Chihuahua oculta datos sobre restos de mujeres desaparecidas, *Proceso*, March 5. Accessed at: www.proceso.com.mx/300097/gobierno-de-chihuahua-oculta-datos-sobre-restos-de-mujeres-desaparecidas.

Tuckman, J. (2015). Murder convictions lift lid on seamy network preying on women of Juarez, *Guardian*, July 21. Accessed at: www.theguardian.com/world/2015/jul/21/juarez-mexico-women-murdered-corruption.

Xinhua, A. (2015). Alerta de género para ocho municipios de Morelos, *El Universal*, August 10. Accessed at: www.eluniversal.com.mx/articulo/estados/2015/08/10/alerta-de-genero-para-ocho-municipios-de-morelos.

CHAPTER SIXTEEN

Justice matters: scaling up the response to sexual violence in areas of conflict and unrest

Hope Ferdowsian

The burden of sexual violence in conflict zones

On average, at least one in three women worldwide experiences physical or sexual violence in her lifetime (World Health Organization, 2013). Sexual violence occurs in every part of the globe, and it is an ancient problem with modern relevance. For centuries to millennia, sexual violence has been used as a means to subjugate, control, or demean women and other vulnerable populations.

The risk for sexual violence is particularly high within areas of conflict and unrest – especially within war zones, after conflict, during political transition, and in times of internal displacement.[1] Evidence of sexual violence has been recorded during ancient warfare, civil wars, including the American Civil War, the First and Second World Wars, and countless other periods of conflict and unrest (Heineman, 2011). During conflict, rates of sexual violence may increase due to war strategies and environmental conditions (Agirre Aranburu, 2010), and the risk for sexual violence can be amplified by gender inequity and pathological socio-cultural norms.

Nevertheless, precise estimates of the prevalence of sexual violence in conflict zones (Palermo & Peterman, 2013) are largely unknown since conditions of conflict undermine efforts to document sexual violence.

Just after the Second World War, there was a relative increase in attention to sexual violence during wartime. For the first time, in 1946, at the Nuremburg Military Tribunal, the occupying powers defined rape under "crimes against humanity." In the same year, under the International Military Tribunal for the Far East (Tokyo), Japanese military officials were successfully prosecuted for abducting women for the purposes of sexual slavery and forced prostitution. Soon thereafter, the Geneva Conventions (1949) and Additional Protocols (1977) resulted in the first explicit mention and prohibition of rape. Women were covered as "protected persons" as civilians outside of combat. However, at the time, rape was still not considered a significant enough offense to be considered a war crime.

Sexual violence during conflict has resurfaced as a modern concern with widespread reports of sexual assaults in ongoing conflicts in Sub-Saharan Africa and the Middle East—including revelations of sexual abuse of prisoners by United States military personnel at the Abu Ghraib prison in Iraq (Heineman, 2011).

Alhough women have historically been the primary targets of sexual violence during or after conflict, men are also targeted, and children comprise a significant number of victims in many areas around the world. Regardless of the age or gender of survivors, sexual violence is a global public health problem resulting in considerable medical and mental health costs for victims, families, communities, and society.

The impact of sexual violence

On the most basic level, sexual violence is a stark form of bodily trespass: disrespect for one's personal sovereignty, one's capacity for consent, assent, or dissent, or one's vulnerability due to a diminished capacity for consent. Sexual violence is an attack on the physical and psychological need to stay free and safe, and it is a distortion of sexual expression, often complicated by personal and cultural expectations.

Sexual violence can have substantial physical and mental health effects on survivors. Health consequences of sexual violence vary from mild to severe medical, gynecological, obstetric, surgical, psychological, and psychiatric trauma. Medical consequences of sexual violence range from injuries involving the sexual organs to other areas of the body and can result in acute or chronic pain, scarring, or disability. Survivors can also acquire sexually transmitted infections, including HIV/AIDS, and they often experience sexual dysfunction, such as painful intercourse and a loss of interest or pleasure. Female survivors can become pregnant, and they face the risk of unsafe abortions where medical or surgical abortion is illegal or unavailable.

The most common sequelae of sexual violence are mental health consequences, and the effects of violence manifest in different ways throughout the life span. Adults commonly experience depression, anxiety, or posttraumatic disorders. For example, rape survivors are more likely to experience posttraumatic stress disorder (PTSD) and contemplate or complete suicide, compared with the general population. Survivors might struggle with these mental health consequences for years.

Mental health sequelae of violence manifest somewhat differently in children, though they are also susceptible to mood, anxiety, and posttraumatic disorders (Beitchman, et al., 1991, 1992; Briere & Elliot, 1994). Young children who have survived sexual violence commonly display abnormal behaviors such as eating disturbances, developmental regression, language delays, or attachment disorders. Less commonly, they may exhibit symptoms consistent with failure to thrive. In school-aged children, it is more common to see psychosomatic complaints, enuresis (bedwetting), behavioral problems, aggression, depression, attachment difficulties, and changes in play. Adolescent survivors of sexual violence may develop depression, suicidal ideation or attempts, and problems forming or maintaining healthy relationships. Like adults, they may also turn to substance abuse as a way to numb their pain.

Regardless of the age of survivors, fear of stigma and rejection is one of the main reasons survivors or their families do not report assault. When survivors disclose a history of assault, they often risk disbelief, blame, stigmatization, isolation, punishment, and a loss of privacy. Survivors commonly fear further harm or retaliation, which can occur as a direct result of the sexual violence incident or as a combination of the trauma and the effects of stigmatization or retraumatization of the survivor. Consequently, fear and stigma can result in delayed medical and mental health care.

Alhough the individual most impacted by sexual violence is the survivor, whole communities are affected. Mass crimes are particularly devastating to communities. Mass rape can result in disruption of social bonds, and it can disrupt access to basic essentials such as food, water, and medical care. Inadequate security and infrastructure can leave communities at risk for repeated attacks by perpetrators. And, when used as a weapon of war, widespread sexual violence can destabilize families and communities and lead to economic instability, further weakening the societal infrastructure and compromising the safety and security of the population.

Despite the many potential adverse consequences of sexual violence, survivors and communities can display remarkable resilience. A sense of agency and hope positively influence resilience, and both of these factors can be influenced by survivors' interactions with clinicians, law enforcement agents, legal experts, and the judicial system.

The international response

In recent history, medical and public health organizations, legal institutions, media outlets, military officials, peacekeeping bodies, scholars, and policymakers have increasingly turned their attention to the problem of sexual violence in conflict zones. A large number of efforts have been launched to address sexual violence during and after conflict, including enhanced data collection and evidence-based response mechanisms (Rowley et al., 2012). Efforts have also centered on screening, assessment, and medical care for survivors of sexual violence (Marsh et al., 2006).

All of these efforts—including finding and treating survivors—are critical. However, until recently, less attention focused on ensuring justice for survivors, which can also have therapeutic benefits.

Changes in international law during the last part of the twentieth century created a legal framework for the prosecution of sexual violence. Although laws against sexual violence in wartime have been in effect for many years, they were largely ignored until the most recent decades. Beginning in 1993 and 1994, the International Criminal Tribunal for the former Yugoslavia and the International Criminal Tribunal for Rwanda established rape as a war crime, a crime against humanity, and an element of genocide. Within five years of these legal decisions, the Rome Statute of the International Criminal Court (ICC) was adopted and, in 2002, following ratification by a critical mass of sixty state parties, formally entered into force. The ICC has since helped to expand the sexual violence crimes that can be prosecuted in national courts. And, in an attempt to establish a uniform medical–legal standard toward greater accountability for sexual violence, in 2014, the Global Summit to End Sexual Violence in Conflict in London launched the International Protocol on the Documentation and Investigation of Sexual Violence in Conflict Zones (International Protocol, 2014).

As a result of changes in international law and political will, adjudicators have increasingly sought justice for sexual violence survivors. In 2012, Charles Taylor was the first former head of state to be convicted of rape as a war crime by an international criminal tribunal. Since then, in February of 2016, a Guatemalan court convicted two former military officers of holding indigenous women as sex slaves during the nation's civil war (Lakhani, 2016) and subsequently ordered them to pay their victims reparations of just over $1 million (Maloney, 2016). In response to the landmark conviction, a news headline published in the *Guardian* read, "Guatemala sexual slavery verdict shows women's bodies are not battlefields" (Ruiz-Navarro, 2016).

About one month after the convictions in Guatemala, the ICC convicted Jean-Pierre Bemba Gombo (Bemba) for his responsibility as commander-in-chief for crimes of murder, pillage, and rape committed by soldiers under his authority in the Central African Republic between 2002 and 2003. Bemba was the first person to be convicted by the ICC for sexual violence crimes committed by troops under his command (Simons, 2016). Then, in late May of 2016, Chad's former president, Hissène Habré, was sentenced to life in prison for responsibility for crimes against humanity, torture, and sex crimes, as Chad's head of state from 1982 to 1990 (Searcey, 2016).

Prior to Bemba's and Habré's convictions, Congolese militia leader Germain Katanga was tried by the ICC in March of 2014 and found guilty of the crime against humanity of murder and the war crimes of willful killing, intentional attack against the civilian population, pillaging, and destruction of property. However, he was acquitted of charges of sexual slavery and rape (Coalition for the International Criminal Court). Nonetheless, the recent cascade of successful prosecutions signals that the international community is now giving sexual violence the global attention it is due.

The therapeutic importance of justice

Clearly, the justice system is a crucial element of a comprehensive response to sexual violence. Perpetrators cannot be held fully accountable without it. When the justice system fails to respond effectively to sexual violence crimes, the risk for recidivism increases. Additionally, a poor or ineffective response from the justice system undermines advocacy and prevention efforts within the legal, medical, and other sectors.

Nonetheless, the majority of sexual assaults are not reported to law enforcement, and the majority of perpetrators will never be held accountable. Even when victims report a sexual assault incident, there are many factors that sway whether the case will be prosecuted. The prosecutor often serves as a gatekeeper, and her or his decision to prosecute is influenced by a number of factors including, but not limited to, the availability of corroborating evidence, victim engagement, legal precedent, resources, the prosecutor's personal biases, and evolution of the law, among other factors (Sellers, 2008; Spohn & Holleran, 2004).

Although research has shown the potential benefits of prosecuting cases through the court system, there is also literature suggesting that common features of the criminal justice system can lead to re-traumatization of victims (Parsons & Bergin, 2010). While prosecution and conviction of perpetrators is an important part of healing for some survivors, this is not always the case: whereas some studies suggest a healing impact of victim satisfaction, others do not (Kunst et al., 2015).

Although there are few studies that incorporate the perspectives of sexual violence victims in conflict zones, victim advocates at rape crisis centers in the United States have reported that victim blaming and distrust of victims are common problems among both police and medical professionals. In studies in the United States, victims and rape victim advocates report that police, medical professionals, and the legal system are a source of re-traumatization (Campbell et al., 2001; Maier, 2008; Ullman, 1996). There could also be important differences among professional sectors. A study in the Eastern Democratic Republic of the Congo (DRC) and the Rift Valley region of Kenya, areas with a high prevalence of sexual violence, showed that law enforcement professionals were more likely than health professionals and lawyers to indicate that survivors should feel ashamed (Ferdowsian et al., 2016a).

Trauma-informed care responds to many of these problems by creating services that are sensitive to the needs of survivors and limiting potential triggers for re-traumatization. Trauma-informed care is also responsive to the possibility that survivors might have experienced repeated episodes of violence and trauma compounded by cultural forces, gender inequity, poverty, and major stressors such as separation from family, disruption of daily life, and migration.

In reality, justice for survivors extends far beyond the prosecution or conviction of perpetrators. Survivors also deserve validation, a transparent, efficient trial process free of corruption, attention to the crime and not the survivor's personal history, external support, and the elimination of barriers to care and justice.

Professionals can also reduce the risk for re-traumatization of survivors by working together to minimize impediments to care and justice. Historically, there has been minimal organized coordination among the medical and legal sectors in response to sexual violence. However, the current legal framework provides doctors and other clinicians with an opportunity to move beyond clinical care for survivors. By providing objective forensic documentation of the physical and mental health effects of sexual violence in individuals and groups of survivors, clinicians can support efforts to secure justice for survivors and hold perpetrators accountable (Ferdowsian et al., 2016b).

Recognizing the importance of cross-sectoral collaboration toward effective care and justice for survivors, Physicians for Human Rights, an international non-profit organization, launched a program in 2011 to enhance cooperation across the medical, legal, and judicial professions (Physicians for Human Rights, 2011). The program is currently being implemented in the Eastern DRC and the Rift Valley region of Kenya, areas with a high prevalence of sexual violence (Anastario et al., 2014; Kelly et al., 2012). In collaboration with local partners, the program addresses systemic challenges such as resource limitations, corruption, and the need for policy reform through a combination of cross-sectoral training and network development efforts, institutional capacity development assistance, and public interest litigation and other advocacy efforts.

Conclusion

Over time, sexual violence in conflict zones has received the needed attention it deserves. However, the scope and severity of the problem demand a continued escalation in the response to sexual violence through cross-sectoral collaboration, trauma-informed care for survivors, and efficient and transparent law enforcement practices and legal mechanisms. Although successful prosecution and ending impunity are important, it is as important to respect the rights of survivors. Accountability, shame, and stigma should be placed where they belong—with the perpetrators who commit and allow such violence. Equally important to securing justice is the acknowledgment that sexual violence occurs because of abuses of power. Justice also requires that we dismantle pathological power dynamics and systems of domination that lead to sexual violence.

Note

1. Although international definitions for sexual violence vary, according to the United Nations Secretary-General, sexual violence within conflict zones refers to: rape, sexual slavery, forced prostitution, forced pregnancy, enforced sterilization, and any other form of sexual violence of comparable gravity perpetrated against women, men, or children with a direct or indirect (temporal, geographical, or causal) link to a conflict. (United Nations General Assembly Security Council, 2013, paragraph 6).

References

Agirre Aranburu, X. (2010). Sexual violence beyond reasonable doubt: using pattern evidence and analysis for international cases. *Leiden Journal of International Law*, 23: 609–627.

Anastario, M. P., Adhiambo Onyango, M., Nyanyuki, J., Naimer, K., Muthoga, R., Sirkin, S., Barrick, K., van Hasselt, M., Aruasa, W., Kibet, C., & Omollo, G. (2014). Time series analysis of sexual assault case characteristics and the 2007–2008 period of post-election violence in Kenya. *PLoS ONE*, 9(8), e106443. doi:10.1371/journal.pone.0106443.

Beitchman, J. H., Zucker, K. J., Hood, J. E., DaCosta, G. A., & Akman, D. (1991). A review of the short-term effects of child sexual abuse. *Child Abuse & Neglect*, *15*: 537–556.

Beitchman, J. H., Zucker, K. J., Hood, J. E., DaCosta, G. A., Akman, D., & Cassavia, E. (1992). A review of the long-term effects of child sexual abuse. *Child Abuse & Neglect*, *16*: 101–118.

Briere, J. N., & Elliott, D. M. (1994). Immediate and long-term impacts of child sexual abuse. *The Future of Children*, *4*: 54–69.

Campbell, R., Wasco, S. M., Ahrens, C. E., Sefl, T., & Barnes, H. E. (2001). Preventing the "second rape": rape survivors' experiences with community service providers. *Journal of Interpersonal Violence*, *16*: 1239–1259.

Coalition for the International Criminal Court (2014). Cases and situations; Democratic Republic of Congo; Katanga and Ngudjolo Chui cases. Accessed at: www.iccnow.org/?mod=drctimelinekatanga.

Ferdowsian, H., Kelly, S., Burner, M., Anastario, M., Gohlke, G., Mishori, R., McHale, T., & Naimer, K. (2016a). Attitudes toward sexual violence survivors: Differences across professional sectors in Kenya and the Democratic Republic of the Congo. *Journal of Interpersonal Violence*, [ePub March 27, 2016], doi: 10.1177/0886260516639257.

Ferdowsian, H., Naimer, K., & Mishori, R. (2016b). Prosecuting sexual violence in conflict: a medical approach. *Angle Journal*. Accessed at: http://anglejournal.com/article/2015–12-clinicians-in-the-prosecution-of-conflict-related-sexual-violence/.

Heineman, E. D. (Ed.) (2011). *Sexual Violence in Conflict Zones: From the Ancient World to the Era of Human Rights*. Philadelphia, PA: University of Pennsylvania Press.

International Protocol on the Documentation and Investigation of Sexual Violence (2014). *Best Standards of Best Practice on the Documentation of Sexual Violence as a Crime under International Law*. London: Foreign & Commonwealth Office. Accessed at: UK Government website: www.gov.uk/government/uploads/system/uploads/attachment_data/file/319054/PSVI_protocol_web.pdf.

Kelly, J., Kabanga, J., Cragin, W., Alcayna-Stevens, L., Haider, S., & Vanrooyen, M. J. (2012). "If your husband doesn't humiliate you, other people won't": gendered attitudes towards sexual violence in eastern Democratic Republic of Congo. *Global Public Health*, *7*: 285–298.

Kunst, M., Popelier, L., & Varekamp, E. (2015). Victim satisfaction with the criminal justice system and emotional recovery: a systematic and critical review of the literature. *Trauma, Violence and Abuse, July 13*(3): 336–358.

Lakhani, N. (2016). Justice at last for Guatemalan women as military officers jailed for sexual slavery. *Guardian*, March 1. Accessed at: www.theguardian.com/world/2016/mar/01/guatemala-sexual-slavery-sepur-zarco-military-officers-jailed.

Maier, S. L. (2008). "I have heard horrible stories." Rape victim advocates' perceptions of the revictimization of rape victims by the police and medical system. *Violence Against Women*, 14: 786–808.

Maloney, A. (2016). Guatemala court orders $1 million in damages to wartime sex slaves. *Reuters*, March 3. Accessed at: www.reuters.com/article/us-guatemala-sexual-slavery-idUSKCN0W50BC.

Marsh, M., Purdin, S., & Navani, S. (2006). Addressing sexual violence in humanitarian emergencies. *Global Public Health: An International Journal for Research, Policy and Practice*, 1: 133–146.

Palermo, T., & Peterman, A. (2011). Undercounting, overcounting, and the longevity of flawed estimates: statistics on sexual violence in conflict. *Bulletin of the World Health Organization, 89*: 924–925.

Parsons, J., & Bergin, T. (2010). The impact of criminal justice involvement on victims' mental health. *Journal of Traumatic Stress*, 23(2): 182–188.

Physicians for Human Rights (2011). Program on sexual violence in conflict zones. Accessed at: http://physiciansforhumanrights.org/issues/rape-in-war/program-on-sexual-violence-in-conflict-zones.html.

Rowley, E., Garcia-Moreno, C., & Dartnell, E. (2012). Sexual violence research initiative. Executive summary: a research agenda for sexual violence in humanitarian, conflict, and post-conflict settings. Accessed at: http://www.svri.org/sites/default/files/attachments/2016-04-13/ExecutiveSummary.pdf.

Ruiz-Navarro, C. (2016). Guatemala sexual slavery verdict shows women's bodies are not battlefields. *Guardian*, February 29. Accessed at: www.theguardian.com/global-development/2016/feb/29/guatemala-sexual-slavery-verdict-womens-bodies-battlefields-sepur-zarco.

Searcey, D. (2016). Hissène Habré, ex-President of Chad, is convicted of war crimes. *The New York Times*, May 30. Accessed at: www.nytimes.com/2016/05/31/world/africa/hissene-habre-leader-chad-war-crimes.html.

Sellers, P. V. (2008). The prosecution of sexual violence in conflict: the importance of human rights as means of interpretation. Accessed at: www.ohchr.org/Documents/Issues/Women/WRGS/Paper_Prosecution_of_Sexual_Violence.pdf.

Simons, M. (2016). Congolese politician, Jean-Pierre Bemba, is convicted of war crimes. *The New York Times*, March 21. Accessed at: www.nytimes.

com/2016/03/22/world/africa/congolese-politician-jean-pierre-bemba-is-convicted-of-war-crimes.html?_r=0.

Spohn, C., & Holleran, D. (2004). Prosecuting sexual assault: a comparison of charging decisions in sexual assault cases involving strangers, acquaintances, and intimate partners. Accessed at: www.ncjrs.gov/pdffiles1/nij/199720.pdf.

Ullman, S. E. (1996). Do social reactions to sexual assault victims vary by support provider? *Violence and Victims*, *11*: 143–156.

United Nations General Assembly Security Council (2013). *Sexual Violence in Conflict*. Report of the Secretary-General. Accessed at: United Nations website: www.un.org/sexualviolenceinconflict/key-documents/reports/.

World Health Organization, Department of Reproductive Health and Research, London School of Hygiene and Tropical Medicine, South African Medical Research Council (2013). Global and regional estimates of violence against women: prevalence and health effects of intimate partner violence and non-partner sexual violence. p. 2.

CHAPTER SEVENTEEN

Women seeking asylum due to gender-based violence

Katalin Roth

In 1999, a psychiatrist colleague asked me if I would do a medical evaluation of a woman asylum seeker who had been tortured in Cameroon; my colleague did these evaluations as a volunteer for the organization Physicians for Human Rights (PHR). Since that first case, I have evaluated many asylum seekers, men and women, well over a hundred by now. I try to do one evaluation per month and usually manage about ten per year. I have met people from all over the world: from Asia, including refugees from China, Myanmar, Afghanistan, Pakistan; from Africa, including Cameroon, Cote d'Ivoire, Ethiopia, Eritrea, Congo, Sudan, Egypt; from Eastern Europe, Ukraine, and Georgia; and from Central America, Guatemala, Honduras, Mexico, and El Salvador. Due to the perspective I have gained from these courageous people, my appreciation for modern history and international news has become much more nuanced and skeptical. I have learned many things, including lessons about how harshly women can be treated. I have met women seeking asylum based on claims of forced marriage, female genital mutilation (FGM), forced domestic slavery and forced prostitution, rape, sexual preference, and domestic violence.

The claim of asylum is derived from international law regarding refugees and their rights under United Nations treaties and U.S. law, including the 1951 Convention Relating to the Status of Refugees and its Protocols. As defined by these agreements, a refugee is a person who is outside his or her country of nationality who, owing to a fear of persecution, on account of a "protected ground", is unable or unwilling to avail herself of the protection of the state. Protected grounds include race, nationality, religion, political opinion, and membership in a particular social group. Grounds for asylum is persecution on account of race, religion, nationality, particular social group, or political opinion. Since 1996, the U.S. added one more ground—forced sterilization or forced abortion or coercive population control, which has mainly applied to persons seeking asylum from China. Around the world, claims of persecution on the basis of female genital mutilation (FGM) and domestic violence have been gradually recognized and, in 2002, the United Nationals High Commission on Refugees (UNHCR) issued gender guidelines.

One can reasonably argue about whether the condition of being a woman qualifies as being a member of a particular persecuted social group. Cultural assumptions about women and culture roles for women differ across the world, and some countries have been reluctant to label traditional customs such as arranged marriage as persecution. When a woman's rights are not protected in her home country, and she becomes a refugee claiming asylum based on violation of those rights, the protection of asylum should be available to her. Of course, many women base asylum claims on non-gendered grounds, such as political or religious persecution, grounds that are likewise available to men.

It is important to point out that in the USA, approximately equal numbers of men and women seek asylum. In Europe, at least until the most recent *tsunamis* of refugees from North Africa and the Middle East, women comprised about 30% of asylum seekers. However, in Australia, up to 80% of asylum seekers in 2012 were women and children.

Women may have a more difficult time articulating the grounds of persecution, especially when the violence is gender based. When a refugee arrives in the United States and seeks asylum, the first step in the process is that the refugee must present a credible claim. Claims that involve sexual privacy and violation, genital cutting, domestic violence, and forced sexual submission might be very difficult for women from traditional, more modest cultures to articulate, especially to an immigration officer who is a complete stranger, and who is likely to be male. People who have been traumatized have great difficulty providing a narrative of their experiences, further intensifying the shame and reserve of these refugees. Some 70,000 refugees are returned to their home countries every year from the United States because they could not state a credible claim to the satisfaction of the first immigration official they encountered.

> *One way that women become involved in political violence is because of indirect associations with men*

Anna, my first client, was a nineteen-year-old woman from Cameroon who was arrested for reasons she never understood. She herself was not political, but her boyfriend was active in an opposition party. It is likely that her arrest was a way of getting at him. In prison, she was brutalized, tortured, and raped. A kindly guard helped her escape from prison but she feared re-arrest and death. After her escape, she learned that her lover had disappeared. Not having strong political convictions herself, she was confused and had no way of understanding her trauma. Being a relative or friend of someone who is involved in opposition politics is an independent risk factor for being tortured, and I have met women from all over the world—Burma, Cameroon, Ethiopia, Congo—who were caught up in torture because their fathers or brothers or husbands or sons were themselves persecuted and tortured.

Membership in a persecuted ethnic or religious group could result in violence against women. Divra, a twenty-five-year-old nurse from Ethiopia was a member of the Oromo ethnic group. When she went out to rural Oromo areas to teach poor women how to improve their reproductive health, she was first harassed, then arrested, beaten, and tortured. Kani was a fifty-year-old single Egyptian woman from a Christian family who worked in her family business. When her father died, she planned to continue the business alone, and was doing well until fundamentalist men began to harass her, seeking to convert her to Islam and seeking to confine her to her home, telling her that it was inappropriate for a woman to walk to work alone. Her home mysteriously caught fire, and she was harassed, beaten, and, finally, forced to flee for her life.

Recently, I met Maryam, a Nubian Sudanese woman who, at age sixteen, was out working in the fields with other women from her village when she and her friends were seized by Sudanese soldiers. Driven miles away, the women were raped and dropped in a ditch. Maryam could not return home because of the shame; she feared that her brothers and father would kill her because of the dishonor. Fleeing north, she was again abused by soldiers because of her Nubian heritage. When these soldiers raped her, they saw that Maryam had been circumcised, and so they then crudely sewed up her vagina to make her "pure again". Having been subjected to traditional female circumcision is no protection against sexual abuse when a woman is outside of her protective community

Being away from one's home and male protectors puts refugee women at great risk. During the exodus of the "boat people" from South Vietnam, after the U.S. troops withdrew, it is estimated that up to one third of the women refugees were raped during their journey. A similarly high rate of sexual abuse and rape has been reported among women fleeing northward to the USA from Central America. Despite these statistics, primary care doctors in the United States rarely ask foreign-born women patients about sexual trauma in their past journeys.

In recent years, I have seen a steady stream of women from Central America who seek safety in the USA because of violence from their partners—the grounds for asylum must include a claim that her own government has failed to protect her.

Sonia is a twenty-eight-year-old woman from Honduras who came to the USA as an illegal eighteen-year-old to work in a Midwestern meat processing plant, where she soon met Jorge. They dated, she became pregnant, and soon they began to live together. Even before their daughter was born, Jorge began to beat her. Physical abuse was frequent, especially when he drank. He became fiercely jealous: she could not go anywhere alone, except to and from work, she was allowed no girlfriends, she could not see her sister alone, and he took all of her money. The abuse continued for two years, during which time she had a second child and they moved several times because of their illegal immigration status. She could not go to the local police for help, fearing that their illegal status would be discovered. Both of her children were born in the USA and are U.S. citizens, yet she could not seek help. Then Jorge was picked up for a traffic violation, his illegal status was discovered, and they were all sent back to Honduras. Back home, Jorge continued to be violent. Despite several visits to the local police station, and several trips to the hospital for injuries, the local authorities refused to help her. One day Sonia threatened to leave Jorge and he began to choke her. She passed out. The next thing she remembers is that she awoke to find her eight-year-old daughter giving her mouth-to-mouth resuscitation. Since that day, she has lost all feeling on the left side of her face because of nerve damage from the choking. Soon after, in fear for her life, her family helped her leave for the USA.

Female genital circumcision, or female genital mutilation, or forced female circumcision (FGC, FGM, FFC) is a traditional practice used in Africa to control women's sexuality and independence. Despite United Nations sanctions and despite lip service to the local laws, this practice continues in many African countries. In most cases, the procedure is performed by medically untrained women, under dirty conditions, without anesthesia or pain medication. The stories are horrific—sometimes daughters are presented to local "cutters", sometimes relatives seize the girls despite the parents' objections. The procedures vary in severity, and can include excision of the labia, removal of all or part of the clitoris, and in the most extreme form, infundibulation, which is a partial sewing up of the vagina. Complications in adulthood include inability to feel sexual pleasure, painful sex, painful menstruation, and increased complications with childbearing. One woman from Ethiopia told me that she was circumcised at age nine, along with her three younger sisters, the youngest of whom was under six months old. A woman from Cote d'Ivoire once told me that she underwent the procedure twice, first at age six and then, because her aunt thought that a vestige of clitoral tissue remained, again at age twelve.

Lila, a woman from Senegal who, as a girl, was traumatized by FGC under terrible conditions, came to the USA with her husband to study; when their student visas expired, she realized that her own eight-year-old daughter would be subjected to FGM if she returned to her home country. She was granted asylum based on her inability to protect her daughter in her native country.

Trafficking and forced labor are also serious issues for women in poor countries. Elizabeth is a woman from Ethiopia who could not support herself when her parents died, and she became a housemaid.

She worked for a wealthy Middle Eastern family, and became a virtual prisoner: she was paid no salary for long hours and hard work, her documents were all confiscated, and she was not able to use the telephone or otherwise contact relatives. In addition, she was routinely subjected to sexual abuse by the oldest son in the family and, when she complained, she was beaten by her employers. She only escaped when the family travelled to New York City on vacation and she escaped their hotel apartment and sought help.

Under the United Nations Charter and the Declaration of Human Rights, women's rights are internationally recognized, and violation of these rights may form the basis for an appeal for asylum.

My volunteer work with refugees who have reached the United States is a meaningful way I can offer support to these incredibly brave women who are seeking a better life for themselves and their children.

Recommended reading

Anker, D. (2002). Refugee law, gender and the human rights paradigm. *Harvard Human Rights Journal*, *15*: 133–154.

Edwards, A. (2010). Age and gender dimensions in international refugee law. Accessed at: www. unhcr.org/419c74784.pdf.

Physicians for Human Rights. Examining asylum seekers. Accessed at: http://physiciansforhumanrights.org/asylum/?referrer=https://www.google.com/.

Siddiqui, S. (2010). Membership in a particular social group: all approaches open doors for women to qualify. *Arizona Law Review*, *52*(2): 505.

CHAPTER EIGHTEEN

Violence against women worldwide: a commentary on Chapters Fifteen to Seventeen

Louis W. Goodman

The three preceding chapters document and discuss violence against women in a range of locales world-wide. They report extraordinary courage to fight against this violence shown by victims of violence, by their families and friends, by technical experts such as doctors and lawyers, by legislators and local leaders, by civil society organizations, and by the international community. In these chapters most, but not all, of those who are described confronting this violence are themselves women.

In Chapter Fifteen, "Combatting femicide in Mexico", Maureen Meyer, of the Washington Office on Latin America discusses femicide in Mexico—the violent and deliberate killing of women in that country. She reports on the dimensions of this crime, how awareness of it has been increased, mechanisms available to address the crime, and what is needed to make these mechanisms effective tools.

In "Justice matters" (Chapter Sixteen), Hope Ferdowsian of Physicians for Human Rights points out that sexual violence during conflict is a historic and global issue beginning to get sustained international attention. While she reminds readers that sexual violence survivors need to be found and treated, she stresses that progress in reducing this horrible crime can only be achieved through the prosecution of perpetrators, ending impunity while respecting the rights of survivors.

In Chapter Seventeen, "Women seeking asylum due to gender-based violence", physician–lawyer Katalin Roth introduces the reader to brave women from around the world who are survivors of extreme violence including physical torture, genital cutting, domestic violence, and forced sexual submission and who have courageously sought remedies. She reports the stories of these women through her work evaluating asylum petitions under the provisions of the United Nations 1951 Convention Relating to the Status of Refugees.

While not comprehensive of all types of violence against women in all countries, these essays remind readers of the dimensions of the problem, the horrors of the crimes that produced this violence, the courage that has been demonstrated to confront it, and some of the things that can be done to reduce its incidence. They also remind readers that the remarkable courage of individuals like Sonia from Honduras, Lila from Senegal, Maryam from Sudan, and Nelly Ledezma from Mexico is indispensable for progress on this issue.

The detail in these chapters reflects the sequelae of many sources of violence, including open warfare and frustrations resulting from less visible, unfulfilled individual aspirations. They also flesh out the consequences of a large scale social structural process described in 1963 by the sociologist William J. Goode in his classic *World Revolution in Family Patterns* (probably the most widely cited book on changes in family patterns written in the twentieth century) and further elaborated and brought up to date by Goren Therborn in *Between Sex and Power: Family in the World, 1900–2000* (2004). The major argument made by Goode is that the pattern of social change described in the mid-twentieth century as "industrialization" and in the early twenty-first century as "globalization" weakens the traditional source of authority in the family and society (patriarchy, or the authority of senior males) and enhances the power of females and youth. In his follow up to Goode's classic, Therborn points out that the forms of change of power relations in families has not been uniform: some have followed the pattern described by Goode, some have reverted to traditional forms, and others have created new arrangements.

As in all processes of social change, those who lose power resist this loss, sometimes through peaceful means and sometimes through violence. As is shown by many of the authors in this volume, this erosion of patriarchy, and its all-too-often attendant violence against women, has taken many forms at different times and places throughout the world. Unfortunately, the end of this process and the end of resistance to this loss of power is not expected to abate in the near term. The nefarious effects of this violence damage the individuals who are its victims and it also weakens society as it restrains women from fully realizing their potential as individual humans and from contributing to their families, communities, and nations. The path ahead, a path that can lead to broader sharing of power among genders, age groups, religions, races, ethnicities, and other groupings, can only be advanced through naming, measuring, analyzing, and proposing remedies for the phenomena involved. That is what the authors of the three chapters I am commenting on have begun to do. This naming, measuring, analyzing, and proposing remedies for violence against women will be critical tasks for citizens, scholars, practitioners, and policy makers for many years to come.

References

Goode, W. J. (1963). *World Revolutions in Family Patterns*. New York: Free Press of Glencoe.

Therborn, G. (2004). *Between Sex and Power: Family in the World, 1900–2000*. London: Routledge.

CHAPTER NINETEEN

Poems on violence against women

E. Ethelbert Miller

Introduction by Louis W. Goodman

Six poems by E. Ethelbert Miller, the renowned Washington, DC based poet and literary activist, are included in this volume. "Ethelbert," as he is known to his friends, is a warm, open man with a broad welcoming smile, encouraging friends and casual acquaintances to express themselves and to realize fully their potential as human beings. He does this one-on-one, in groups, and in the public media, where he hosts *The Scholars* on UDC-TV and is frequently heard on PBS and other public radio stations. For many years I have appreciated Ethelbert's support of the humanities in Washington, DC and worldwide, as well as his steadfast promotion of social justice, exemplified by his service as Board Chair of the progressive Institute for Policy Studies. Ethelbert and I share a special "guys'" bond as fervent baseball fans, although we welcome both women and men to join us in our appreciation of "the thinking person's sport."

The six poems presented below portray a range of circumstances in which violence against women can be perpetrated. They include violence against women by parents, by lovers, by siblings, by men, by other women, by agents of the state, by religious zealots, and by individuals who are themselves damaged by violence. The poems are haunting and disturbing. They contain lessons about the prevalence of violence against women, about the possibilities for any of us to commit such violence, and the importance of recognizing and blocking such behavior.

* * *

Women Surviving Massacres and Men

> *"I want time to look for my children and see how many of them I can find. Maybe I shall find them among the dead. Hear me my chiefs, I am tired; my heart is sick and sad. From where the sun now stands. I will fight no more forever."*
> Chief Joseph

she was beaten
she was blue
her man had hit her
and he had run

she said she now found comfort
in watching tv westerns

said she felt like an indian
surviving massacres
and men

E. Ethelbert Miller

Elaine Beckford

when the dog needed walking
we would walk the dog
out near the river where the johnsons lived
and the rich folks had summer homes
and maybe a few of us like ginger and eddie
would toss rocks into the water
take our shoes off
splash each other and try to scoop

small fish up with our hands
our world was perfect
like sunlight coming through the curtains
and finding a special spot on the wall or floor
i never had goosebumps until the summer the
body of elaine beckford was found in the water
near the big rock and police came and told my daddy
to keep us indoors and it was three weeks later
that they shot a colored man
a few miles from where we lived
some of our neighbors said he was innocent
but most folks said he was only colored
and someone had to pay for doing what they did
to elaine beckford let it be the colored
my daddy said and no one knew but me
that my daddy was real sweet on elaine
and i caught them twice together in the barn
she no older than i
and i don't know what they doing
cause i ain't old enough to know

E. Ethelbert Miller

The Equator

So what's that line around your nose
the equator or something? I'm in the playground
sitting next to Omar and in between him and Natalie.

She's the new girl
with the old clothes who moved into
the corner house one month ago.

What you talking about? she squeaks.
Her voice has that little girl sound
like she could sing high notes

and maybe call herself Mariah
but she's just Natalie
from down the street.

Why you staring at my nose? You just
a silly looking boy with one of those
Mooslem hats on your head.

You shouldn't even be looking at me.
Why should I let you look at me?
Why? You tell me why?

I'm between Omar and Natalie and this
is what my Momma means when she says
If you make your bed you gotta lie in it.

Or maybe this is just a hard place
and the rock is here too.
I don't know.

It was me who decided not to do my homework,
so here I am listening to Omar trying to talk
all smart and talk about geography

like he knows where he is.
Omar don't know nothing about no equator.
You can't see the equator fool! I tell him.

You just want to mess with Natalie's nose.
In between my words, her tears gather like
clouds coming from behind the big buildings

and telling us it's time to go.
But it's Natalie's crying which makes me shiver.
She stutters and tries to find her own rain of words.

My daddy broke my nose when I was small
because I didn't stop crying.
He broke my nose and it left a mark.

Natalie's words catch Omar and me like we
were running and now we both out of breath.
Omar pushes me out the way and puts his arm

around Natalie's shoulder like he's the equator.
I guess this was the right thing to do
if we added our ages together.

Sometimes Omar does things I wish I could do.
Sometimes he just sees things
I'm too young to see.

E. Ethelbert Miller

I Have Always Wanted a Woman to Be My Lover

How can it be morning in two places at once?
I was so happy when I moved into this house.
Finally a place where I can grow and hang my plants.
Finally a lover to love my difference and my sex;
her tongue discovering the secret parts of me.
I have always wanted a woman to be my lover.
How many men find this strange?
Once, my father found his way to my bed.
He was not lost. I did not surrender.
I fought and was beaten and wet my bed with his blood.

Now a woman holds a knife to my throat
and I am speechless . . .

I did not know she would do such things.
How unnatural for a woman to beat another woman
after being lovers. Did she not whisper one night
when I was in her arms—no man would ever treat me
better?

E. Ethelbert Miller

Throwing Stones at the Porno Star

It was I who threw the first stone
at her head. I said a prayer to Allah
asking for forgiveness. For a moment
I wanted to see her body. I wanted to
see sin close-up. In the prison courtyard
she was buried with only her head exposed
and naked like a breast. I threw a second
and third stone. I turned to find a fourth.
Even when her eyes closed and her blood
flowed like piss, I did not stop. How could
I? Is this not the blessing of believers?

E. Ethelbert Miller

After She Told Me This Her Husband Killed the Kids

trapped. you ask how i feel or how i felt. trapped.
well that's the only word i can
find that would capture or define
what it is i can't explain.
three years maybe more, i forget unless i count the jobs.
the part-time ones and the night-time ones.
the ones i'm ashamed of and the ones i rather not recall.
i did all right by myself with
three kids, the youngest not too smart
and the oldest, a girl and getting prettier every day.
i think she knows more than i did or more than i know now.
i lose count of days and the nights i subtract from where i ache,
the place where a man is supposed to be.
i started writing to him in prison when he didn't come home,
and when he returned home i didn't know him.
i once knew his eyes. i fell in love with his eyes,
now i'm afraid of this man with the look, the glance, the stare
too strange to forget. i'm afraid he will tear into me and open
my insides and i'll bleed leaving the sound of a heart beating
in search of a vacancy for love. trapped. it's the only word i
can think of. the kids need this and they need that and i cook,
clean, wash and everything i would give away for romance,
for music, for happiness tonight,
or a moment when we kiss like this,
and i fly into the air.
when we kiss like this and i fly into
the air.

E. Ethelbert Miller

CHAPTER TWENTY

Violence against women in the work of women artists

Janice S. Lieberman

In this book you are reading many *words* that describe the horrific treatment of women in various parts of the world. In this chapter, I describe and, at times, illustrate *visual* images in order to deepen your understanding of this difficult topic. As they say, "One picture is worth a thousand words". Most of these images are difficult to think about and to look at. The art of the 1970s and 1990s especially is very concrete and "in your face". This art does not hide behind beauty to tell its story. As I have noted elsewhere, "contemporary artists feel free to express visually ideas that were once forbidden, and to show what never before could be seen, at least in public" (Lieberman, 2000, p. 223). These artists concern themselves with issues of human conflict and human paradox. Each artwork and artist I discuss is well known and well established in art history, past and present.

I focus on contemporary art, but first I want to go back as far as seventeenth century Italy to a painting done by the great woman artist, Artemesia Gentileschi, the daughter of artist Orazio Gentileschi (Image 20.1). This was painted when she was just seventeen years old. The Old Testament tale she depicts, that of "Susannah and her Elders" (1610), is an ancient one about sexual coercion. Susannah was threatened with execution for an infidelity she did not commit unless she

Image 20.1. Artemesia Gentileschi (1610) *Susannah and Her Elders*.

consented to the Elders' sexual demands. Susannah refused and was brought to trial. In the cross-examination that followed, the Elders were shown to have lied and were stoned to death. Susannah is a self-portrait of Artemesia. We see her cringing with unbearable pain under the leering looks of the two older men. They are fully dressed, giving them power, their stare gives them power and their positioning above her gives them power. She, on the other hand, is naked except for a small flimsy cloth. Her feet are red—they have been literally and figuratively in "hot water" and are "blushing" instead of her cheeks. Her cringe is clearly that of an adolescent girl, and seems very much like the cringe of girls we know today subject to the prurient gaze of older men. It is uncanny that Artemesia herself was raped a year after painting this picture by her father's friend Tassi, whom she tried to stab in self-defense. Here, too, as in the Old Testament tale, there was a trial.

Artemesia grew up in a rather lawless home characterized by overstimulation and visual traumata. Supposedly, she witnessed her parents in intercourse and the bloody birth of her brother, resulting in her mother's death when she was twelve. She had posed nude for her father and had seen many nude male models. At the trial, Tassi tried to present proof that she was not a virgin when he trapped her by deducing from her drawings of men that she had "seen" male genitalia.

In that same seventeenth century, a number of artists depicted rape in mythological images so familiar to us that we tend to admire the art and artist and tend to ignore the violent subject matter of rape. How many of us have admired Bernini's *Rape of Persephone* (1622) in the Villa Borghese in Rome, its baroque grace and pure white marble evoking beauty, rather than feeling horror or indignation at her tears. Persephone was the vegetation goddess and was the daughter of Zeus. She was abducted by Pluto, the god-king of the Underworld. Similarly, in the case of Poussin's (1634) *Abduction of the Sabine Women* and Rubens' (1618) *Rape of the Daughters of Leucippus*, mass rape was considered to be part of war, all fair, and not to be thought about or challenged, very much as is the case today in too many parts of the world. We admire these paintings for their grace and beauty, ignoring the violent subject matter.

For the sake of time, I must skip a few centuries to the twentieth century, in which women artists began to have a voice about violence in their own lives as well as in others. Frida Kahlo's (1935) painting *A Few Nips: Passionately in Love* (Image 20.2) was done after Frida read of a woman stabbed to death by her boyfriend, who alleged that he dealt her "only a few small nips" with his knife. This woman could be a stand-in for the artist herself. Frida's small body was savaged by a bus accident, her life one of physical pain. According to Knafo (2009),

> Frida said two things destroyed her: the accident and Diego (Rivera, her artist husband). Frida twice married Diego, who was double her age and three times her size, and she was deeply distressed by his numerous infidelities. (For example, he had an affair with her sister.) Just as she struggled with the many assaults to the integrity of her damaged body, so too she refused to give up on the tempestuous

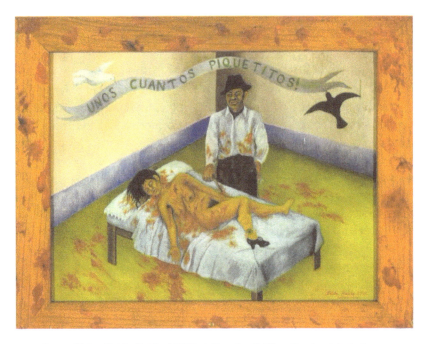

Image 20.2. Frida Kahlo (1935) *A Few Small Nips: Passionately in Love.*

relationship with Diego which was the source of so much heartache and pain. (p. 73)

In this painting she seems to be unconsciously depicting not just the incident of which she had read, but also the sadomasochistic bond she had with Diego by showing them both bloodied. He is clothed, wearing a hat, standing over her, clearly the powerful one. The banner says "Unos Cuantos Pique Titos" (a few small nips), the doves ironic symbols of peace.

The rise of the feminist movement in the 1970s resulted in much politicized art. A number of twentieth century women artists chose to depict violence against women in ways they said were not necessarily autobiographical. Marina Abramović, for example, in her various performances, asked her audiences to abuse her, sometimes with knives or with scissors (*Rhythm 0*, 1974). To test the limits of the relationship between performer and audience, Abramović developed one of her most challenging (and best-known) performances. She assigned a passive role to herself, with the public being the force that would act on her. Abramović placed on a table seventy-two objects that people were allowed to use (a sign informed them) in any way that they chose. Some of these were objects that could give pleasure, while others could be wielded to inflict pain, or to harm her. Among them were a rose, a feather, honey, a whip, olive oil, scissors, a scalpel, a gun, and a single bullet. For six hours the artist allowed the audience members to manipulate her body and actions. This tested how vulnerable and aggressive the human subject could be when hidden from social consequences. By the end of the performance, her body was stripped, attacked, and devalued into an image that Abramović described as the "Madonna, mother, and whore". Additionally, markings of aggression were apparent on the artist's body; there were cuts on her neck made by audience members, and her clothes were cut off of her body.

Abramović's art also represents the objectification of the female body, as she remains motionless and allows the spectators to do as they please with her body, pushing the limits of what one would consider acceptable.

The women artists I discuss next give us a window into the shattered psyches of those who have been abused and raped. Unlike the images of Artemesia, Bernini, Poussin, Rubens, and Kahlo, the men are not depicted. Ana Mendieta (1973) recreated the crime scene of the rape and murder of fellow University of Iowa student Sara Ann Otters. For the performance, spectators found Mendieta crouched, bloody and still, naked from the waist down. She did additional tableaux of rape that year. She did not announce them but let them be discovered by unsuspecting passersby. In one, she spread blood on the sidewalk and observed people walking on by, indifferent to the violence they had just seen. A number of Mendieta's performances, which she photographed, depict she herself as abused, her face bloodied. You might know that in her personal life she either jumped or fell out of a window and died. Her partner, the prominent artist Carl Andre, was brought to trial, but exonerated from having committed the brutal act.

Also autobiographical are the photos and films of Nan Goldin, who had a series of sadomasochistic relationships with men. In *Nan One Month After Being Battered* (1984) she shows what was a considerable improvement upon her physical condition after have been battered. In 1980, less horrific, she photographed her *Heart-shaped*

Bruise, as if bruises and affairs of the heart necessarily belong together. Goldin, in her ongoing film series *The Ballad of Sexual Dependency* (1981–) said, "I wanted it to be about every man and every relationship and the potential of violence in every relationship". I find this to be sadly accepting. Nevertheless, today showings of her photos are used to effect change.

I first saw Sue Williams' (1992) autobiographical sculpture *Irresistible* on the floor of the Whitney Museum. The pain of the crouched figure and the writing on it go right to your heart. She cringes as if in a catatonic cocoon. The words of her batterer are: "YOU DUMB BITCH. I DIDN'T DO THAT. HAVE YOU BEEN SEEING SOMEONE ELSE? SLUT. I THINK YOU LIKE IT MOM. LOOK WHAT YOU MADE ME DO. ETC."

In my opinion, the woman artist whose oeuvre most poignantly depicts violence against women is Kiki Smith. Her father was the prominent sculptor Tony Smith. His three daughters all became artists. Kiki says little about her relationship with her father. I saw *Tale* (1992a) (Image 20.3) also on the floor of the Whitney Museum. A naked woman crouches on the floor, her rear end covered with

Imagee 20.3. Kiki Smith (1992a) *Tale*.

excrement and leaving a long t-a-i-l that is concrete evidence of the t-a-l-e she could tell. Art critic Linda Nochlin (2015) reports a "visceral shock" when she wrote, "I still remember the intensity of the feeling, as though the bottom had dropped out of the sedate world of the gallery and my own place in it, to put it more physically, I felt it in my guts" (p. 290).

Kiki did *Bloodpool* (1992b) (Image 20.4) in the same year. What could be a more wretched image than this fetal image with its prominent spine? And, in the same year, *Pee Body* (1992c) (Image 20.5), a humiliating image of an abused woman sitting on the floor surrounded by yellow glass beads (pee), a quintessential image of "abjection" as conceptualized by Julia Kristeva (1982) in her book *Powers of Horror*. (Evidently some male art critics wrote that Smith degraded art itself by calling attention to such low bodily functions as peeing.) Kristeva says this about "abjection":

> The body's inside . . . shows up in order to compensate for the collapse of the border between inside and outside. It is as if the skin, a fragile container, no longer guaranteed the integrity of one's "own and clean self" but, scraped or transparent, invisible or taut, gave way before the dejection of its contents. Urine, blood, sperm, excrement then show up in order to reassure a subject that is lacking its "own and clean self".

Image 20.4. Kiki Smith (1992b) *Bloodpool*.

Image 20.5. Kiki Smith (1992c) *Pee Body*.

The abjection of those flows from within suddenly become the sole "object" of sexual desire—a true "ab-ject" where man, frightened, crosses over the horrors of maternal bowels and, in an immersion that enables him to avoid coming face to face with another, spares himself the risk of castration. (p. 53)

A most compelling explanation of rape, to my mind.

The early 1990s were a time of unearthing tales of violence during wartime. Judy Chicago of *The Dinner Party* fame worked on a book called *The Holocaust Project: From Darkness into Light* (1990). In "Double jeopardy: everybody raped" she found that in the camps, not just the Nazis but the liberators too—American, British, and Soviet soldiers—raped women Bergen-Belsen survivors.

Kara Walker, one of our most prominent African-American women artists, chronicled in her powerful silhouettes the sexual misuse and abuse of black slave women by their white masters on Southern plantations during those infamous years of American history. In her incredible mural (1995) *The Battle of Atlanta: Being the Narrative of a Negress in the Flame of Desire*, we notice a flung chicken leg. Walker's work bitingly satirizes the white man's desire for black women: "I like my coffee like I like my women, any number of combinations, 'hot, black and sweet', 'black with a touch of cream'." The black female body as both subject and repository of sexual fantasies, phobias, and taboos prevails as the locus of a major portion of Walker's work with the hope that, as she exposes it, it will lose its menacing power.

Fast forward to today. Emma Sulkowicz, a performance artist, decided to not forget about and keep "hidden under the mattress" a date rape incident at Columbia University. For her senior thesis, called "Carry that Weight", she carried the offensive mattress wherever she went and even disregarded university authorities by bringing it with her to graduation. University President Lee Bollinger turned away from her, refusing to shake her hand. She was harshly criticized for creating publicity that could promote her career, but she did bring awareness to the public about the prevalence of date rape, a backlash to the growing independence and success of young women.

I end with glorious images of bronze sculptures by Kiki Smith called *Rapture* (2001) and *Genevieve and the May Wolf* (Images 6 and 7a,b). It recalls the story of St. Genevieve, who saved her people from

Image 20.6. Kiki Smith (2001) *Rapture.*

Images 20.7(a,b).. Kiki Smith (2000) *Genevieve and the May Wolf.*

Attila the Hun. She is standing erect, the wolf is powerless, lying on the ground. Smith also refers to the story of Little Red Riding Hood and the Wolf. She is not crouching, bent over or beseeching. She shines in the light just as women all over the world will shine as a result of efforts such as this one.

References

Abramović, M. (1974). *Rhythm 0*. Performance at Studio Morra, Naples, Italy.
Bernini, G. L. (1622). *Rape of Persephone*. Villa Borghese, Rome, Italy.
Chicago, J. (1990). "Double jeopardy: everybody raped", in: *Holocaust Project: From Darkness into Light*. New York: Viking Adult/Penguin, 1993.
Gentileschi, A. (1610). *Susannah and her Elders*. Schonborn Collection, Pommersfelder, Germany.
Goldin, N. (1980). *Heart-shaped Bruise*. Museum of Modern Art, New York.
Goldin, N. (1984). *Nan One Month after Being Battered*. Museum of Modern Art, New York.
Kahlo, F. (1935). *A Few Small Nips: Passionately in Love*. Collection of D. O. Patino, Mexico City, Mexico.
Knafo, D. (2009). *Dancing with the Unconscious: The Art of Psychoanalysis and the Psychoanalysis of Art*. New York: Routledge.
Kristeva, J. (1982). *Powers of Horror: An Essay on Abjection*. New York: Columbia University Press.
Lieberman, J. S. (2000). *Body Talk: Looking and Being Looked at in Psychotherapy*. Northvale, NJ: Jason Aronson.
Mendieta, A. (1973). *Rape, Murder Scene*. Iowa City, Iowa, April 1973.
Nochlin, L. (2015). Unholy postures: Kiki Smith and the body. In: M. Reilly (Ed.), *Women Artists: The Linda Nochlin Reader* (pp. 290–300). New York: Thames and Hudson.
Poussin, N. (1634). *Abduction of the Sabine Women*. Metropolitan Museum, New York.
Rubens, P. P. (1618). *Rape of the Daughters of Leucippus*. Alte Pinakothek, Munich, Germany.
Smith, K. (1992a). *Tale*. Photograph courtesy of the artist and Pace Gallery, New York.
Smith, K. (1992b). *Bloodpool*. Art Institute of Chicago, Chicago, Illinois.
Smith, K. (1992c). *Pee Body*. Harvard Art Museums/Fogg Museum Cambridge, Massachusetts.

Smith, K. (2000). *Genevieve and the May Wolf*. Photograph courtesy of Shoshana Wayne Gallery and the Denver Art Museum, Denver, Colorado.

Smith, K. (2001). *Rapture*. Photograph courtesy of Richard-Max Tremblay and Pace Gallery, New York.

Sulkowicz, E. (2014–2015). *Carry That Weight*. Performance at Columbia University, New York.

Walker, K. (1995). *The Battle of Atlanta: Being the Narrative of a Negress on the Flame of Desire*. Nexus Contemporary Arts Center, Atlanta, Georgia.

Williams, S. (1992). *Irresistible*. 303 Gallery, New York.

CHAPTER TWENTY-ONE

Woman: power and representation in pre-Columbian societies in the Andean region*

Moisés Lemlij

Introduction

In the mid 1980s, three psychoanalysts, Max Hernández, Alberto Péndola, and I, an anthropologist, Luis Millones, and a historian, María Rostworowski, founded the Interdisciplinary Seminar of Andean Studies (SIDEA) with the aim of studying Peruvian society and history by applying the conceptual tools of history, the social sciences, and psychoanalysis. Our first publications, *Entre el mito y la historia* (Between Myth and History) and *El umbral de los dioses* (The Threshold of the Gods) were the result of intense work sessions in which our interdisciplinary research methodology was refined; in addition to this, our research of the *Taki Onqoy*, a collection of influential studies on Andean society, was published in a book entitled *El retorno de las huacas* (The Return of the *huacas*), in partnership with the Instituto de Estudios Peruanos (IEP).

---

* I hereby declare that I have been authorized by the photographers and/or owners of the photos included in this chapter to submit them with the purpose of being published in the book *The Courage to Fight Violence Against Women* on the condition that their credits are duly included.

In the mid-1990s, Luis Millones and I published the book *En el Nombre del Señor: Shamanes, Demonios y Curanderos del Norte del Perú* (1994) (In the Name of the Lord. Shamans, Demons and Healers of Northern Peru), which built on the research carried out a decade earlier with psychiatrist Mario Chiappe. We also explored the theme of death, based on funerary rituals and myths, and on its representation in the arts, which led us to compile several papers by specialists of various disciplines in a book entitled *Al Final del Camino* (1996) (At the End of the Road). We worked together again in the early 2000s to study the Sarhua board paintings, which depict the impact of violence in the Ayacucho region, in a book entitled *The Tablas of Sarhua: Art, Violence and History of Peru* (2004), published in Spanish and English.

Here, I would like to introduce our upcoming publication, *Mujer: Poder y Prestigio en las Sociedades Andinas* (Woman: Power and Prestige in Andean Societies), which is to be published in a digital edition, and will be available and accessible worldwide on Amazon books. This study focuses on the historic societies of the northern coast of Peru—specifically on the Moche society. By contrast, the book also examines female representations (or the lack of them), as well as the place of women in power relations, in the Andean societies of the valleys of the Cusco region and its surrounding areas, the territory in which the *Tawantinsuyu* emerged, developed, and eventually declined.

Before I present the subject of my chapter, I would like to refer briefly to our interdisciplinary way of working. As we all know, Sigmund Freud realized that clinical facts can be regularly represented through universal cultural symbols, which led him to examine myths, historical phenomena, and cultural structures from a psychoanalytical perspective. Since then, psychoanalysis has refined its tools, and its complex hermeneutics has been submitted to the scrutiny of internal criticism and to questioning from other disciplines. Towards the end of the 1960s, psychoanalysis came to be closely related to the social sciences, when the writings of several Middle European psychoanalysts of the inter-war period were revisited: Otto Fenichel, Siegfried Bernfeld, Wilhelm Reich, and Erich Fromm. When Levi-Strauss defined ethnology as a science dealing with the unconscious structures of culture, he opened up the possibility of a new link with psychoanalysis. In those days, William L. Langer, Chairman of the American Academy of History, suggested that historians had to reconstruct the subjective universe of historical actors, a task in which they could be aided by a remarkably useful instrument: psychoanalysis.

So, the idea that our understanding of cultural, social, or political phenomena can be significantly expanded when approached within the framework of interdisciplinary collaboration is not a new one. In the case of the Andean world, the difficulties that arise from the analysis of documents that gather the oral tradition, but based on the perspective of the Spaniards and using the linear code of writing, are difficulties that can be interpreted—from a psychoanalytic perspective—as "resistances" to translating the Quechua worldview into Spanish, thus opening up an interesting point of entry into the material. As psychoanalysts, we try to interpret the text of the Spanish chronicles "by listening" while also seeking to comply with the requirements of historical and anthropological methods when comparing them. In addition, we have had to resort to other disciplines in order to corroborate the data and to rectify recurrent prejudice that appears in the written records. Art history and iconography, for instance, have allowed us to better understand the ideology of the Andean nations that were forced, following the conquest, to use the European system of concepts, but who, when painting or sculpting images—including the Christian ones—reworked the message of the Spaniards and made it their own.

This psychoanalytic approach allowed us to identify several recurrences or subtle decenterings in the narratives in order to gain access to latent realities. Clearly, interpreting historical material is not exactly the same as interpreting the material that a patient brings. In the former case, we interpret something that remains fixed; what changes is not the subject who brings the material, but the context in which it is interpreted. There is no transference relationship as there is in the consulting room, where what matters is the clarification and working through of this transference. Neither can we evaluate the effects of our interpretations: the text remains immutable; what changes is the way in which we understand it. On more than one occasion, the interpretations we offered led to insight within the group, and subsequently to a consensus of opinion.

In short, psychoanalytic thought is the thread running throughout the reflections and interpretations that emerge in the process. It has allowed us, for instance, to identify changes in the kinship systems described in the chronicles, the manner in which relationships between those in government and those governed change, the transition from a cyclical version of origins to a more dynamic and linear view of historical time, and the shift from an organization based on narcissistic and dyadic relationships to the outline of a triangular structure.

Pre-Columbian societies of the northern coast of Peru

In order to understand pre-Columbian societies, one must take into account the geographical features of the regions in which they developed. The societies of northern Peru spread out along the stretch of the Pacific desert coastline lying between northern Lima and the Tumbes region, bordering Ecuador. Shallow rivers cross the arid dryland here and there, most of them not fit for navigation, their waters descending from the Western Andean mountain chain to flow into the ocean. In these narrow valleys created by the flowing of the rivers, the Mochica, or Moche, society flourished and organized in a number of autonomous political entities governed by religious elites.

The origins of the Mochica society date back 1,900 years. Fishermen and other collectors of the abundant marine resources found in the area met with people who arrived from the mountains, following the river course; the highlanders contributed with their agricultural knowledge and complemented the skills of the people from the coast. As they expanded and refined their technical abilities, the Moche, or Mochica, people soon excelled in the art of pottery and goldsmithing.

However, the scarcity of drinking water sources in a region with a dry and arid climate made it difficult to expand the farmlands, and this promoted rivalry between the communities and the confederations. Neverthess, in its 800 years of conflictive coexistence the Mochica cultural formations came closer gradually as they achieved technical improvements with the materials they worked with. With regard to religious practices, the communities that occupied the Mochica space shared a similar line of thought and worshipped the same deities.

Early on, researchers' attention was drawn to the Mochica pottery, which represented human beings, the living and the dead, deities, animals, and a number of scenes of daily life. These naturalistic representations provide evidence of their knowledge of perspective and geometry, which will be expressed later, and conclusively, in the monumental temples, palaces, or ceremonial spaces built by them. Such buildings render account of the man/hours employed in the construction, which implies that the laborers were conscripted and controlled by a ruthless system.

Mochica communities are particularly interesting for being a social organization in which both males and females are found at the top of the power structure. These Mochica women are currently described as priestesses. According to archaeologist Ulla Holmquist (1992), it is possible to distinguish between three different types of female images in Mochica art: the mythical, the dead, and the "natural". Mythical images have fangs and serpents around their bodies or necks, while dead women are depicted with deathlike features in their faces or bodies. It should be noted that the activities of the dead women portrayed are not any different from those in which "natural" women are involved; in other words, they carry out the same activities as those performed by any living person in their daily lives: child care, sexual intercourse, dancing, participating in a ceremony, and so on. Finally, "natural" women are identified as those who do not display any deathly or supernatural features, are dressed in long tunics, and generally wear their hair in two braids.

A large number of Mochica pots and *huacos* represent anthropomorphic images related to sexuality and sexual intercourse, and they stand out for their originality. Genitals appear in different shapes, and with such a conspicuous display that a number of vessels were modeled expressly after them, so that liquids (generally *chicha*) can be poured and drunk directly from them. This denotes a peculiar—rather aggressive—sense of humor, probably intended to offend and mock those who drank from the vessels. Mochica potters often attributed functions to genitals that differed from the usual functions: a vagina may function like a mouth, a mouth, like a vagina; a penis penetrates a body through the mouth, and so on (Images 1–4). The mix and substitution of body orifices and their functions has also been a motif in classical works of art such as Bosch's *Garden of Earthly Delights* or the painting *Rape* by René Magritte.

This representation of genitalia is not exclusive to the Mochicas. Some pots displaying genitals to which teeth and thorns have been added (by drawing or modeling) can also be seen in more ancient societies of Peru such as the Chavin (1,000 BC), as well as in other

194   THE COURAGE TO FIGHT VIOLENCE AGAINST WOMEN

Image 21.1.   Representations of genitalia and sexual pleasures related to life and creation for women and men in Mochica art: male.

Image 21.2.   Representations of genitalia and sexual pleasures related to life and creation for women and men in Mochica art: female.

WOMAN: POWER AND REPRESENTATION IN PRE-COLOMBIAN SOCIETIES   195

Image 21.3.   Ceramic plate with representation of women with genitalia.

Image 21.4.   Representations of genitalia and sexual pleasures related to life and creation for women and men in Mochica art: male and female.

societies of the same period as the Mochicas, such as the Nazca, which flourished in southern Peru. According to Maria Rostworowski et al. (2000), it is possible to establish an evolutionary sequence between the Chavin representations and the Mochica vessels: the Chavin would "represent the *vagina dentata* of an anthropomorphic being carrying batons ... which suggests a powerful being associated with the horrific", while the Mochica representations of the vagina depict

> the vulva standing out predominantly ... oversized and fully dilated. This image would be the counterpart of the Chavin's *vagina dentata*, with its teeth as sharp elements appearing as evil and violent powers which prevent any penetration. The immense and open vagina in Mochica art is shown in a powerful pose, as if priding itself, probably in connection with intercourse and birth, both as situations related to life and creation. (p. 8, translated for this edition).

Huaco portraits are another set of outstanding work among the Mochica pottery; they are tridimensional reproductions of the facial features of humans. These heads are generally decorated with a hairband or some other kind of similar adornment with meaningful emblems, which has led Bawden (1999) to consider them as portraits of the elite. Most of them were found in burial sites, which may suggest that such adornments could have been worn by these people in ritual ceremonies.

The Mochica pictorial representations have particular characteristics. Similar to the relationship between content and structure, a reciprocal relation is established between particular elements in images and the cultural universe of the community. The desire to serve as testimony must not be overlooked. Every human being wishes to express his feelings, his life and history in a way that might be shared and understood not only by those who belong to his immediate world. In this sense, human beings are inclined to eternity. It is possible to find this intention present in men from cave paintings to graffiti scattered on the walls of every modern city. This will to give testimony seeks to perpetuate a moment that is perceived to be perishable. It is portrayed on an object that might not have the individual artist's characteristics, but, from the first moment, it has a sort of corporative will to leave a testimony of the artist's condition as a member of the community. The Mochica paintings, carvings, or sculptures are a cultural testimony, not an individual one.

The theme of death is incessantly repeated in all its artistic manifestations, where it is common to see people interacting with skeletons, and engaged in various activities that may even include sexual intercourse. War motifs and human sacrifices are predominant in all pictorial representations; the owl, the fox, the boa constrictor, and the vampire are frequently represented. Many depict systematic brutality, with mutilated faces or prisoners tied with a rope on their way to being sacrificed. The walls painted with such motifs would mark a great distance between subjects and the governing elites while their authority and the harsh punishment inflicted on those who disobeyed would be justified by their divine status. Without doubt, these representations were used to consolidate a social and political structure that was organized according to a strict hierarchy.

I would like to draw your attention to a piece of pottery with painted scenes of what we know as the "ceremony of sacrifice" (Image 21.5). In the upper part, we can see the participants in this ceremony, who are wearing lavish clothes and adornments. The lower part depicts smaller figures, which correspond to the sacrificial victims to be offered to the deities. The "warrior priest", who presides over the ceremony and drinks the blood of the victims from a cup, is wearing more elaborate clothes and headbands. To his right, in order of importance, a person

Image 21.5. Scene of sacrifice on a piece of Mochica pottery showing the preeminence of a priestess.

known as the "bird priest" is wearing a bird mask that covers his head. Next to him, the woman wearing elaborate attire and adornments, which are similar to those worn by the previous individuals, is the "priestess", who precedes the "priest", usually identified by the feathers in his headdress. The fact that the priestess is one of the four sacred characters in the representation is a sign of her pre-eminence in government.

The scene can be compared with the Dionysian festival, although the Mochica ceremony features a woman who plays an active part: she engages in the beheading and in the collection and drinking of blood. What we know about Dionysius, about Pentheus's mother and aunts, is that they died in the middle of a Dionysian frenzy, and we also know what happened to Pentheus. We can compare the myth, as recounted by Euripides in *The Bacchantes*, with what we see in this pictorial representation of the Dionysian festival. However, we do not know the story behind the Mochica ceremony of sacrifice depicted on this pot.

The Lady of Cao dates back to 450 AD and it stands out among the Mochica female funerary sites. The well-preserved remains are those of a twenty-five-year-old adult woman, a member of the privileged classes, who probably died during childbirth. She was buried along with her officiants and guards. To the left of her funerary bundle, remains were found of a teenage girl who had been strangled; to the south of the tomb, archaeologists found the remains of a male who was nicknamed the "guard of the tomb". Three other funerary bundles found at the foot of the site's southern wall revealed the remains of three individuals who wore various items of personal adornment. Gold jewels and needles as well as other sewing devices and traces of unbleached cotton were found inside the tomb. The lady's body was also surrounded by a number of spears, maces, and other combat weapons.

This evidence led to the hypothesis that the woman was a political–religious figure whose duties included the celebration of human sacrifices, which would explain why she was buried with her servants, and also with her dogs. The feet of some of her carers were cut off to prevent them from escaping their terrible fate. The body of the Lady of Cao was buried

> naked, with her arms folded, one foot on top of the other. She is wearing earrings and has a set of necklaces made of tumbaga (an alloy of gold or silver and copper), silver, quartz, coralline, turquoise, and

lapis lazuli. Near her neck, a case was found containing forty-four nose ornaments (and two in her mouth) made of the materials mentioned earlier . . . She wore her hair in braids, a custom of the Mochica women, and had a flattening at the back of her skull, which may indicate that she had been tied up to her bed as a child. (Franco, n.d., pp. 6–8) (Image 21.6)

A remarkable detail of the mummy is that her arms were covered with tattoos of snakes, spiders, and land snails as well as designs of plants, curves, lozenges, triangles, and lines. In addition to being obvious symbols of sexuality and the phallus, tattoos of snakes also represent renewal, knowledge, and immortality in the Andean world. The spider is a hard-working creature, a feminine figure, and a diligent weaver, but she is also the black widow that devours the male. The tattoos of the Lady of Cao were an exhibition of her magical powers. Tattoos are fashionable nowadays, but they are regarded as pathological in most psychoanalytical studies. In my opinion, the main point is that tattoos are always the expression of something, and they also confer a quality or a specific power. We might think about the importance that tattoos have, for instance, in the Yakuza groups.

In the same *Huaca Cao Viejo*, we can see a remarkable wall painting that depicts a group of naked men with erect penises that are walking

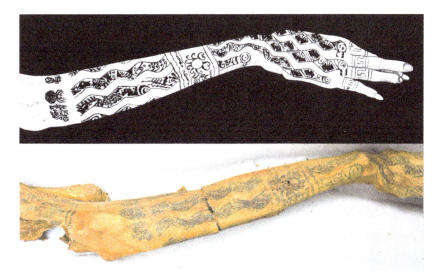

Image 21.6. Arms.

in a row, with a rope tied around their necks, as if they were warriors who had been made prisoners. What was the intention of the artists when they painted such a scene, which is recurrent in the Moche society? Bourget (2006) proposes that there is a clear relation between the heads of those about to be slaughtered and their penises, or, in his own words, "between strangulation and an erection."

The tawantinsuyu

Tawantinsuyu means "the four parts" in Quechua. The Inca state expanded across a vast territory (comprising present-day Peru, Ecuador, Colombia, Bolivia, Chile, and Argentina) which was divided into four *suyus* and covered deserts and coastal valleys, high mountains and desolate plateaus, as well as fertile Andean valleys and rainforest mountains and basins. Such geographical diversity was interconnected by a road system of 30,000 kilometers called *Qhapaq Ñan*, or "Inca road", used by the army and state administrators to transport crops and foodstuffs from the conquered territories and store them in "tambos".

Cusco was the cradle of the Inca State and its capital city. Located in the basin of the Huatanay river, on the eastern side of the Andes Mountains, the region is fit for farming and animal husbandry. The Incas exploited the grasslands and built terraced fields on the mountainsides, which were irrigated through a system of channels and aqueducts. The terraced fields, aqueducts, roads, and bridges attest to the outstanding engineering skills of the Incas. This ability allowed them to overcome the challenges of a rugged geography that posed hurdles to the expansion and flourishing of the Inca society.

Their architecture is also remarkable for its restrained and symmetrical style, characterized by its harmony with the landscape. This differs from the buildings of the societies of the northern coast, which are profusely painted and decorated, as we have seen. The Incas developed a technique to build huge walls that look like gigantic mosaics made of carved stone blocks that fit together perfectly.

Inca pragmatism and severity are also reflected in the mass-production of mainly utilitarian pieces of pottery with plain and rather unpolished shapes decorated with geometric designs (Image 21.7). Unlike that from the societies of the northern coast, Inca pottery was not employed to portray or artistically represent daily life, beliefs, or attitudes towards sexuality and eroticism. One wonders if it would be possible to paraphrase Freud and say that geography is destiny. For it is evident that people who lived 2,000 meters (6,500 feet) above sea level and contemplated mountains which are over 13,000 feet high had a totally different worldview from that of people who settled on the coast and lived at the edge of an immense ocean where they saw the sun set on the distant horizon every evening. The weather of the northern coast is warm, and the fact that coastal people are closely related to sea life (they sailed out to collect seafood and swam to cool off) rendered them more in contact with their bodies, in their own nakedness or semi-nakedness and that of their peers, aroused by the caress of sea waters. This probably would have led to a more open enjoyment of sexual pleasures and eroticism. Inversely, the people from Cusco were always forced to wrap up in order to survive in the freezing temperatures of the high Andean plateau; this probably would have made them develop a more distant and controlled attitude toward their own bodies.

Image 21.7. Inca pot, with geometric design.

In its approach towards art, and painting in particular, psychoanalysis puts a special emphasis on content. In other words, it stresses men's vocation to symbolize their work, their actions, and also objects of nature. Furthermore, psychoanalysis puts aside structural or formal aspects in artistic creation. Nevertheless, in diverse cultural contexts, this representative vocation has shown remarkable variations. There have been times when some cultures sanctioned the intention to reproduce images of nature, as they were seen as an attempt to replace their god. They had great fear of the possibility that representations could transform into concrete objects and that any of them could then have the omnipotent power of transforming into a god. This could have been the case of the Incas.

There is also a big difference between northerners and the Incas with regard to the role of women in their respective societies, particularly in the way women have a share in power. We base our assertion on very specific evidence for each case. Neither the Mochicas nor the Incas had a writing system. What we know about the pre-Columbian societies of the northern coast comes from archaeological research based on the remains found in burial sites and other monuments. These have been collated with research carried out by anthropologists and linguists (one of the regional dialects was still in use in northern Peru until the mid-1950s, and there is a number of vocabulary lists drawn up as early as the eighteenth century), while, in the case of the Incas, sources also include written documents. As was mentioned in the introduction, in spite of there being remarkable primary sources, our reading of them is faced with the problem of a biased description of the Andean world, with its legends and narratives markedly influenced by the Christian perspective of the sixteenth-century Spaniards who wrote them.

In the various narratives about the mythical origins of the Incas collected by the chroniclers, women appear as mere companions of the founding heroes, except for the case of the legend of the Ayar brothers, in which Mama Huaco, sister and wife of Ayar Auca (one of the four brothers) is depicted as a bold and independent female warrior. On the other hand, Mama Ocllo, sister and wife of Ayar Manco or Manco Capac, the first Inca, is described as a homely woman in charge of her household, who raises her children and tends to the crops and the production of textiles. However, Garcilaso de la Vega describes in his chronicle how, on their arrival in Cusco, Manco

Capac and Mama Ocllo summoned their people and divided them into two halves: those who rallied to the call of Manco Capac became a part of the *Hanan Cusco*, the upper part, while those who heeded the call of his wife became a part of *Hurin Cusco*, the lower part. Although Garcilaso is at pains to explain that there is no difference between the halves with regard to hierarchy or authority, he contradicts himself when he says that people from Hanan Cusco were the "first-born", the "elder brothers" and the "right-hand men of the population" (Garcilaso, 1985, I: 40). The female deities of the Inca pantheon have a lesser role in a universe that is dominated by males. The Moon, or *Quilla*, presides over female activities, but the description of the rituals of the female deity is succinct when compared with the description of the rituals of the principal male deity, such as those dedicated to *Inti* or Sun, *Illapa*, or Viracocha himself. Similarly, there is very little mention in the chronicles of the cult to *Pachamama* (mother earth), which is still worshipped in the Peruvian Andes to this day, or to Mamacocha (mother of the waters), and we do not have an artistic representation of them.

The authority of the Inca sovereign—who kept his distance from his subjects, who barely spoke to him and could not look him in the eye—did not seem to consider a place for women during the time of his reign, but they became especially important in times of succession conflicts, when they exhibited their power. On the death of the sovereign, the noble families of the *panacas*, who claimed the privilege of being the founders of Cusco by a mandate of the father Sun, vied for the right of one of its members to bear the *mascapaicha*, the Inca crown. Alliances were established between the families, but there was also jealousy, competition for power, and murder plots in which women played a central role. *Panacas* were powerful enough to claim the right of any of their children to succeed to the throne, which opened a wide range of possibilities and outcomes. The mothers of the candidates to the Inca throne were behind the doing or undoing of alliances, as long as their power derived from their being the mothers of the would-be Inca, not the widow of the Inca.

The events following the death of Huayna Capac, the penultimate Inca, illustrate how things unfolded during the periods of succession. Atahualpa was in the mountains of northern Peru in Cajamarca, where he met his historic demise at the hands of the Spaniards. While traveling from Quito (Ecuador) to Cusco for his coronation as the Inca sovereign, he stopped over in Cajamarca. He had previously sent ahead a company of his soldiers, who imprisoned his brother Huascar, with whom he competed for power, and imprisoned and killed all of Huascar's wives and children, including the pregnant women and the families that had been on his brother's side. It is said that Huascar had tried to legitimize his right to be a candidate to the throne after his father's death by celebrating the wedding of his own mother with the mummy of the Inca. However, this story lacks credibility, and it seems to have been an interpretation of the way Spaniards understood succession rights (Images 21.8–21.10).

With regard to the girls and the women of the *hatun runa*, or ordinary people, some of them were picked out at the age of eight to serve as *acllas*, at the service of the deities, the Inca, and his wives and relatives. Some others were picked out to be exchanged with the chiefs of ethnic groups that were conquered or in the process of being conquered. But they were also reserved for human sacrifices, which were customary in the Inca ceremonies, occurring nearly as frequently

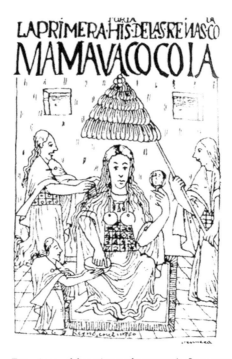

Image 21.8. Drawings of functions of women in Inca representations.

Image 21.9. Drawings of functions of women in Inca representations.

Image 21.10. Drawings of functions of women in Inca representations.

as sacrifices with llamas, which were a substitute for human beings in the Andean mind. Such slaughters were linked to the calendar of rituals or to dramatic events such as plagues or the illness of an Inca, which were interpreted as the deities' claim for blood, in which children played a special role. Their bodies were rubbed against the body of the ailing monarch in order to revitalize him, but the victims were never spared after this ritual of transmission of vitality, and they were eventually sacrificed.

The case of the capullanas

Francisco Pizarro recounts the fantastic story of his encounter with the capullanas during his third voyage (1532). First of all, we should point that the name is of Spanish origin:

> our people called them capullanas after the name of the dress they wore to cover themselves from their throats to their feet, and which (1603–1609) Indians wear presently almost everywhere in the flatlands [that is, on the Pacific coast]; some of them tie it up on their waists while others prefer to wear it loosely. (Lizárraga, 1968, pp. 9–10)

The same chronicler completes his description of these female chieftains of the north as follows:

> These capullanas were like lords because of their lack of fidelity; they married as many times as they wished as long as they were not satisfied with the husband they had, whom they dismissed to find a new spouse. On the day of the wedding, the husband-to-be would sit next to the lady in a gathering of great merriment and drunkenness; the discarded husband would sit on the floor in a corner, crying for his misfortune, and not even getting a sip of water from anyone. The bride and the groom would express their joy and make fun of the poor creature. (Lizárraga, 1968, p. 10)

Most probably, the capullanas had an important role in the political structure of a number of chiefdoms that must have re-emerged after the fall of the Gran Chimu kingdom. While Incas were able to move large contingents of people to the conquered territories, they generally preferred to negotiate with those who were to be their subjects. As long as the societies that were subdued complied with their duties, such as paying tax or accepting the symbols of the Cusco Empire (the temple of the sun, the *acllawasi*, the mitimaes, and so on), they did not seem interested in modifying the local customs. We do not know whether the Chimor rulers acted in the same manner, but, in any case, they had already disappeared when Pizarro arrived in these territories.

The power of the capullanas declined after the Spanish domination, especially after a new type of chief or ethnic leader emerged; the new leaders were better adapted to the colonial system, and were in a position to negotiate their rights of ancestry in commercial terms. There was no space left for the capullanas. However, the cult of minor female deities, such as Pachamama or Mamacocha, has prevailed up to the present day, probably due to syncretic rituals devoted to the virgin Mary and Saint Rosa of Lima. Religious syncretism can also be observed in the images that were painted by the Indians or the *mestizos*; these techniques, acquired from the Spaniards, merged the representation of the holy virgin with that of the *Apu*, a mountain or hill associated to masculine or feminine deities.

References

Bawden, G. (1999). *The Moche*. Massachusetts: Blackwell Publishers.
Bourget, S. (2006). *Sex, Death, and Sacrifice in Moche Religion and Visual Culture*. Austin: University of Texas.
Franco, R. (n.d.) *El Brujo*. 5000 años de historia.
Garcilaso de la Vega, Inca ([1609]1985) *Comentarios reales*. Caracas: Fundación Biblioteca Ayacucho.
Holmquist, U. (1992). El personaje mítico femenino de la iconografía mochica. Tesis de Bachiller en Humanidades. Lima: Pontificia Universidad Católica del Perú.
Lemlij, M., & Millones, L. (1994). *En el nombre del señor: shamanes, demonios y curanderos del norte del Perú*. Lima: Biblioteca Peruana de Psicoanálisis.
Lemlij, M., & Millones, L. (1996). *Al final del camino*. Lima: Sidea.
Lemlij, M., & Millones, L. (2004). *The Tablas of Sarhua: Art, Violence and History of Peru*. Lima: Sidea.
Lizárraga, R. (1968). *Descripción breve del Perú*. Madrid: Biblioteca de Autores Españoles, Tomo CCXVI.

Rostworowski, M.. Ramos, M., & Ortiz de Zevallos, P. (2000). Los genitales femeninos en la iconografía andina prehispánica. Paper delivered at the XXI Congreso Latinoamericano de Psiquiatría "*Carlos Alberto Seguín: hacia un lenguaje compartido*". Lima.

CHAPTER TWENTY-TWO

Maternal imago and bodily symptoms*

Rosine Jozef Perelberg

This chapter argues that, in the analysis of women by women, one might be confronted by a melancholic core in the relationship to a frightening, internal, maternal imago that has not been elaborated. These analyses powerfully evoke the relationship to the somatic. The internalization of the body of the mother, which is a requirement in the development of a woman, can take on frightening, fragmented qualities. The mother's body and sexuality need to be kept at bay while, at the same time, preserved in oneself. These somatic experiences tend to be expressed in fragmented, part object terms, so that what emerges in the analysis are bodily parts such as the breasts, the uterus, ovaries, and anus (see Cournut, 2010). An image of a submersion in the maternal body—or maternal waters—is that of an endless orgasm (Perelberg, 2015) The process of bodily fragmentation that takes place in the course of the analysis makes it difficult at times to differentiate this melancholic core from hysteria. The differentiation, as I argue, will be given by the analyst's countertransference: the issue at

---

* This paper was previously published as Introduction 1 in: Raphael-Leff, J., & Perelberg, R. J. (Eds.) (2008). *Female Experience: Three Generations of Women Psychoanalysts on Work with Women* (pp. 21–35). London: The Anna Freud Centre.

stake is not expressed in terms of a battle between love and hate (as in hysteria), but, more accurately, between life and death (that points out a melancholic core).

The primitive tie to the mother

It was in *Group Psychology and the Analysis of the Ego* (1921c) that Freud defined the concept of "primitive tie" as a type of identification where a distinction between self and object has not been firmly established. "Identification", at this point in Freud's work, was viewed as the process by which the individual was constituted. It is an unconscious process, which takes place in phantasy. In the early modalities of identification, mental processes are experienced in bodily terms such as ingesting or devouring. Already, in his work on "Mourning and melancholia" (1915e), Freud had discussed the role of incorporation whereby the individual would identify in the oral mode with the lost object; the constitution of the internal world was made through identifications. In the "Wolf Man" (1918b, see also Wolheim, 1984), Freud discussed the shifting identifications in the primal scene, which go towards constituting the individual's character. If, in Freud's first model of the mind, the topographical model, the emphasis is on the conflict between the drives, where the object may appear to be accidental, in the structural model, the object becomes "theoretically crucial" (Kaes et al., 1993, p. 172). Freud progressively concentrates on how it is that the external is "taken in" and, thus, is constituted into psychic reality. The concept of a "primitive type of identification" became relevant in his discussions on female sexuality in that he postulated the little girl's primitive attachment to the mother.

To quote Freud,

> Everything in the sphere of this first attachment to the mother seemed to me difficult to grasp in analysis – so grey with age and shadowy and almost impossible to revivify – that it was as if it had succumbed to an especially inexorable repression. (1931b, p. 227)

In "Female sexuality" (1931b), Freud indicated the fear the little girl has of being devoured by her mother. The importance of the "pre-oedipal"[1] relationship with the mother has been more fully discussed since Freud's time (for example, Brunswick 1940; Chasseguet-Smirgel, 1985a,b; Deutsch, 1925, 1930; McDougall, 1985). More recently interest in the nature of female identity can be found in the works of Person (1974), Fast (1979), and Benjamin in the USA (1995), as well as in the works of Chasseguet-Smirgel (1985b), Luquet-Parat (1985), Torok (1985), and McDougall (1985) in France. The powerful character of the primitive maternal imago is experienced by children of both sexes. Both boys and girls desire to be the object of their mother's desire: both would like to give her a baby.

Langer (1989) has suggested that it is at *this* level that one can find an explanation for the stress on matriarchy in early attempts to outline the history of society. Matriarchy, thus, becomes a myth arising from the personal history of every individual. In the beginning there is an all-powerful mother who nourishes the infant. The father then makes his appearance as the embodiment of the law, interrupting that duality (Langer, 1989, p. 196).

In England, psychoanalytic work from an early stage started to concentrate on primitive states in infancy and attention was paid progressively to the impact of these primitive states in the transference. Klein's work brought an emphasis on the relationship between the infant and the maternal body. The little girl's earliest anxiety is of "having the inside of her body robbed and destroyed" (1975, 1977), as she believes her mother's body contains everything that is desirable, including the father's penis. As a consequence, the little girl is filled with hatred towards her mother and wishes to attack and rob the inside of her body in turn. Klein's views on this early relationship between mother and baby had an impact on some of the early writings on femininity in the British society, such as the work of Riviere (1929) and Payne (1935).

Some of these views on early infancy, however, have been challenged and viewed as an attribution of sophisticated mechanisms to the mind of the infant: the innate character Klein attributes to unconscious phantasies, her reduction of all mental life to unconscious phantasies (thus flattening the distinction between thinking, memory, perception, and phantasy), and her belief in constitutional knowledge. Klein was also criticised for her neglect of the role of experience in the constitution of the unconscious phantasies. These challenges to Kleinian theory were raised by Glover, Foulkes, Brierly, and Anna Freud (in King & Steiner, 1991, also Yorke, 1973, and Hayman,

1989). Klein's work, however, has had an important impact through its emphases on the early relationship between the infant and her mother.

The idea that the psychoanalytic situation reproduces the early mother–infant situation has been explored since by many other authors, such as Balint (1950, 1952). The functions of the original maternal environment as being empathic (Kohut), mirroring (Winnicott), facilitating (Mahler), and containing (Mahler) are seen as being re-enacted in the analytic situation. Progressively, psychoanalysts from all the groups in the British Society, inspired by the works of Winnicott, Brierley, and Bion, have emphasized the connection between primary affective development and object relationships. Winnicott believed in a state of primary identity between the little girl and her mother: "... this primary identity can be a feature from very early, and the foundation for simple being can be laid (let us say) from the birth date, or before, or soon after ..." (1971, pp. 80–81).

For Winnicott, affective development has to include the mother's affects and her capacity to tolerate, sustain, and relay affective messages to the baby in a way that allows the baby to integrate them. Winnicott postulates a primary identification with the mother for both sexes. In the earliest years, it is the mother who provides the infant with a reflective and containing environment that allows the infant to go on being. When this containment does not take place, mental and emotional functioning are not facilitated and development in the internal relationship between subject and object is arrested.

More recent emphases have been given to the role of the father as interposing himself on the imaginary mother–infant dyad (Lacan, 1966), and as representing the beginnings of the cultural order (Lévi-Strauss, 1947). In the mother, the child sees a mirror of herself. It is the father who interposes himself between the dyad, thus presenting the child with the experience of the relationship between the couple. The denial of this third object is one of the tenets of the modern understanding of perversion. The impact of the absence of the father, either literally or emotionally, for the child's emotional development has been discussed and understood in terms of not helping the creation of the internal boundaries in the relationship between mother and child and inserting the child in a chain of reciprocity which requires the presence of the third object.

The phallic mother and the emergence of femininity

An imago present in this early relationship is that of the phallic mother. Kulish (1984) has reviewed the literature on this concept and indicates that, in his writings on perversion, Freud stressed that the little boy has the phantasy of a woman with a penis in order to deal with his fear of castration (1927e, 1940e). Later, Stoller (1975), Greenacre (1968), and Glasser (1979) emphasized the importance of this phantasy. All these authors stressed the relevance of the environment in the construction of phantasies such as that of a seductive mother and an absent father (Limentani, 1977).

In my clinical practice, I have found that the phantasy of a phallic, all-powerful mother is commonly present for both men and women. A patient of mine, a young single woman, was, at the beginning of her analysis, very addicted to daydreaming. In these states, she masturbated and had images of scenes of enormous aggression in love-making with a violent man. In these daydreaming states, she experienced herself as both male and female, and, thus, not needing a sexual partner. Her aggression was encapsulated in these daydreams and she could not find a creative alternative for it. Several years of analysis allowed her to work through her feelings of guilt towards both her mother and father for finding each lacking and for her wish to be more successful than them. This allowed a process of mourning to take place, enabling her to give up the phantasy of being all powerful and both male and female. She was then able to take on a position that allowed her creativity to be expressed through painting.

There are several images that express in an analysis the phantasy of the phallic mother, or a combined primitive couple, such as vampires, sharks, piranhas, or werewolves. In one session, a woman who struggled with her wish to be both male and female told the story of a werewolf, derived from a film she had seen, where a woman, at the time of a full moon, transformed herself into a wolf. This had first happened when she had been raped and had killed the man who had raped her. This story seems to contain some of the primary phantasies I have been discussing, such as the imago of the phallic, all-powerful castrating woman and the primal scene as the scene of a murder, a sadistic encounter between a rapist and a murderer.

The imago of a phallic mother is present in the women discussed in the book, *Female Experience: Four Generations of Women on Work with*

Women (Raphael-Leff & Perelberg, 2008). Such cases include the image of the ugly hunchback brought by Mrs. Y (E. Balint, 1997), the imago of the monster in Cara's dream (Burgner, 1997), and the sadistic all-powerful queen in Maria's analysis (Perelberg, 1997, 1998b).

Hypothesis: the core conflict and bodily symptoms

One of the hypotheses derived from my work with women is that a same gender therapeutic relationship (i.e., female patient and female analyst) might be an aid in the re-enactment of aspects of an early relationship between mother and infant. I am not assuming that there is a replication of this relationship in the sense of the present being isomorphic with the past, since, over time, changes occur in the meanings and functions of conflicts (Sandler, 1988; Sandler & Sandler, 1994), and other layers of experiences and phantasies are added.

It is, perhaps, not surprising that so many women struggle to turn away and separate from their mothers involves a bodily symptom. I have come to understand many of the bodily experiences of some of the women whom I have seen in my clinical practice as representing attempts to have a body and a sense of self that is separate from the mother. At the same time, these symptoms seem to represent an aspect of the relationship with the mother that has not been properly internalized. I think that the aspect of the mother which has not been internalized is the mother as a protector against the child's own sexual and destructive phantasies (as in the story of the woman–werewolf killing the man).

These bodily experiences might range from severe symptoms, such as anorexia or ulcerative colitis, to vertigo, asthma, eczema, or states of anxiety, such as insomnia and gastric disturbances. I have found that symptoms may present themselves as a solution to the conflict between longing for and fear of fusion with the mother. The girl, says Irigaray, "has the mother, in some sense, in her skin, in the humidity of the mucous membranes, in the intimacy of her most intimate parts, in the mystery of her relation to gestation, birth and to her sexual identity" (1989, p. 133).

This is the conflict that Glasser has discussed at the core of perversions, but which I think might have a wider relevance, as being found at the core of each individual's relationship with their mother. Felman

(1987) has suggested that the mother (or the mother's image) stands for the first object of the child's narcissistic attachment (an object and an image of the child's self love, or love for his own body—for his own image), inaugurating a type of mirroring relationship.

In her analysis of the literature on female sexuality, Breen (1993) has pointed out the conflict between those psychoanalysts who stress a more positive, "biologically based experience of femininity" and those who define it in terms of a lack (a positive femininity), indicating that some other authors stress the existence of both. If one postulates that natural biological differences are both culturally and psychically reinterpreted, however, one might potentially find a solution for the debate. Birksted-Breen herself argues for "an understanding of femininity which encompasses both an unconscious representation of a lack and an unconscious representation of its 'concentric' aspects" (1993, p. 37).

It is, thus, not by chance that several chapters of the book I edited with Joan Raphael-Leff, entitled *Female Experience* (1998), focus on anorexia, although other bodily symptoms, such as diabetes (which is being managed in a destructive way), ulcerative colitis, or other forms of attacks on the body such as self cutting, are also present. In these cases, it is essential for the analyst to keep in mind what Brierley pointed out all these years ago, "that the processes of introjection and projection are psychic processes which must be distinguished from concomitant phantasies and bodily efforts to cope with concrete objects" (1936, p. 174). I suggest that these are attempts to attack thoughts, feelings, and desires which, by definition, occur in the mind, through the body (Perelberg, 1998a).

I would suggest that the transference to a female analyst allows for an identification with a primitive maternal imago to explode more vividly in the transference. At times, this might lead to impasses in the analysis, and, perhaps, this is because the "as if" so necessary for a therapeutic alliance is broken and a patient might become more deluded about being in a real fusion with the mother.

The effect of the sex of the analyst on the transference

Many writers have argued that the sex of the analyst has no major influence on the development of the analysis (Chasseguet-Smirgel, 1985b; Glover, 1955; Greenacre, 1959). If bisexuality is a characteristic present in both sexes, it should be possible, in the transference situation, for both the femininity and the masculinity of the analyst to be the vehicle for the expressions of their patients' sexuality. In 1920, however, Freud was the first to point out the relevance of the gender of the analyst when treating a case of a female homosexual who developed a negative transference to him. Later, in 1931, he also emphasized the importance of women analysts as being able to have more access to the pre-oedipal transference in female patients. He said,

> It does indeed appear that women analysts – as, for instance Jeanne Lampl-Groot and Helene Deutsch – have been able to perceive these facts more easily and clearly because they were helped in dealing with those under their treatment by the transference to a suitable mother substitute. (1931b, pp. 226–227)

I think that the belief of the relevance of the gender of the analyst–patient pair is present in the training of psychoanalysts, as it is recommended that the first training case should be of the opposite sex of the analyst, as the identification might not be as powerful. Obviously, this is a complicated issue. As Kulish has pointed out in her review of the literature (1984, p. 93), "to isolate one aspect, in this case the sex of the analyst, from such a complex, multidetermined phenomenon as the transference is to run the risk of distortion and superficiality" (Kulish, 1984, p. 96). She also raises an important question for writers who put forward the notion that female analysts promote a specific type of transference, whether there is an "active" process that takes place on the part of the analyst or whether one is just talking about the fact that the analyst is female (Kulish, 1984, p. 100).

Many analysts have agreed that the sequence of material presented in the transference might reflect the sex of the therapist, early pre-oedipal material being more frequently identified in the analysis with female analysts. Glover (1955), Blum (1971), Pines (1993), and E. Balint (1973) also point out in their work with female patients that there are specific issues that arise in the transference to female analysts. Pines believes that "a woman analyst's physical capacity to be a mother appears to facilitate the transference of primitive feelings arising from partial maternal deprivation" (1993, p. 24). This is in contrast with the transference to male analysts, which often tends to be reported as presenting itself in an erotised pseudo-heterosexual way (see Lester, 1993).

Karme (1979) has suggested that a possible reason for an emphasis on a maternal, as opposed to a paternal, transference to female analysts is related to the fear of a phallic mother and suggests that maternal transference reported by male analysts is of the pre-oedipal mother. However, Kulish (1984) feels that there is no evidence to support these points. In a later paper, she reports the result of interviews with seventeen senior female analysts who mostly felt that the analyst's gender particularly affects the sequence of the emergence of the material and that female analysts might pull pre-oedipal material into the transference more quickly.

In all this, one must not lose sight of the eminently oedipal configuration of the analytical situation. Chasseguet-Smirgel (1986) has pointed out that, in analysis, the analysand is offered a womb, a potential for regression, but, in the setting itself with its framework and rules, the limits are also indicated, in the same way as the father separates the mother and the child. She prefers to discuss the issue in terms of how the femininity of the analyst—whether male or female—affects their professional practice. I would suggest, however, that the presence of a female analyst facilitates the phantasy that Chasseguet-Smirgel has called the archaic Oedipus complex, a smooth universe, without obstacles, representing the mother's insides to which one would have free access (Chasseguet-Smirgel, 1986, p. 30).

Transference and countertransference

The other aspect that needs to be taken into account when examining the mutual impact of gender in the analytic process—not present in the American discussion—is the countertransference of the analyst. This is a dimension present in every chapter in this section of the book.

In the British School, the inclusion of the analyst's affective states in the sessions—the understanding of the countertransference—became increasingly part of the central analytical task. It is in the process of holding, containing, and transforming feelings that cannot be elaborated by the patients themselves that the analytic work is carried out. Klein had already suggested that there are "pre-verbal emotions . . . [which are] revived in the transference situation . . . [and which] appear . . . as 'memories in feelings'", which are reconstructed and put into words with the help of the analyst (Klein, 1961, p. 318).

A group of analysts have addressed themselves to specific modes of communication present in analyses that impinge on the analyst in the countertransference. Starting with Heimann (1950), this line of inquiry has been developed by Money-Kyrle (1978), Bion (1967), Racker (1968), Grinberg (1962), Joseph (1998a,b), Segal (1986), and Brenman Pick (1988). For these authors, the countertransference became a way of gaining access to patients' unconscious communication. In the analytic situation, it is the analyst who has to be able to take in and reflect on her patients' feelings and desires and return them in a more digestible form. Sandler (1976) has coined the term "actualization" to indicate the patient's attempts to re-establish with the analyst an early object relationship. This approach combines an experience of the transference as actualized in the consulting room as well as a comprehension of the unconscious phantasies. To my understanding, this actualization is not only of wished-for patterns of relationships, but also of experiences that were not previously understood.

In the British Society, the understanding of the countertransference has become the main area of work from which the understanding of feeling states in the analytic session is derived. This has marked a shift in terms of a stress on the emotional quality of the experience in the analytic process.

This is the way in which I also understand Bion's formulations. There is an equivalence, for Bion, between emotions and knowledge. He writes,

> Before an emotional experience can be used for a model its sense data have to be transformed into alpha elements to be stored and made available for abstraction. In minus K the meaning is abstracted, leaving a denuded representation. (1962, pp. 74–75)

By thinking about emotional experiences and by understanding them, the mind comprehends meanings. All knowledge is assumed to have its origins in primitive "emotional experience". The incorporation of feelings into the psychic sphere, in early life, presupposes the experience of having had a caregiver able to reflect on the mental states of the infant, able to be both a witness of, and a participant in, a child's emotional development. When this process does not take place, there can be emotional arrest and a disavowal of the need for the object.

In the analytic process, aspects of the internal world, parts of the internal self-representation, are projected onto the analyst and re-enacted in the transference. The analyst is invited to take on these different aspects and re-enact these different roles to the patient, who will then "take on" other aspects. The process is characterized by the fluidity with which these various parts present themselves, although, in the cases presented in this section, because of the severity of the psychopathologies, there is a tendency for some interactions to become more fixed and to last for a long period of time. In several cases, one can identify different stages in the process.

Enid Balint, in her work, is concerned with the "dark continent" of a woman's early attachment to her mother. Balint is referring to Freud's discussion of the little girl's prolonged attachment to her mother (Freud, 1925j, 1931b) and presents two women patients who had not been able to identify with their mothers, although they did manage to establish sexual relationships with men. Balint points out that these women's preoccupation remained with women whom they attempted to care for. In their analyses, this was expressed by these women's wish to satisfy their analyst, one in an erotized way, while in the other the relationship with the mother was represented in a frozen way, un-integrated into the patient's ego. It "seemed a foreign body frozen and untouchable inside her". Balint suggests that, in both women, there was a denial of castration and an undervaluation of their husbands as representing their fathers. Balint does not think her patients are latent homosexuals, but are, rather, driven by a wish to keep their depressed mothers alive. She further puts forward the idea that a woman needs to feel that she was satisfied by her mother's body as an infant in order to feel that her own body satisfied her mother. The early relationship between mother and daughter is, thus, expressed in the experience of the body itself and the way it is represented.

In a previous paper, I examined some of the problems raised in the analysis of Maria (Perelberg, 1996), a patient who has to adhere to a version of reality that emphasizes processes in her body as opposed to processes in her mind. This assumed a concrete dimension in the two accidents she suffered on the two first anniversaries of the start of her analysis. I suggested that my patient's experience of these two accidents and the way she brought them into the transference revealed her beliefs about her internal primary relationship to her maternal object. Both accidents became a screen on which she projected her beliefs about relationships in her life, more specifically her beliefs about her early catastrophic relationship with her mother and her beliefs about sexual intercourse as a violent and catastrophic encounter. It is because any encounter between two people is potentially violent, sexual, and murderous that Maria had to retreat into a timeless world where people did not exist as whole persons and, thus, were unable to differentiate from each other. The analytic process presented her with an impossible dilemma: to be in a relationship with me implied the risk of this violent and dangerous encounter; not to be, however, meant remaining trapped in a two-dimensional, timeless world. This patient also adhered to a representation of herself close to the somatic, and her various experiences in the analysis for a long time took the pathway of her body. It was only *après-coup* that one could construct these earlier experiences, through the vicissitudes of the transference and countertransference (Perelberg, 2006).

Burgner (1997) discussed the analysis of a seventeen-year-old bulimic girl who had attempted suicide. In her analysis, Cara expressed her conviction that bingeing and vomiting were her only possession, the thing that she felt that she did for herself and to herself, separately from a mother who was experienced as intrusive and invasive. It was also an omnipotent attempt to avoid any feelings of need and, therefore, of abandonment. Cara experienced no sense of separation from her mother, that they were bound to each other through crazy and addictive sexuality. She was caught in the conflict between her struggle to separate from her mother on the one hand and a yearning for a state of no-separation from the breast/mother/analyst on the other. In the analysis, Cara brought to the transference this sadomasochistic relationship with both her parents. In this, as in other accounts in this book, the analyst's countertransference was an important source of information on the patient's affective states, and one which allows for pre-verbal states of mind to be understood in the analytic process. Burgner suggests that what is palpable in the transference are primitive, pre-oedipal relationships.

This literature, reviewed in Perelberg (1998a) pointed out certain central themes:

1. All the women patients seem to express a core conflict between a longing for fusion with a pre-oedipal, idealised mother, on the one hand, and a terror of this mother, on the other.
2. Pre-verbal and pre-oedipal experiences are centrally brought to the transference.

3. There is a recurrence of bodily symptoms as vehicles for the expressions of conflicts.
4, The setting includes a female patient and female analyst.
5. The primary transferential conflict is focused on the issue of giving up an omnipotent phallic position towards a position of femininity, which is experienced as an impossibility.
6. The use the analyst makes of the countertransference feelings is central to the understanding of the clinical presentation.

Note

1. One should note that, from the analyst's perspective, there is no such thing as a pre-oedipal mother because any mother–child relationship presupposes the existence of the father. The term is, thus, used as shorthand to express the perspective of the patient's phantasies and experiences. The analytic encounter takes place, by definition, within a triadic constellation, because the third element—whether the father or the analytic process—is present in the conceptual framework of the analyst. In an earlier work, where I discussed feminist writings in the field of psychotherapy in the 1970s and 1980s (Perelberg, 1990), I pointed out the misleading emphasis on the mother–daughter relationship at the exclusion of the father. I then said, "However, it is that very triangle that makes the relationship between mothers and daughters possible: there can be no mother and daughter unit without the existence of a father" (Perelberg, 1990, p. 37). Another aspect that tends to be neglected in the literature that emphasizes the early experience between mother and infant is the role of oedipal sexuality. Lebovici has pointed out in a recent interview that the woman/analyst who appears in the psychoanalytic literature is represented in terms of the "good breast" or the "bad breast" and never in terms of the "woman's breast". The erotic relationship with the breast disappears (in Baruch & Serrano, 1996).

References

Balint, E. (1973). Technical problems found in the analysis of women by a woman analyst. *International Journal of Psychoanalysis*, 54: 195–201.
Balint, E. (1997). The analysis of women by a woman analyst: what does a woman want. In: J. Raphael-Leff & R. J. Perelberg (Eds.), *Female Experience: Four Generations of Women on Work with Women* (pp. 36–45). London: The Anna Freud Centre, 2008.

Balint, M. (1950). Changing therapeutical aims and techniques in psychoanalysis. *International Journal of Psychoanalysis, 31*: 117–124.
Balint, M. (1952). On love and hate. *International Journal of Psychoanalysis, 33*: 355–362.
Baruch, E. H., & Serrano, L. J. (1996). *She Speaks, He Listens*. London: Routledge.
Benjamin, J. (1995). Sameness and difference: toward an "overinclusive" model of gender development. *Psychoanalytic Inquiry, 15*: 125–142.
Bion, W. R. (1962). *Learning From Experience*. London: Karnac.
Bion, W. R. (1967). *Second Thoughts*. London: Maresfield Library.
Birksted-Breen, D. (1993). General introduction. In: *The Gender Conundrum: Contemporary Psychoanalytic Perspectives on Femininity and Masculinity* (pp. 1–43). London: Routledge and The Institute of Psycho-Analysis.
Blum, H. P. (1971). On the conception and development of the transference neurosis. *Journal of the American Psychoanalytic Association, 19*: 41–53.
Brenman-Pick, I. (1988). Working through in the counter-transference. In: E. Spillius (Ed.), *Melanie Klein Today, Vol. 2* (pp. 34–47). London: Routledge.
Brierley, M. (1936). Specific determinants in feminine development. *International Journal of Psychoanalysis, 17*: 163–180.
Brunswick, R. M. (1940). The pre-oedipal phase of the libido development. *Psychoanalytic Quarterly, 9*: 293–319.
Burgner, M. (1985). The Oedipal experience: effects on development of an absent father. *International Journal of Psychoanalysis, 66*: 311–320. Reprinted in: J. Raphael-Leff & R. J. Perelberg (Eds.) (1998) *Female Experience: Three Generations of British Women Analysts on Work with Women* (pp. 93–103). London: Routledge.
Burgner, M. (1997) Analytic treatment of an adolescent with bulimia nervosa. In: J. Raphael-Leff & R. J. Perelberg (Eds.), *Female Experience: Four Generations of Women on Work with Women.* (pp. 93–103). London: The Anna Freud Centre, 2008.
Chasseguet-Smirgel, J. (Ed.) (1985a). *Female Sexuality*. London: Maresfield Library.
Chasseguet-Smirgel, J. (Ed.) (1985b). Feminine guilt and the Oedipus complex. In: *Female Sexuality* (pp. 94–134). London: Maresfield Library.
Chasseguet-Smirgel, J. (1986). *Sexuality and Mind*. New York: New York University Press.
Cournut, M. (2010). The feminine and femininity. In: D. Birksted-Breen, S. Flanders & A. Gibeault (Eds.), *Reading French Psychoanalysis* (pp. 623–640). London: Routledge.

Deutsch, H. (1925). The psychology of women in relation to the functions of reproduction. *International Journal of Psychoanalysis*, 6: 405–418.

Deutsch, H. (1930). The significance of masochism in the mental life of women. *International Journal of Psychoanalysis*, 11: 48–60.

Fast, I. (1979). Developments in gender identity: gender differentiation in girls. *International Journal of Psychoanalysis*, 60: 443–455.

Felman, S. (1987). *Jacques Lacan and the Adventure of Insight*. Cambridge, MA: Harvard University Press.

Freud, S. (1917e). Mourning and melancholia. *S. E.*, *14*: 239–258. London: Hogarth.

Freud, S. (1918b). *From the History of an Infantile Neurosis*. *S. E.*, *17*: 7–121. London: Hogarth.

Freud, S. (1921c). *Group Psychology and the Analysis of the Ego*. *S. E.*, *18*: 67–143. London: Hogarth.

Freud, S. (1925j). Some psychical consequences of the anatomical distinction between the sexes. *S. E.*, *19*: 241–258. London: Hogarth.

Freud, S. (1927e). Fetishism. *S. E.*, *21*: 152–158 London: Hogarth.

Freud, S. (1931b). Female sexuality. *S. E.*, *21*: 225–243. London: Hogarth.

Freud, S. (1940e). Splitting of the ego in the process of defence. *S. E.*, *23*: London: Hogarth.

Glasser, M. (1979). Some aspects of the role of aggression in the perversions. In: I. Rosen (Ed.), *Sexual Deviation* (pp. 278–305). Oxford: Oxford University Press.

Glover, E. (1955). *The Technique of Psychoanalysis*. New York: International Universities Press.

Greenacre, P. (1959). Certain technical problems in the transference relationship. *Journal of the American Psychoanalytic Association*, 7: 484–502.

Greenacre, P. (1968). Perversions: general considerations regarding their genetic and dynamic background. *Psychoanalytic Study of the Child*, 23: 47–62.

Grinberg, L. (1962). On a specific aspect of countertransference due to the patient's projective identification. *International Journal of Psychoanalysis*, 43: 436–440.

Hayman, A. (1989). What do we mean by 'phantasy'? *International Journal of Psychoanalysis*, 70: 105–114.

Heimann, P. (1950). On counter-transference. *International Journal of Psychoanalysis*, 31: 81–84.

Irigaray, L. (1989). Equal to whom? *Differences*, 1/2: 59–76.

Joseph, B. (1988a). The patient who is difficult to reach. In: E. Spillius (Ed.), *Melanie Klein Today*, Vol. 2 (pp. 48–60). London: Routledge.

Joseph, B. (1988b). Projective identification: some clinical aspects. In: J. Sandler (Ed.), *Projection, Identification, Projective Identification* (pp. 65–76). London: Karnac.

Kaes, R., Faimberg, H., Enriquez, M., & Baranes, J. J. (Eds.) (1993). *Transmission de la Vie Psychique Entre Generations* (Intergenerational Transmission of Psychic Life). Paris: Dunod, Collection Inconscient et Culture.

Karme, L. (1979). The analysis of a male patient by a female analyst: the problem of the negative oedipal transference. *International Journal of Psychoanalysis*, 60: 253–261.

King, P., & Steiner, R. (Eds.) (1991). *The Freud–Klein Controversies 1941–45*. London: Routledge and The Institute of Psycho-Analysis.

Klein, M. (1961). Narrative of a child analysis. *International Psycho-Analytic Library*, 55: 1–536. Hogarth Press and the Institute of Psychoanalysis.

Klein, M. (1975). Love, guilt and reparation. In: *Love, Guilt and Reparation and Other Works, 1921–1945* (pp. 306–343). New York: Delta.

Klein, M. (1977). The importance of symbol-formation in the development of the ego. In: *Love, Guilt and Reparation and Other Works, 1921–1945* (pp. 219–232). New York: Delta.

Kulish, N. M. (1984). The effect of the sex of the analyst on transference: a review of the literature. *Bulletin of the Menninger Clinic*, 48: 93–110.

Lacan, J. (1966). *Ecrits*. Paris: Seuil.

Langer, M. (1989). *From Vienna to Managua: Journey of a Psychoanalyst*. London: Free Association.

Lester, E. P. (1993). Boundaries and gender: their interplay in the analytic situation. *Psychoanalytic Enquiry*, 13: 153–172.

Lévi-Strauss, C. (1947). *The Elementary Structures of Kinship and Marriage*. Boston, MA: Beacon Press, 1969.

Limentani, A. (1977). Affects and the psychoanalytic situation. *International Journal of Psychoanalysis*, 58: 171–182.

Luquet-Parat, C. (1985). The change of object. In: J. Chasseguet-Smirgel (Ed.), *Female Sexuality* (pp. 84–93). London: Maresfield Library.

McDougall, J. (1985). Homosexuality in women. In: J. Chasseguet-Smirgel (Ed.), *Female Sexuality* (pp. 171–212). London: Maresfield Library.

Money-Kyrle, R. (1978). Normal counter-transference and some of its deviations. In: D. Meltzer (Ed.), *The Collected Papers of Roger Money-Kyrle* (pp. 330–342). Strathtay, Perthshire: Clunie Press.

Payne, S. (1935). A conception of femininity. *International Journal of Psychoanalysis*, 15: 18–33.

Perelberg, R. J. (1990). Equality, asymmetry and diversity: on conceptualisations of gender. In: R. J. Perelberg & A. M. Miller (Eds.), *Gender and Power in Families* (pp. 34–62). London: Routledge.

Perelberg, R. J. (1996). To be or not to be here: that is the question. Ce qu'une femme croit d'elle-meme, de ses objets et de ces accidents. *Revue Francaise de Psychosomatique, 10*: 59–80.

Perelberg, R. J. (1997). "To be or not to be" – here: a woman's denial of time and memory. In: J. Raphael-Leff & R. J. Perelberg (Eds.), *Female Experience: Four Generations of Women on Work with Women.* (pp. 60–76). London: The Anna Freud Centre.

Perelberg, R. J. (1998a). Introduction 1 and 3. In: J. Raphael-Leff & R. J. Perelberg (Eds.), *Female Experience. Three Generations of British Women Analysts on Work with Women* (pp. 21–35; 218–227). London: Routledge.

Perelberg, R. J. (1998b) "To be or not to be" – here: a woman's denial of time and memory. In: J. Raphael-Leff & R. J. Perelberg (Eds.), *Female Experience. Three Generations of British Women Analysts on Work with Women* (pp. 60–76). London: Routledge.

Perelberg, R. J. (2006). Controversial discussions and *après-coup*. *International Journal of Psychoanalysis, 87*: 1199–1220.

Perelberg, R. J. (2015). On excess, trauma and helplessness: repetitions and transformations. *International Journal of Psychoanalysis, 96*: 1453–1476.

Person, E. (1974). Some new observations on the origins of femininity. In: J. Strouse (Ed.), *Women in Analysis* (pp. 250–261). New York: Grossman.

Pines, D. (1993). The relevance of early psychic development to pregnancy and abortion. In: J. Raphael-Leff & R. J. Perelberg (Eds.), *Female Experience: Four Generations of British Women Psychoanalysts on work with Women* (pp. 131–143). London: The Anna Freud Centre.

Racker, H. (1968). *Transference and Countertransference.* London: Karnac.

Raphael-Leff, J., & Perelberg, R. J. (Eds.) (1998). *Female Experience: Three Generations of British Women Psychoanalysts on Work with Women.* London: Routledge.

Raphael-Leff, J., & Perelberg, R. J. (2008). *Female Experience: Three Generations of Women Psychoanalysts on Work with Women.* London: The Anna Freud Centre.

Riviere, J. (1929). Womanliness as a masquerade. *International Journal of Psychoanalysis, 10*: 303–313.

Sandler, J. (1976). Countertransference and role-responsiveness. *International Review of Psycho-Analysis, 3*: 43–47.

Sandler, J. (1988). Introduction to the First Plenary Discussion. *EPF Bulletin, 31*: 68–75.

Sandler, J., & Sandler, A.-M. (1994). Phantasy and its transformations: a contemporary Freudian view. *International Journal of Psychoanalysis, 75*: 387–394.

Segal, H. (1986). Countertransference. In: *The Work of Hanna Segal* (pp. 81–88). London: Karnac.

Stoller, R. J. (1975). *Perversion*. New York: Random House.

Torok, M. (1985/ 1964). The significance of penis envy in women. In: J. Chasseguet-Smirgel (Ed.), *Female Sexuality* (pp. 135–170). London: Maresfield Library.

Winnicott, D. W. (1971). *Playing and Reality*. London: Tavistock.

Wolheim, R. (1984). *The Thread of Life*. Cambridge: Cambridge University Press.

Yorke, C. (1973). Some suggestions for a critique of Kleinian psychology. *Psychoanalytic Study of the Child, 26*: 129–158.

CHAPTER TWENTY-THREE

Discussion of Lemlij and Perelberg: women of power

Arlene Kramer Richard

Lemlij tells us that images of women in the ancient Peruvian society of Mochica display three kinds of power: the mythical with fangs and serpents, the dead with unanimated features but lifelike activities, and the natural, with long tunics and hair in two braids. Both the dead and the living are depicted doing the daily activities of child care, sexual intercourse, dancing, participating in a ceremony, and so forth. In these communities, both males and females are shown as leaders.

A prominent feature of the woman represented in this art is the fully dilated, completely exposed vulva. This powerful image is not the *vagina dentata*, nor is it the dreaded image of the vulva known as the Medusa, which is seen in the West as capable of paralyzing anyone who looks at it. Rather, it is a proud display of power to experience sexual pleasure and to give birth. Pleasure and creativity are displayed in this image.

Death, the opposite of birth, is dealt with creatively in this art. The priestess who kills drinks the blood of the victim. The power of men and women to take the life of others is the counterpart of the power to create new life. And the woman who gives birth can give death. And the power of women is the power of life and death, the ultimate power.

These images of women as mothers and as death givers are supplemented by images of women weaving, creating body coverings that protect against the cold, the wind, and the rain. Images of women preparing food, the images of daily life, emphasize the continuity of female caring, an ongoing expression of female power. They contrast with the high drama of moments of birth and death, and they emphasize the basic necessities of continuing the family, the tribe, and the species.

To me the importance of Lemlij's contribution is the description of violence against women in the burial of an aristocratic young woman. Another young woman was found in the grave of the aristocrat. The second young woman had been strangled, presumably so that she could serve her mistress in a later rebirth. The use of the servant as if her own life was not valuable, use of her as an instrument for the purposes of the aristocrat, was the epitome of using some people as mere artifacts, not people whose lives were valuable for their own pleasure and productivity. Their family and clan relationships were not valued, only the relationship with the person of power who had died. The aristocratic lady had the opposite of the parental power. She did not give life. She gave death.

Perelberg's paper focuses on the mother–daughter relationship in cases where the daughter comes to analysis to deal with the uncanny relationship with her mother. The relationship involves the daughter's perception of the mother's intrusiveness on, and control over, her daughter. The treatment Perelberg describes involves lowering the perception of the mother as omnipotent and seeing her as powerful, but not so powerful that the daughter cannot identify with her. Perelberg cites Balint as saying that the early relationship with the mother is replicated in the daughter's experience of her own body. Where the mother gives life, the daughter treats and represents her body as she felt her mother treated her. This becomes apparent in cases of anorexia where the daughter starves her body, thus doing violence to herself as she saw the mother as violent.

Perelberg sees the desire for fusion with the pre-oedipal, all-powerful mother as the counterpart to the terror of that mother. If the baby is torn between these images, the fear of the mother can lead to retaliatory violence against the mother, or other women whom the daughter sees as like the mother. This view can easily be expanded to include the relation of the pre-oedipal boy baby to his all-powerful, pre-oedipal mother.

In my view, the near universal denigration and devaluation of women that leads to violence against women stems from the experience of that early mother. This is exacerbated by the inevitable failures of the separation–individuation phase and the toddler's disappointment when the mother is not always present to protect. It can only be exacerbated by the oedipal rage at the mother for not allowing the child to displace father in order to sleep in her bed. In addition, the latency developmental push to be more rational makes the emotional tie to the mother more dangerous yet. Adolescence brings both boys and girls to differentiate from the opposite sex and to find a counterpart to love—someone other than mother. At all of these stages, the push to be less attached to mother and to keep her from intruding and controlling becomes ever more urgent. The result in adulthood, in my view, is that the powerful, adult, motherly woman must be denigrated, devalued, and becomes a fair target for abuse.

Beating one's wife or girlfriend is beating on the image of the omnipotent mother, is carried over from earliest infancy, and is transformed and solidified at each developmental stage. That makes violence towards women a tendency in every known society and culture, more extreme in some, but to be expected in all. It is my belief that the developed world has brought a measure of restraint over this tendency toward condoning violence towards women, but we have a long way to go in taking account of this in our analytic work.

CHAPTER TWENTY-FOUR

Introduction to *Traces in the Wind*

Robin Dean

> NOCTURNE VOICES
> Words connect us—tell their story
> Onward with our soulful cry
> Pain and suffering haunting moments
> Memories walking side by side
> Please remember, hear, and listen
> Art upholds us even now
>
> NARRATOR: Who will carry the word?

These are the opening lines from the staged reading of *Traces in the Wind*, written and conceived by Gail Humphries Mardiosian, with original music by Tom Andes. The first production was presented at the COWAP Conference on Courage to Fight Violence Against Women in Washington, DC in March 2016, and will soon be presented in Prague at the Embassy of the Czech Republic for Holocaust Remembrance. *Traces in the Wind* tells the story of three women survivors of the Holocaust who used art in an effort to maintain their sense of identity while healing from, and bearing witness to, violence. These three women's words and stories echo the experience of contemporary women who are victims of violence and cruelty and need this to be seen and heard. The beautiful lines above capture several themes running throughout this book, including the challenge of seeing and hearing the trauma of violence against women. Moreover, the staged reading highlights the role of art in connecting memory with words and understanding. In addition, it underscores the need for one's experience of violence to be received and acknowledged by others. Charlotte Delbo, one of the three survivors and a poet, remarks "Pure cruelty, pure horror" and the Narrator responds, "Who could bear to face the truth in that cruelty?" This exchange artfully echoes the challenge that contributors to this Book put forward: that of seeing and bearing the truth of the cruelty of violence against women today.

Dr. Humphries Mardirosian's staged reading is an effort to use theatre to reach us in a deep way. In the following chapter, Dr. Humphries Mardirosian outlines an effort following the staged reading to measure how empathy, aroused through theater, will call the audience to thought and action. A quote in Dr. Humphries Mardirosian's following chapter captures the parallel goals of psychoanalysis and theatre: "Storytelling induces deep listening, deep imagining, and an experience of deep time." As psychoanalysts, we strive for these depths in our efforts to see and hear our patients' trauma and pain. Dr. Humphries Mardirosian's hope, and the hope of this book, is to generate an empathic response in theater audiences and the readers of this chapter which will then engender thinking and action to help prevent violence and protect women.

Dr. Humphries Mardirosian is the Dean of the Stephens College School of Performing Arts in Columbia, Missouri. *Traces in the Wind* arose out of Dr. Humphries Mardirosian's time as a Fulbright Senior Scholar in the Czech Republic. She felt the writings of these three women survivors of the Holocaust, Charlotte Delbo, Rosalina Glaser, and Eva Kavanová, called out to her.

CHAPTER TWENTY-FIVE

A staged reading for remembrance, reminder, and inspiration:
Traces in the Wind

Gail Humphries Mardirosian

> "This will be my response to violence: to make music more intensely, more beautifully, more devotedly, than before. And, with each note, we will honor his spirit, commemorate his courage, and reaffirm his faith in the triumph of the mind"
>
> (Leonard Bernstein, Nights of the Stars, Madison Square Garden, November 25, 1962)

Of course, Maestro Bernstein was referring to the violence against John F. Kennedy when he made this statement, but his words resonate resoundingly for me, when looking at the very notion of violence. This chapter is about coping with violence with a specific perspective that embraces the arts, as espoused in Bernstein's quote, as a means of speaking, even shouting out, as an artist. The writings of three women of courage, survivors of the Holocaust, who possessed an amazing depth of spirit, as well as an affirmation of faith in the triumph of the mind and the arts, were explored as readings for remembrance, reminder, and inspiration. This chapter charts and explores the possibilities afforded by theatre in concert with music, to generate empathic responses, and, ultimately, to precipitate thinking and action from audiences regarding specific situations of violence against women during the Holocaust. It is presented with a hopeful and cautionary outlook about the importance of rebellion against oppression and violence against women, alongside a reminder about the potent power of the arts.

Background and context

When invited to present at the International Psychoanalytical Association COWAP Conference focusing on "The Courage to Fight Violence Against Women" on March 5 and 6, 2016 in Washington, DC at the American University, I began to explore the idea of presenting a "living paper," that is, to present provocative readings by women who had survived the Holocaust, presented with a goal of precipitating dialogue and action. The words of three extraordinary women who were betrayed, humiliated, deprived of normal living conditions, incarcerated, and experienced the depth of psychological and physical abuse and, yet, survived, were used as the matrix for the presentation. It seemed as if each of these exceptional women—Charlotte Delbo, Rosalina Glaser, and Eva Kavanová—had used their art as some form of sustenance and it gave them some renewal, at least for the soul. The circumstances under which they suffered are impossible for me to fully comprehend. Yet, as an artist, I found there was such a compelling empathy generated from reading their writings that I felt an extraordinary desire to share their words. At times, when reading their words and embracing their stories, it was almost unbearable, and, often, when hearing them aloud, there was a depth of interconnected pain. However, in spite of it all, there was an underlying outreach of hope because each of them survived to tell their stories with a different perspective and this was the compelling, propelling force to generate the presentation that ultimately was entitled *Traces in the Wind*. Through our staged reading, I hoped to bring their voices to life to generate reflection, connections to contemporary situations, and, ultimately, as a call for action.

In fact, the young women who read their words—undergraduate students at Stephens College, a women's college in Columbia, Missouri—became connected to these women. There was a timeless resonance in the spirit of each one of these survivors, although remarkably different as individuals, each possessing an underlying depth of courage that generated a natural linkage for the actors in the staged reading. Actors give life to texts and endow the words with their own personification and interpretation, but there was a truthfulness in the writings of each woman that was guiding and undeniable through the readings.

The selection of the three women who were chronicled through their writings was a process that this author can only note as *bashert* (meant to be). The scars and everlasting haunting resonance, as I heard their words spoken aloud, was as if they were speaking directly to me across time and space.

In 2009, I was introduced to the writing of Eva Kavanová, a Czech survivor of Terezín (a Nazi transit camp that was located forty-five miles outside of Prague) when preparing for a Fulbright appointment to teach at the Academy of Performing Arts (AMU) in Prague. A fellow Fulbrighter, Dr. Lisa Peschel, a theatre scholar and professor who has conducted research and developed publications around theatre in Terezín (currently lecturer in the Department of Theatre and Dance at York University in the UK) shared Kavanová's paper and interview with me. The paper was written by a woman who was a Terezín survivor who studied, and then later taught, at the Academy of Performing Arts (AMU). The interview was Professor Peschel's translation of a 1995 interview with Ms. Kavanová. I was captivated by the personality of Eva Kavanová, as expressed in both the paper and the interview. I became drawn to the stories of individuals sent to Terezín, subsequently interviewed survivors from the transit camp, and pondered the exceptional artistry that apparently thrived in the camp despite horrific circumstances of duress.

Eva Kavanová was born in Prague in 1924 and was only eighteen when she was deported to Terezín. She was sent to the Terezín ghetto, along with her mother, and survived to become a dramaturge, professor, and costume designer in Prague. Eva's survival, as chronicled in her paper and interview, was an astonishing and deep testimony about the potency of the arts. She described words in theatre performances as providing essential sustenance in times of little medicine and as a catalyst for hope. Around 144,000 prisoners entered Terezín and in the end only 17,247 survived. Eva Kavanová was one of them.

While in the Czech Republic on my Fulbright appointment, I also directed the play *Smoke of Home*, written by two young men while incarcerated at Terezín, performed both in Prague and then on-site at

Terezín. Subsequently, the play was presented at American University in Washington, DC, with performances sponsored by the Embassy of the Czech Republic. I chronicled my work on the project in *The Power of Witnessing* (Goodman & Meyers, 2012) in a chapter entitled "Giving Voice to the Silenced Through Theatre" (Humphries Mardirosian, 2012). Following this, I continued to pursue my interest in theatre at Terezín. At American University, I directed *I Never Saw Another Butterfly*, the story of children of the Terezín ghetto and the poetry and artwork that they created in a horrific world. Then, I was asked to direct a production of an original musical entitled *Signs of Life* (Ullian, Schiff, and Derfner), a story of artists imprisoned in the Terezín Ghetto, who were coerced to create a performance for the visit of the International Red Cross, a one-time visit that actually took place on June 23, 1944. The musical was presented in Washington, DC and also in Prague at Divadlo Inspirace (a theatre located at the Academy of Performing Arts) as part of the International Psychoanalytical Association's Congress in the summer of 2013. At this time, I began to think again about Eva Kavanová and I reread her paper and her interview.

A few years later, another colleague, Professor Susan Taylor Lennon at the University of Tampa, knowing of my interest in women artists who connected to their artistry in circumstances of oppression, introduced me to the searing story of the women of Convoy 31000 through a compelling book entitled *A Train in Winter: An Extraordinary Story of Women, Friendship, and Resistance in Occupied France* (Moorehead, 2011). I experienced deep admiration as I read the chronicle (Delbo, 1997) of these astonishing women of the French resistance, who sang "Le Marseillaise" as they marched through the gates of a concentration camp. Of the 229 Frenchwomen who were in the group that was finally sent to Auschwitz, only forty-nine survived. I was compelled to read and explore more about the individual women and read works by one of the survivors, the trilogy of Charlotte Delbo entitled *Auschwitz and After* and her play *Qui Rapportera Ces Polores?* (Who Will Carry the Word?). Her work was a harsh and poignant testimony to all that she and so many other women had suffered during their incarceration.

The same colleague introduced me to Rosalina Glaser just one year later. It was staggering for me to read the incredible story of her nephew's encounter with her past. Another amazing woman leapt across time for me. I looked at her pictures and saw a vitality that was captivating. Rosalina Glaser was born in 1914 in the Netherlands. She was a ballroom dancer who was betrayed by her ex-husband, was arrested and sent to a series of seven different concentration camps, the last of which was Auschwitz. She survived by teaching dance and etiquette to her captors in the camp. After the war, her story was written by her nephew, Paul Glaser, in his book *Dancing with the Enemy* (2011). There were 1,200 prisoners in her group that was sent to Auschwitz and she was one of the eight that survived.

The reading aloud of the selected writings of these three eventually did become the "living paper" that I had envisioned for the conference in Washington, DC. Each of them personified a different perspective: one of hope, joy, and survival with optimism, the other embodying intellectual determination, while the third expressed anger and cynicism after her survival.

When I arrived at Stephens College in August, 2014. I announced my thoughts about developing a staged reading and presenting the spoken words of these women. Student actors stepped forward and, over the course of a year, fifteen different women read aloud the writings of the women. The writings by and about these women were explored with a view towards developing the fifty-minute reading of their writings for the conference presentation. A student dramaturge, Jayme Brown, worked carefully with all of us as a script unfolded. As the reading evolved, a composer–musician (Professor Tom Andes) was asked to join the ensemble and a movement consultant, a visiting professor of dance (Brandi Coleman), was involved to help us selectively reinforce the content with gestures and minimal movement. A trusted colleague at another institution, Dr. Barbara Korner, Dean of the College of Arts and and Architecture at Pennsylvania State University, also provided invaluable feedback throughout the process. The final casting included four Stephens undergraduate women, Clara Bentz, Lauren Hardcastle, and Katherine Moore, representing the three incarcerated women and Abilen Olsen functioning as the narrator.

Intertextuality

Ultimately, an "intertextuality" occurred in the sharing of the presentation, as evidenced in the response of the audiences. In her book,

Roles in Interpretation (2002), Judy E. Yordon addresses ingredients of interpretation that are significant when analyzing the impact of the staged reading. Yordon describes interpretation as "a process" that involves the overlap of the "literary text," "the texts of the performers," and the "texts of the audiences." The matrix of this chapter is to view the use of theatre and music through these three lenses.

Working with a backward design, I examined the response of the audience first, because theatre is only fully realized with the presence of the audience in that ephemeral connection of actors as the conduit to text communicated in the shared moment with the audience. The famous theatre writer, philosopher, and actor, Constantin Stanislavski, called this connection "communion"—a type of spiritual connection that occurs between actors and then extends to the audience as they embody text. In this case, it was an unusual amalgam as young women spoke aloud the words of women who were reckoning with personal violence.

Next, the intertextuality of the actors is explored, and, finally, the impetus for the entire presentation, the stories of three amazing women, are discussed.

As professional storyteller Dr. Milbre Burch recently asserted to me, "Storytelling induces deep listening, deep imagining and an experience of deep time." Those of us involved with this project entitled *Traces in the Wind* certainly experienced that trilogy of depth.

Texts of audience

When I worked on the production of "Signs of life" in Prague, our discussant, Batya R. Monder spoke, and then subsequently wrote, about "what Dori Laub and Daniel Podell called the 'art of trauma,' a special kind of art that can imaginatively recreate traumatic events that defy representation" (Monder, 2013; Laub & Podell, 1995). She addressed Gilbert Rose's statement that "the art of trauma does not simply communicate meaning, it generates meaning in receptive minds." It "urges the mind beyond experience and gives us license to feel more" (Monder, 2013). Monder discussed the role of creative activity as it "facilitated survival and transformed the external world, a world that threatened to become devoid of meaning." She also commented that "art helped survival by widening one's vision and offering alternative perspectives and ways of seeing things." This viewpoint is relevant when examining the audience reaction to the staged reading.

Through audience surveys and talkbacks, I attempted to gather audience impressions and responses with the hope that the experience of the staged reading would afford deeper thinking about the particular violence against these women and the audience would, indeed, feel more.

The staged reading was presented in three completely different environments within a single week: (1) a small recital hall on the Stephens College campus; (2) a larger recital hall as part of the international conference on the stage at American University; (3) in the living room of a host from Stephens College for alumnae in Washington, DC. The return rate on the post-performance audience questionnaire was approximately 60%.

The survey was designed to afford both qualitative and quantitative feedback with both forced response items and open-ended questions.

The age and gender demographics of the respondents were revealed as follows: 39% in the 17–28 age range; 16% in the 29–53 age range; 25% in the 54–77 age range, and one respondent in the 78–89 age range (Figure 25.1).

The audience gender was 69% female and 13% male, according to the voluntary self-reporting (Figure 25.2). This response appears to provide an appropriate baseline of responses for the given audiences, since two of the three audiences were connected to the women's college.

Respondents were asked three questions that directly related to their actions as a result of viewing the performance. The first set of questions was framed to relate directly to the content of the staged reading.

"As a result of this performance, I intend to:" (please select all that apply):

1. Seek out other theater pieces that tell the stories of women who survived the Holocaust with the arts as refuge.
2. Seek out more information on the women protagonists.
3. Seek out information on women and the Holocaust in different countries other than those presented (Figure 25.3).

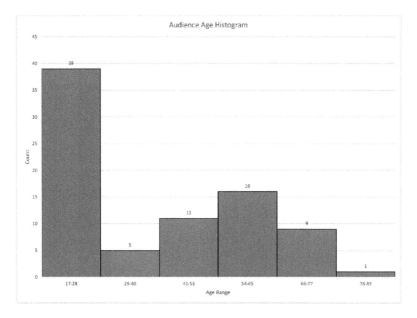

Figure 25.1. Audience's ages.

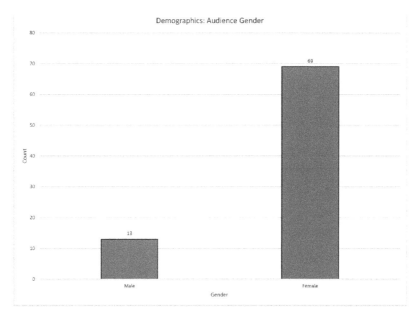

Figure 25.2. Audience's gender.

A STAGED READING FOR REMEMBRANCE, REMINDER, AND INSPIRATION   241

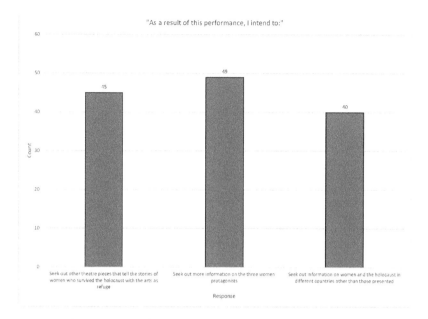

Figure 25.3.   Audience responses to the first set of questions.

Responses ranged from forty-five for number 1 to forty-nine for number 2 and forty for number 3. As such, audiences appeared to have reacted in a constructive manner to the content of the reading.

The second set of questions was framed to capture the emotional responses to the reading and to discern identification with the characters. Audience members were asked if they felt emotionally connected to the stories of the women (Figure 25.4), if music evoked an empathetic response (Figure 25.5), and if viewing enactment of the writings as a staged reading generated emotional responses (Figure 25.6). There was a strong majority of responses in each of these major categories ranging from eighty-eight "yes" to seven "no" for the first area, from ninety-four yes and three no in the second, and, finally, ninety-four yes and one no to the third question. Specific emotions that were identified in a given menu included strong responses in compassion, empathy, inspiration, anger, appreciation (Figure 25.7).

The final section of the questionnaire dealt with overarching themes for the reading: the arts as a strategy for survival, spiritual resistance, and individual response to violence. All three categories indicated an audience connection with favorable responses at seventy-one for questions 1 and 3 and sixty for question 2.

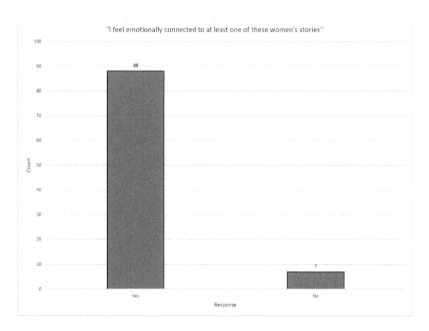

Figure 25.4. Reponse to whether the stories evoked emotional connection.

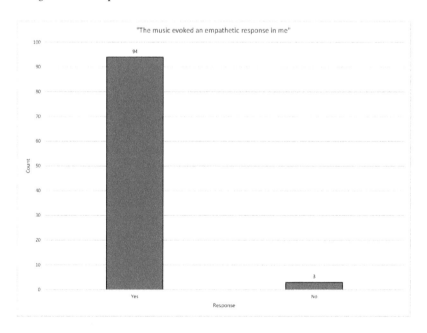

Figure 25.5. Response to whether the music evoked empathy.

A STAGED READING FOR REMEMBRANCE, REMINDER, AND INSPIRATION   243

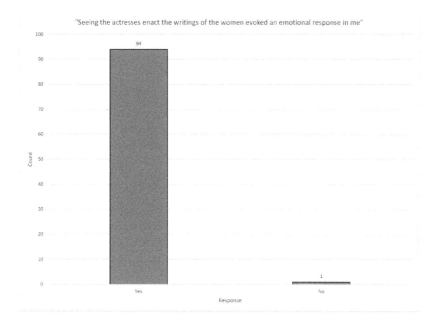

Figure 25.6   Response to whether enactment of the writing generated emotional reactions.

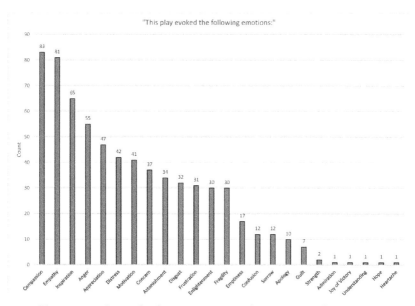

Figure 25.7.   Strength of reactions in specific categories of emotions.

With open-ended responses regarding audience identification with the characters, there was a revelation about connection to personal feelings, to specific characters that generated a strong response, as well as to connections to the stories of all three women (Figure 25.8). Audience members identified connections to:

Charlotte's anger;
Rosie's betrayal;
Eva's life in the theatre world.

Respondents also noted that the reliance on art as a means to "keep them going," noted reactions to the witnessing of the "power of survival," and the "inner strengths" of the women. One response included recounting a profound experience involving Auschwitz, while another noted "being in a place just like one of the characters with vulnerability and without control over what could be done."

Audience talkbacks affirmed similar responses. "It was very powerful, as if I was transported to another day and time in your 'bubble' of the story and place."

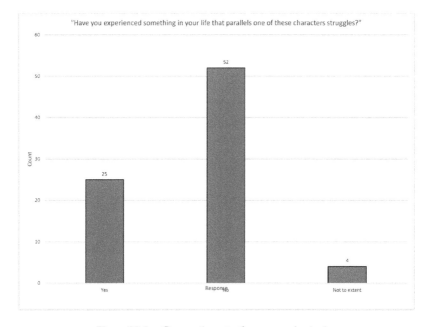

Figure 25.8. Connections to the women's stories.

Additional insightful and telling comments included:

* "Without music it would be more than I could bear. Music lifts the performance and completes the story telling."
* "I have experienced nothing as tragic as the characters, yet I could definitely identify with their struggle for identity and meaning in the fire of adversity."
* "I found myself so engaged with the women that the 'system' was mostly a given for me—perhaps reflective of my age (71) and life experience—the actors, I believe, did an extraordinary job of portraying women whose experience they are only able to imagine—kudos to them."
* "The play awakened thoughts about generating a strategy for clarifying one's faith—spiritual survival."
* "This was very informative and very powerful. Really incredible, this performance was very emotional. Music added so much. Very effective with no staging to speak of, just the actors. Wishing this is never repeated again."

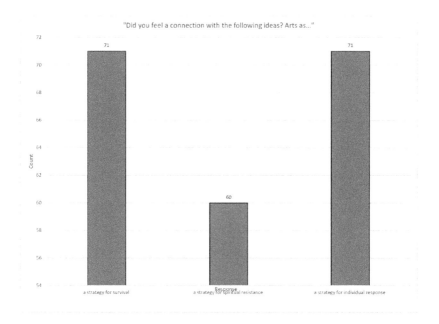

Figure 25.9. Responses to how the arts contributed to the audience members' connection.

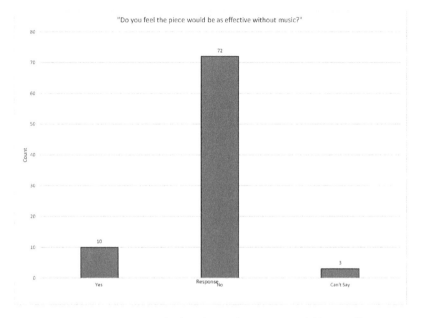

Figure 25.10. Response as to whether the performance would be as effective without music.

* "I have been inspired to have even more courage to establish a life filled with courage, art and hope."

Several individuals identified themselves as having relatives who were survivors and one individual noted that she, herself, was a survivor.

In composite, the findings from the audience response indicate the potential for theatre and music to ignite audience connections to this important content.

Texts of actors

In an effort to glean an understanding of the impact of the rehearsal–performance processes for the students, a focus group was organized two weeks after the staged reading with the four female performers (three actors and one narrator) and the student stage manager. They were asked three questions related directly to the process of generating the staged reading and the experience of sharing the readings with the audience.

1. What did you learn?
2. What worked in the process?
3. What would you improve?

Their responses revealed the emotional power of the stories, the importance of delving deeply into realistic connections with the stories and circumstances, as well as the significance of working beyond normal comfort zones as actors.

What worked for everyone was the unity of connection to the struggles the women had faced, the significance of art in their lives, and sharing these stories with an audience. They also commented on the importance of presenting the work as a staged reading, noting that the simplicity of the presentation with a minimalist approach to costumes, the basic use of stools and music stands, afforded an emphasis on the stories that they were revealing. They each emphasized an underlying connection to the women whose words they were retelling and the personal journey that they discerned for each woman. The parallel connection of age and gender from the actors connecting to the women whose work they were reading seemed to be an important factor.

An interesting discussion point revolved around the functioning of the group as a unit, a true ensemble united through the significant messages that they were imparting. They spoke about a trust that developed with the entire ensemble, trust among actors, the stage manager, the composer–musician, the movement consultant, and the director, commenting that this trust allowed them an ability to embrace the challenging material with even greater depth. They also commented on personal emotional involvement and engagement. One actress aptly noted the difficulty and beauty of being a "bridge between the past to the present."

All of the actors commented on the importance and influence of the music in telling the stories and capturing the emotional life of the individual characters, as well as the composite message. Each actor noted the effective use of basic movement and minimalistic choreography to enhance story content. All agreed that there was an inherent group dedication to serve the integrity of the stories and the significance of the retelling.

When discussing what needed improvement, all agreed that they wanted to include more music, increased content for each woman, and perhaps just a few more moments of brightness in the lives of these women. Actors also suggested the use of a short passage for each woman presented in their native language, followed by an English translation. Finally, there was also a suggestion that some theatrical lighting could have been used that would retain the simplistic approach of the reading, and enhance particular moments for ambience.

Literary texts along with music and lyrics

The resources for the literary text were:

1. *About Terezin Theater A Little Bit Differently*, a personal interview with Eva Kavanová (1995), translated by Peschel.
2. Letters of Rosalina Glaser, as presented in *Dancing with the Enemy: My Family's Holocaust Secret* (Glaser, 2013).
3. *Auschwitz and After* (Delbo, 1997[1965]) and *Who Will Carry the Word*? (Delbo, 1983).

The reading included an intertwining of selected writings of these three women, along with commentary from a narrator to provide historical context, music to afford ambience, and original songs to represent a collaborative voicing of the three women. The women's words are personal accounts of historical events, sometimes chronicling and analyzing memories and, at other times, simply observing and reporting experiences while incarcerated. Often the writings are reflections of past and recent experiences, recounting relationships with family members in the past or interactions in the present. The source for each woman's writings was quite different: Eva Kavanová's was a paper written over twenty years after her release from Terezín and then an interview in later years. Rosie Glaser's writings were through her letters written while a prisoner. Charlotte Delbo has written several books and a play that were important in this recounting. In each case, the speaker mode is lyric—someone very much like the composer is speaking. In fact, the musical compositions with lyrics allowed for the convergence of the three voices. Generating the lyrics for the music was not difficult. There were themes and threads in the writings of the women that allowed us to speak in sound and song with numbers that ranged from the opening "Nocturne" to "Melancholia" and the main motif of *Traces in the Wind*. The musical underscoring and the vocal numbers seemed to unfold.

The music ranged from original pieces composed in the past years by Professor of Music Tom Andes at Stephens College to pieces that he composed specifically for the reading. As Professor Andes noted,

> When we began to read through "Traces" the opening music and the dialogue synced up so perfectly on the first reading that I knew something special was about to happen. My music flowed out effortlessly because the exposition was so intensely moving to me. Putting words to some of my existing music was equally cathartic. It was as if these piano pieces written years ago were meant to be in *Traces in the Wind.*

Lyrics were written for three of the vocal numbers as a joint venture between Professor Andes and me, and we readily discovered lyrics that represented a merged voicing for the three women. Music was also composed to underscore sections through the entire reading, creating a soundscape that captured the subtext of the stories. The title number for *Traces in the Wind* had no lyrics. It was a wistful, haunting piano piece that was also used as a leitmotif throughout the performance. Professor Andes actually created a soundscape completely synchronized with the wordscape of the reading.

The first vocal number, entitled "Nocturne" was a melody sung by each woman individually, and then as a round with all of the women and the narrator. It was delivered as an invocation to the audience.

> Words connect us—tell our story
> Onward with our soulful cry.
> Pain and suffering, haunting moments
> Memories walking side by side.
> Please remember, hear and listen,
> Art upholds us even now.

The second vocal number, entitled "Melancholia" was an introspective reckoning by each woman about their situation in the camps:

> I'm longing for home, family, friends,
> Days of past memory abound.

Hard to find in this word gone awry . . . ghosts of my past standing by.
Strength and tenacity,
Stretching capacity
Try to stay calm, yet, barely alive.
This meager existence wore down by resistance
I hardly survive though my confidence thrives,
I'm longing for home and family and friends . . .
Days of past memory abound . . . days of past memory abound.

The final vocal number, entitled "Perchance to Dream," was also sung by all of the women. It was presented as an anthem and call to the audience, with solo and ensemble voicing as well as a descant.

> I'm holding fast to my art with complete inspiration
> I'm holding tight to my heart and creative design
> With determination, I won't resign.
> I must hold on to the creative spirit within me,
> I mustn't waiver and never begin to give in,
> They will not break me.
> Strong to the end.
>
> I hope the dream goes on and on,
> I hope the dream goes on and on,
> They will not break me [round of voices].
> I will endeavor, art is forever.
>
> Hear our traces, see our faces,
> Art embraces all the races . . . all.

Summary: fighting violence with our work and the arts

My storyteller colleague, Dr. Milbre Burch, was recently talking with me about the willingness to give over to the trance that is the essence of her work, the trance that is the ultimate and unique connection between the story, the storyteller via the performance/presentation, and the audience. This particular project validated the potency and impact of the human-to-human connection, as demanding and challenging issues were presented and the trance ensued for the actors connecting to the audiences. Ultimately, it is my hope that as we connect to stories of the past, our "trance" that harshly reminds us of parallel contemporary connections will precipitate and yield further thinking and action. I hope that our presentation was a proclamation against moral transgression and that we validated an important thought of the Czech playwright, world leader, and humanist Vaclav Havel—"Art has the capacity . . . to be stronger than death."

Acknowledgment

Special thanks to Devon Whetsone, Director of Assessment, Stephens College, for the creation of the graphs of audience response.

References

Delbo, C. (1983). Who will carry the word? In: Skloot, R. (Ed.), C. Haft (Trans.), *The Theatre of the Holocaust, Volume 1*. Madison: University of Wisconsin Press.

Delbo, C. (1997)[1965]. *Convoy to Auschwitz: Women of the French Resistance* C. Cosman (Trans.). Boston, MA: Northeastern University Press.

Glaser, P. (2011). *Dancing with the Enemy. My Family's Holocaust Secret*. New York: Random House.

Goodman, N. R., & Meyers, M. B. (Eds.) (2012). *The Power of Witnessing: Reflections, Reverberations, and Traces of the Holocaust*. New York: Routledge.

Humphries Mardirosian, G. (2012). Giving voice to the silenced. In: N. R. Goodman & M. B. Meyers (Eds.), *The Power of Witnessing: Reflections, Reverberations, and Traces of the Holocaust* (pp. 255–266). New York: Routledge.

Kavanová, E. M. (2007)[1967]. *About Terezín Theater A Little Bit Differently*, L. Peschel (Trans.), a paper and an interview in 1995.

Laub, D., & Podell, D. (1995). Art and trauma. *International Journal of Psychoanalysis*, 76: 871–1081.

Monder, B. (2013). Signs of life. International Psychoanalytical Association Congress in Prague.

Yordon, E. (2002). *Role in Interpretation*. New York: McGraw Hill.

INDEX

Abramović, M., 180–181
Abrams, K., 122
abuse, xxxii, xxxiv, xl, 3–4, 6, 9, 13,
    19, 21, 32, 35–36, 74, 79, 100, 109,
    110–111, 119–120, 164, 180–181,
    183, 229
    childhood, 76
    domestic, 3
    emotional, 19
    history of, 4
    human rights, 66, 120
    mental, 37
    past, 118
    physical, xxxii, 4, 18, 22–23, 66, 123,
        164, 234
    of power, 17, 156
    psychological, 23, 234
    sexual, 3, 13, 19, 23–24, 107–123,
        131, 150, 164, 166
    spousal, xxxvi
    substance, 151
    verbal, xxxii
    violent, 4
    of women, xxxix, 115–116, 123
Adhiambo Onyango, M., 155
affect(ive), 212
    development, 212
    experiences, 2
    states, 217, 220
aggression, xl, 3, 5, 43–44, 52–54, 88,
    91, 93, 119, 129–130, 151, 181,
    193, 213
    behavior, 129
    child's, 100, 130
    eroticism of, 94, 101
    hostile, 26
    libidinalization of, 94
    manifestation, 52

    physical, 44
    primary, 92
    ruthless, 92–95, 100
    sadistic, 92, 95
    self-preservative, 92, 94, 100
    sexual, xxxix
Agirre Aranburu, X., 149
Agosin, M., 66
Ahrens, C. E., 154
Akman, D., 151
Alcayna-Stevens, L., 155
Amar, A., 113–114
American Federation of State, County
    and Municipal Employees
    Newsletter, 112, 120
Amnesty International, 135–137
Anastario, M. P., 155
Anaya, A., 138
Anderson, G., 112
anger, 19, 32, 37, 43, 55, 78–79, 130,
    237, 241, 244
Anna Freud Centre, 100
anxiety, xxxii, 18–19, 44, 48, 53,
    76–77, 93–94, 151, 214
    annihilation, 54
    earliest, 5, 211
    group, 51
    intense, 43
    underlying, 52
Arlington County Detention Facility,
    120
Arlow, J., 6
art, xli, 6, 10, 13, 35, 38, 42, 84, 177,
    179, 181, 183, 192–193, 202, 227,
    231–232, 234, 236, 238, 244, 246,
    249–251
    contemporary, 177
    history, 177, 191

Mochica, 193–196
  performance, 185
  politicized, 180
  significance of, 247
  therapy, 70
  of trauma, 238
Aruasa, W., 155
Aslanian, S., 26
asylum, xxx, xl, 64, 162, 164–166, 168
  interviews, 12
  protection of, 162
  -seekers, xl, 64, 161–162, 168
attachment, 4, 27, 210
  early, 4–5, 219
  difficulties, 151
  disorders, 151
  insecure, 21
  meaningful, 27
  narcissistic, 215
  painful, 5
  primitive, 210
  prolonged, 219
  relationships, 129
  symbiotic, 56
autonomy, 48, 50, 56–57, 59, 64, 192

Bach, S., 4
Balint, E., 214, 216, 219, 228
Balint, M., 212
Baranes, J. J., 210
Barnes, H. E., 154
Barrick, K., 155
Bartlett, K., 111
Baruch, E. H., 221
Basch, N., 111
Basseches, H. B., 3–5
Bawden, G., 196
Becerra, L., 135
Beck, M., 25
behavior(al), 24, 54–55, 78, 84, 95, 172
  see also: aggression
  abnormal, 151
  concerns, 51
  problems, 151
  sexual, 25, 27
Beitchman, J. H., 151
Belknap, J., 108
Benjamin, J., 211
Bergin, T., 154

Bernini, G. L., 179, 181
Bion, W. R., xxxiii–xxxiv, 212, 218
Birksted-Breen, D., 215
Blanck-Cereijido, F., 44
Blue Campaign, xxxv
Blum, H. P., 216
Bourget, S., 200
Bourne, J., 110
Brenman-Pick, I., 218
Bridgewater, P., 109, 111–112
Briere, J. N., 151
Brierley, M., 211–212, 215
Brooke, J., 112
Brooks, R., 112
Browne, A., 116
Bruch, E., 116
Brunswick, R. M., 211
Buchanan, K., 111
Burgner, M., 214, 220
Burner, M., 155
Butler v. Perry, 114

California Department of
  Corrections, 120
Cámara de Diputados del Congreso
  de la Unión, 139
Campbell, R., 154
Cannon, W. B., 92
Canterino v. Wilson, 117
Carrigan v. Davis, 111, 113
Carver, C. S., 76
case studies
  Anna, 163
  Blanca, 74–75
  Cara, 214, 220
  Carla, 75–76
  Cotton Field Murders, 140, 142
  Divra, 163
  Kani, 163
  Lila, 165, 168
  Maryam, 164, 168
  Mr. Giles, 95–96, 100–102
  Ms. M., 4
  Nelly, 168
  Norma, 144
  Rosa, 73–74
  Sonia, 164–165, 168
  Surita, 63
  Wolf Man, 210

Cason v. Seckinger, 119
Cassavia, E., 151
Center for Justice and International
    Law, 140
Centro de Estudios Sobre Impunidad
    y Justicia, 145
Chasseguet-Smirgel, J., 5, 45, 211,
    215, 217
Chicago, J., 184
Clark, A. E., 11, 105, 131
Clyatt v. United States, 114
Coalition for the International
    Criminal Court, 153
Cohen, R., 65, 84–85
Comisión Mexicana de Defensa y
    Promoción de los Derechos
    Humanos, 143, 144
Comité de América Latina y el
    Caribe para la Defensa de los
    Derechos de la Mujer
    (CLADEM), Caso Campo
    Algodonero, 145
Common Threads (CT), 70–72, 74,
    76–80, 83–85
conscious(ness), 85 *see also*:
    unconscious
  accessibility, 13
  beliefs, 44
    legitimating, 42
    identifications, 42
    gender, 44
  intent, 84
  realities, 1
  sabotage, 51
  shared objectives, 51
contact, 50, 113, 166, 201
  eye, 69
  skin, 26
Convention Against Torture,
    114
Cornelius, G., 119
Corrections Corporation, 112
countertransference, 217–218 *see also*:
    transference
  analyst's, 209, 220
  feelings, 221
  vicissitudes, 220
Country Reports on Human Rights
    Practices, 119, 124

Cournut, M., 209
Covi, L., 76
Cragin, W., 155
Cronholm, P. F., 25

Dabney, J. D., 19
DaCosta, G. A., 151
Danto, E. A., 59
Dartnell, E., 152
Daskalea v. District of Columbia, 111,
    114
Decker, M. R., 19
Delbo, C., 232, 234, 236, 248
Department of Homeland Security,
    xxxv
depression, 18–20, 55, 74, 76–77, 151,
    219
  position, xxxii
  reactions, 53
Derogatis, L. R., 76
Deutsch, H., 211, 216
development(al), 5, 9, 12, 14, 94,
    99–100, 123, 138–139, 155, 209,
    212, 215, 229 *see also*: affect
  child, xli, 94, 100
  commentary, xxxix
  of courage, 3
  economic, 112
  efforts, 155
  emotional, 212, 218
  female, 59
    adolescent, 83
  human, xli
  of internal strengths, 6
  policy, 119
  regression, 151
  of resilience, 11
  sexual, 27, 94
    perverse, 101
  social, 36
Dick, K., 104
Dinos, A., 111, 122
Dirks, D., 103, 111
discrimination, 56, 108, 117, 139, 142
    see also: gender
  non-, 139
  prejudice, 142
  treatment, 110
  violence, 142

disorder, 18 *see also*: attachment
    addictive, 19, 23
    personality, 19
    posttraumatic stress (PTSD), 76–77, 151
    psychiatric, 22
dominance, 4–5, 11, 26, 43, 110, 122, 156, 203, 207
    sexual, 122
    of women, 42–43
Doretti, M., 137
Dovydaitis, T., 38
dynamics, 44, 192 *see also*: gender
    balance, 91
    family, 55, 129
    group, 48, 84
    power, 156
    psycho-, 13
    sadomasochistic, 12

ego, 58, 91–92, 100, 219
    ideals, 50, 58
    strength, 19
    super-, 56
    support, 55
El Diario, 134
Elliott, D. M., 151
Ellman, P., xxxix, 2–6
enactment, 2, 5, 121–122, 241, 243
    re-, 214
End Rape on Campus (EROC), xxxix, 11, 103, 131–132
Enriquez, M., 210

Faimberg, H., 210
fantasy, 3–6, 21, 24, 43, 55, 94, 101
    see also: unconscious
    internal, 3
    life, 24
    masturbation, 94, 101
    of omnipotence, 3
    perverse, 24
    sadomasochistic, 3
    sexual, 185
    violent, 24, 102
Fast, I., 211
Felman, S., 214–215
female genital
    circumcision (FGC), 165
    mutilation (FGM), 3, 5, 161–162, 165

femicide, 11–12, 53, 59, 133–135, 137–139, 141–144, 167
    cultural, 3
femininity, 211, 215–217, 221
    positive, 215
Ferdowsian, H., 155
Fishman, C., 87
Fox, L., 118
Fraiberg, S., 130
Franco, R., 199
Franke, K., 111, 122–123
Freedman, E., 108
Freud, S., 4, 6, 26, 43, 59, 91, 100, 190, 201, 210–211, 213, 216, 219
    see also: case studies

Garcia-Moreno, C., 152
Garcilaso de la Vega, Inca, 202–203
Garvey, S., 107, 112
gender, xxxv, 43, 47–49, 52, 59, 105, 108–109, 115, 150, 169, 216–217, 239–240, 247 *see also*: unconscious
    -based
        killings, 133–134
        violence, 63–65, 70, 80–81, 103, 133, 138–139, 141–142, 144, 162, 168
    capacities, 84
    crimes, 140
    cross-, 109
    demographics, 239
    differences, 129
    discrimination, 25, 57
    diversity, 48
    dynamics, 42, 44
    equality, 48, 84–85
    essentialism, 116
    expression, 105
    feminine, 43, 52
    guidelines, 162
    identification, 44
    identity, 42, 105
    inequalities, 52, 149, 155
    issues, xxxvii
    masculine, 43
    norms, 81
    parity, 57
    perspective, 142
    stereotyping, 43–44

therapeutic relationship, 214
violence, 140
Gentileschi, A., 177, 178
Giddings, P., 110
Gilmore v. Salt Lake City, 115
Glaser, P., 237
Glaser, R., 232, 234, 236–237, 248
Glasser, M., 92, 99–100, 213–214
Glocer Fiorini, L., 43
Glover, E., 211, 215–216
Gohlke, G., 155
Goldin, N., 181–182
Goode, W. J., 168
Goodman, N. R., xxxix, 2–6, 10, 88, 236
Goodwin, J., 110
Gratz v. Bollinger, 114
Greenacre, P., 215
Grinberg, L., 218
guilt, 21, 49, 70, 78, 95, 96, 123, 153, 213
Gupta, J., 19
Gurrea, C. J. A., 141

H.R. 1707, 108th Cong., 121
H.R. 4943, 121
Haider, S., 155
Harris, A., 111
Hayman, A., 211–212
Heimann, P., 218
Heineman, E. D., 149, 150
Herman, D. S., 76
Herman, J., 68–69, 79
Hernandez, M., 189
Hewitt, N., 109
Hindus, M., 112
Hodge, D. R., 38
Holleran, D., 154
Holmquist, U., 193
Hood, J. E., 151
hooks, b., 115, 123
human rights, xxxvii, 6, 118, 122, 138–139 *see also*: abuse
activists, 136
female, 54, 59
implementation of, 48
international, 114, 118, 137
organizations, 139, 144
physician, 13

problem, 64
violations, 137
Humphries Mardirosian, G., 231–232, 236
Huska, J. A., 76

Ice v. Dixon, 123
identification, xxxviii, xl, 36, 42, 210, 215–216, 241, 244 *see also*: gender, unconscious
alternative, 3
destructive, 3
empathic, 3
internal, 3
primary, 212
projective, 55
trial, 3
Igra, L., xxxii–xxxiii
imago, 213–214
maternal, 209, 211, 215
Instituto Nacional de Estadística y Geografía (INEGI), 134–135
Inter-American Commission on Human Rights (IACHR), 137, 139–140, 144
Inter-American Court of Human Rights, 137, 140, 142
Interdisciplinary Seminar of Andean Studies (SIDEA), 189
International Covenant on Civil and Political Rights, 114
International Protocol on the Documentation and Investigation of Sexual Violence, 153
International Psychoanalytical Association, xxxvii, 40, 143, 234, 236
International Rescue Committee (IRC), 64
International Union of Sex Workers, 21
intervention, 10–11, 15, 20, 24, 48, 50, 77, 80, 84, 101, 129, 131
comprehensive, 70
early, 102, 130
effective, 12
informed, 47
meaningful, 12

ongoing, xl
psychodynamic, 13
Irigaray, L., 214
Isaacs, S., 6

Jacobs, H., 109, 123
Jordan v. Gardner, 123
Joseph, B., 5, 218
Judgment Day, 110–111

Kabanga, J., 155
Kaes, R., 210
Kahlo, F., 179–181
Kapur, R., 116
Karme, L., 217
Kavanová, E. M., 232, 234–236, 248
Keane, T. M., 76
Kelly, J., 155
Kelly, S., 155
Kibet, C., 155
King, P., 211
Klein, M., 5–6, 211–212, 217
Knafo, D., 179
Knufken, D., 22
Koppelman, A., 114
Kristeva, J., 183
Kulish, N. M., 213, 216–217
Kunst, M., 154

Lacan, J., 212
Lakhani, N., 153
Langer, M., 211
Laplanche, J., 6
Laub, D., 238
Lax, R., 5
Lemlij, M., 189–190
Lerner-Kinglake, J., 121
Lester, E. P., 216
Levi-Strauss, C., 190, 212
Lieberman, J. S., 177
Limentani, A., 213
Lipman, R. S., 76
Litz, B. T., 76
Lizárraga, R., 206
Luquet-Parat, C., 211

Maheshwari, A., 19
Maier, S. L., 154
Maloney, A., 153
Mariner, J., 110, 121

marriage, 31, 57, 111
arranged, 162
childhood, xl, 5, 13
forced, 161
Marsh, M., 152
masochism, 4, 96 *see also*: dynamics, fantasy
position, 43, 53
sado-, xli, 1, 3, 5, 93–94, 100–101
bond, 180
relationship, 3, 94, 181, 220
solutions, 101
Mayorga, P., 145
McConnell, J. C., 113
McCormack, G. L., 69
McDougall, J., 211
McFarlane, L., 121
McHale, T., 155
Medina Rosas, A., 142
Mejía Piñeros, M. C., 142
Mellon, J., 111
Mendieta, A., 181
Meyers, M. B., 88, 236
Michigan Department of Corrections, 120
Millones, L., 189–190
Mishori, R., 155
Molina, J., 134
Monárrez Fragoso, J., 136
Monder, B., 238
Money-Kyrle, R., 218
Moya-Raggio, E., 65
Mukamal, D., 123
Muthoga, R., 155

Naimer, K., 155
National Center for Missing and Exploited Children, 24
National Sheriffs Association, Resolution, 119
Navani, S., 152
Nochlin, L., 183
Nordic Model, 26–27
Notman, M., 5
Nyanyuki, J., 155

object, 4, 25, 92–94, 196, 202, 210–212, 215, 218
concrete, 215

constant, 20
degraded, 6
depersonalized, 25
internal, 10
lost, 210
maternal, 5, 219
of pain, 4
part, 209
relations, xli, 5, 212, 218
sexual, 26, 43, 184
third, 212
threatening, 93
transitional, 69
objective, 51, 59
forensic documentation, 155
main, 51
original, 48
positive, 53
shared, 51
Observatorio Ciudadano Nacional del Feminicidio (OCNF), 138, 142
oedipal *see also*: transference
configuration, 217
pre-, 210, 216–217, 220–221, 228
rage, 229
sexuality, 221
Oedipus complex, 43–44, 217
Offen, K., 111
Office of Justice Programs Fact Sheet, 18
Ogden, P., 68
Omollo, G., 155
oppression, xxxiv, 13, 110, 116, 234, 236
sexual, 116
Ortiz de Zevallos, P., 196

Palermo, T., 149
Parsens, J., 154
Patel, V., 19
Payne, S., 211
Pender, V., 25–26
Pendola, A., 189
Perelberg, R. J., 209, 214–215, 219–221
Person, E., 211
Peterman, A., 149
phantasy, 210–211, 213, 217
Cinderella, 50

sexual, 214
unconscious, 211, 218
phenomena, 169 *see also*: transference
cultural, xli, 191
historical, 190
multidetermined, 216
political, 191
social, 24, 191
structural, 135
Phillips, S., 111
Physicians for Human Rights (PHR), 155, 161
Pimlott, S., 108
Pines, D., 216
Pino, A., 11, 105
Plata v. Davis, 118
Podell, D., 238
Pontalis, J.-B., 6
Popelier, L., 154
pornography, 23–25, 53
child, 24
industry, 23
Poussin, N., 179, 181
pregnancy, 11, 49, 51, 134, 151, 164, 204
adolescent, 48, 50, 58
early, xl, 13, 49
forced, 156
prison *see also*: rape
guards, 130
male, 108
officials, 108
reformers, 108
system, 12, 112–113
women's, 109
Prison Rape Elimination Act (PREA), 121–123
ProCon.org, 18
prostitution, 17–18, 23–25, 31, 35, 53, 108, 150, 156, 161
psychic *see also*: rape
creation, xxxii
energy, xxxiv
equivalent, 94
groundwork, 94
helplessness, 3, 11, 15
life, 10
mechanisms, 12
narrative, 4

necessity, 14
pain, 55
processes, 1, 215
realities, xlii, 6, 10, 210
scripts, 4
sphere, 92, 218
structure, 27
Purdin, S., 152

Racker, H., 218
Rafter, N. H., 107–108, 117
Raj, A., 19
Ramos, M., 196
rape, xxxviii–xl, 3, 5, 10–12, 14, 20, 31, 35, 37, 39, 54, 66, 69, 74–75, 87, 89, 112, 115, 121, 129–130, 150, 152–153, 156, 161, 163–164, 178–179, 181, 184, 213
    actual, 54
    attempted, 54
    crisis centers, 154
    culture, 105
    date, 185
    gang, 63
    mass, 152, 179
    physical, xl
    prison, xl, 121–122
    psychic, xl, 11
    rampant, xxxix
    state-sponsored, 18
    survivors, 151
    victims of, xl, 11, 154
    violation of, xli
Raphael-Leff, J., 209, 214
Reebye, P., 129
refugee, 64–66, 161–164, 166
    camps, xxx, xl
    communities, 12, 71
repetition compulsion, 2–3
resilience, xxxviii–xli, 3, 9–12, 14, 64, 67, 70, 83, 85, 152
Rhodes v. Chapman, 113
Richards, A. K., 5–6
Rickels, K., 76
Riley v. Olk-long, 114, 119
Riviere, J., 211
Robertson v. Baldwin, 114
Robertua, V., 136
Rohrer, F., 23

Rostworowski, M., 189, 196
Rothschild, B., 68
Rowley, E., 152
Rubens, P. P., 179, 181
Rubenstein, G., 123
Ruiz-Navarro, C., 153
Russell, K., 19

sadism, 4, 43, 93–94, 96, 99–101, 214
    see also: aggression, dynamics, fantasy, masochism
    anal-, xxiii
    attack, 93–96
    control, 94
    encounter, 213
    exchange, 94
    instinct, 43
    subjective, 43
Sahay, S., 87
Salisbury, E. J., 19
Sandler, A.-M., 92, 214
Sandler, J., 92, 214, 218
Sarri, R. C., 108
Scales-Trent, J., 114
Scheier, M. F., 76
Searcey, D., 153
Secretaria de Gobernación (SEGOB), 134, 143
Sefl, T., 154
Segal, H., 218
self, 4–5, 13, 27, 71, 84, 92–93, 101, 183, 210 *see also*: aggression
    -aggrandizement, 56
    -assertion, 77
    -blame, 70
    -confidence, 20, 77
    cutting, 215
    defense, 179
    -esteem, 19–20, 51, 56–57, 91
    -expression, 70, 79
    -hating, 4
    -hood, 102
    -injury, 21
    -limits, 51
    love, 215
    -preservation, 91–94, 100, 102
    -protection, 68, 100–101
    -recognition, 56
    -regulation, 78

-reported, 77, 239
-representation, 21, 218
ruthless, 92
-sabotage, 58
-sacrificial, 53, 55, 57
sense of, 21, 101, 214
-soothing, 69
Sellers, P. V., 154
separation, 93, 155, 220
 –individuation, xli, 50, 58, 229
Serrano, L. J., 221
sex trafficking, xxxix–xli, 3, 5, 17–18, 24–26, 31, 34–38, 41
sexual(ity) (*passim*) *see also*: abuse, aggression, behavior, development, dominance, fantasy, object, oedipal, oppression, phantasy
 act, 43
 activity, 26
 arousal, 26
 assault, xxxvi, xxxix, 2, 103–104, 121–122, 129–131, 135–136, 150, 154
 attacks, xxix
 attraction, 23
 being, 5
 bi-, 215
 bodies, 22, 25
 coercion, 177
 degradation, 109
 demands, 178
 desire, 111, 184
 diversity, 49
 drive, 27
 dysfunction, 151
 enjoyment, 21
 exploitation, 17–18, 35–36, 109, 114, 141
 expression, 122, 150
 female, 48, 57, 210, 215
 genital, xxxiii
 gratification, 43, 94, 101
 harassment, 25, 48, 54
 hetero-, 58, 216
 homo-, 21, 216, 219
 identity, 49, 214
 intercourse, 193, 197, 220, 227
 interest, 25
 male, xxxiii
 maternal, 23
 misconduct, 112–113, 119–122, 131
 misuse, 184
 molested, 19
 needs, 18, 23, 27
 organs, 151
 orientation, 105, 116
 partner, 213
 performance, 23
 phobias, 185
 pleasure, 5, 165, 194–195, 201, 227
 preference, 161
 privacy, 162
 relations, 48, 111–112, 219
 security, 48
 services, 17, 21, 41, 114
 servitude, 18
 slavery, 31, 38, 63, 150, 153, 156
 status quo, 26
 submission, xl, 162, 168
 taboos, 185
 trauma, 53, 83, 164
 victimization, 107
 violation, 162
 violence, xxix, xxxiii, 18, 25–26, 53–54, 64–65, 68, 79, 83, 103–104, 110, 114, 116, 119–120, 122–123, 131, 136, 142, 144, 149–156, 167
 of women, xli
Sheldon, R., 112
Shumate v. Wilson, 118
Sigal, P., 119
Silverman, J. G., 19
Simon, J., 109
Simon, R., 109
Simons, M., 153
Sirkin, S., 155
slavery, 12, 17, 109–115 *see also*: sexual
 abolition of, 108, 113
 African, 114
 chattel, 113–114
 Convention, 110, 114
 forced domestic, 161, 165–166

Sluzky, C., 44
Smith, B., 108–109, 112–113, 120, 123–124, 131
Smith, K., 13, 182–187
Soh, C., 110
Spohn, C., 154
Stanley, D., 108
Stanton, E., 109, 115
Steiner, R., 211
Stockholm Syndrome, 35, 38, 53
Stoller, R. J., 213
Sulkowicz, E., 185
symbolization, xl–xli

The Fabric of Healing, 80
The National Center for Biotechology Information, 36–37
Therborn, G., 168
Thomas, D. Q., 109, 118, 120
Torok, M., 211
Torres Ruiz, G., 137
transference, 13, 55, 191, 211, 215–220
    see also: countertransference
  conflict, 221
  idealizing, 55
  maternal, 217
  moment, 56
  negative, 216
  oedipal, 216
  phenomenon, 59
  relationship, 191
  situation, 216–217
  vicissitudes, 220
trauma(tic), xxx, xxxviii, xl, 2, 5, 9–10, 14–15, 18, 21, 24, 51, 55, 59, 65–66, 68–70, 72, 74, 76–77, 79–80, 83–85, 87, 100, 151, 154–156, 163, 165, 232 see also: art, disorder, sexual
  complex, 20–21
  consequences of, 63
  events, xxxv, xxxviii, 21, 50, 54, 68, 85, 238
  experience, 39, 68, 70, 83, 85, 88
  helplessness, 101
  imaginary, 6
  impact, 6
  information, xxviii
  intergenerational, 101
  memories, 49, 68, 70, 72
  mind, xlii
  narratives, 72
  overwhelming, 85
  post-, 69, 81, 151
  psyche, 84
  psychiatric, 150
  recovery, 68
  repetitive, 2, 5, 14
  secondary, 25
  stories, xxxviii
  symbolizing, xl
  terrible, xxx
  unbearable, 10
  unnamed, xli
  unrecognized, 10
  victim, 2
  violence, xxxviii, xlii, 12, 84–85, 232
  visual, 179
Tricked: *The Documentary*, 22–23
Tuckman, J., 141

U.N. Economic & Social Council, Commission on Human Rights, 110
U.S. Constitution Amendment
  Eighth, 115, 117–118
  Fifth, 117
  Thirteenth, 113–114
U.S. Department of Justice, 119, 122
Uhlenhuth, E. H., 76
Ullman, S. E., 154
unconscious(ness), 2, 55, 58–59, 85, 180 see also: conscious, phantasy
  beliefs, 44
    legitimating, 42
  communication, 218
  effort, 5
  fantasies, xxxviii, xl, xlii, 1, 3–6, 13
    primitive, 13
  identifications, 42
    gender, 44
  mind, 4, 12
  motivations, 5
  power of, xxxviii
  processes, 2, 210
  psychic
    narrative, 4
    processes, 1

representation, 215
resistances, 51
sabotage, 51
scripts, xxxix, 4
structures, 44, 190
vicarious interest, 25
United Nations High Commissioner for Refugees (UNHCR), 64–65, 162
United Nations Human Rights: Office of the High Commissioner, 17
United Nations Office on Drugs and Crime, 17
United Nations Population Fund (UNFPA), 63–64
United States Department of Urban Housing (HUD), 18
United States v. Arizona, 120

Van der Kolk, B., 68
van Hasselt, M., 155
Vanrooyen, M. J., 155
Varekamp, E., 154
victim, xxxix, xl, 2–6, 9, 11, 19, 21–23, 25–26, 34, 38, 41–42, 55, 65, 69–70, 80, 95, 116, 118, 130, 136, 138–141, 150, 153–154, 169, 197, 206, 227, *see also*: rape, trauma
 of crime, 116
 engagement, 154
 -hood, 122
 potential, xxxvi
 sacrificial, 197
 satisfaction, 154
 subject, 116
 trafficked, 19, 25, 35–36
 of violence, xl, 6, 14, 135, 138, 142, 167, 231
violation, xxxiv, xli, 3, 113, 115, 118, 137, 139, 162, 164, 166

Violence Against Women Act (VAWA), 116, 120–121, 123
Volpp, L., 116

Walker, K., 184–185
war, 53, 79, 83–85, 110, 150, 152, 168, 179, 184, 237
 aftermath of, 64
 American Civil, 149
 civil, 64, 74, 89, 149, 153
 crime, 150, 152–153
 First World, 149
 inter-, 190
 motifs, 197
 post-, 64, 70
 Second World, 66, 149–150
 strategies, 149
 weapon of, 152
 zones, 149
Wasco, S. M., 154
Weathers, F. W., 76
Weintraub, J. K., 76
White, D., 111
Williams, S., 182
Winnicott, D. W., 92, 100, 212
Wisconsin Department of Justice, 22
witnessing, xxxviii, xl, 3, 9–11, 32, 51, 244
 community, 2
 process, 2–3
Wolheim, R., 210
Women Prisoners of the D.C. Department of Corrs. v. District of Columbia, 114, 116–117
World Health Organization, 18, 149
Worley, R., 111, 116

Xinhua, A., 143

Yordon, E., 238
Yorke, C., 211

Ziering, A., 104
Zucker, K. J., 151